Gintarė Grigonytė

Building and Evaluating Domain Ontologies: NLP Contributions

Logos Verlag Berlin

 λογος

Bibliografische Information Der Deutschen Bibliothek

Die Deutsche Bibliothek verzeichnet diese Publikation in der Deutschen
Nationalbibliografie; detaillierte bibliografische Daten sind im Internet
über http://dnb.ddb.de abrufbar.

Gedruckt mit Unterstützung des Deutschen Akademischen Austauschdienstes

ISBN 978-3-8325-2657-3

Logos Verlag Berlin GmbH
Comeniushof, Gubener Str. 47,
10243 Berlin
Tel.:   +49 (0)30 / 42 85 10 90
Fax: +49 (0)30 / 42 85 10 92
http://www.logos-verlag.de

Logos TITLE

Building and Evaluating Domain Ontologies: NLP Contributions

Gintarė Grigonytė

IMPRESSUM

Abstract

An ontology is a knowledge representation structure made up of concepts and their interrelations. It usually means shared understanding delineated by some domain. The building of ontology can be addressed from the perspective of natural language processing.

In this thesis I have discussed the validity and theoretical background of knowledge acquisition from natural language. I have also presented the theoretical and experimental framework for NLP- driven ontology building and evaluation tasks.

This thesis reports the contributions to the state-of-art of NLP-driven ontology learning and evaluation. First, the framework for automatic detection of ontology building blocks: domain terms and their semantic relationships is presented. In addition, the approach of thesaurus-based evaluation of the pragmatic quality of ontologies is reported. Finally, the experimental investigation of proposed methodology has been evaluated on two different domains.

Section 1 briefly discusses the motivation of ontology building. Ontology is perceived differently, depending on the point of view of the research domain, as presented in section 2 that outlines the main perspectives on ontology derived from domains of philosophy, computer science and linguistics. The major interest of the thesis is to investigate the task of ontology building and evaluation from the standpoint of linguistics and an NLP perspective. Section 3 summarizes theoretical premises of a bottom-up ontology building approach and presents the arguments defending this perspective.

Additionally, section 4 overviews the techniques of NLP that have proved to be sufficient for the tasks of term extraction and semantic relationship extraction. Domain terms and their semantic interrelations are building blocks of an ontology. Section 5 reports state-of-art ontology evaluation approaches and explains how NLP can contribute to the strategy of the glass-box ontology evaluation.

Section 6 presents the hybrid methodology for domain terminology extraction and termhood assessment, which is based on linguistic NP pattern preprocessing and statistical termhood filtering. The proposed method achieved 79% of accuracy and has improved the baseline AUTOTERM approach (Hong et al. (2001), Haller (2006)) by 4%. In addition, the proposed method organizes domain terms into hypernym-hyponym hierarchies .

Regarding automatic relationship extraction, a novel method for utilizing monolingual paraphrase alignments and detecting synonymy has been developed. The approach does not use any language processing tools. The extended Cordeiro et al. (2007) method showed 72%-89% performance of accuracy in extracting synonymous word pairs, and synonymous MWU (multi-word unit) pairs.

In addition to unsupervised synonymy detection section 6 presents an SVO pattern matching approach that extends the KURD (Carl and Schmidt-Wigger (1998)) procedure.

The tasks of domain term extraction and semantic relationship extraction are major contributions to ontology building from NLP-driven standpoint. Yet another field where the role of natural language and NLP recently started to be explored is the evaluation of domain ontologies. A methodology for evaluation of a pragmatic property of domain ontologies is proposed. Evaluation of domain coverage of an ontology with specialized domain thesauri is an innovative attempt to assess other than syntactic properties of the quality of domain ontologies. Ultimately, section 7 demonstrates that the developed methodology has proved to be useful because it was successfully applied and evaluated in two different research domains.

A thorough overview of related work is introduced throughout all the sections.

Zusammenfassung

Eine Ontologie ist eine Struktur zur Darstellung von Wissen, die aus Konzepten und deren Beziehungen zueinander aufgebaut ist. Gewöhnlich meint dies ein gemeinsames Verständnis, welches durch einen Gegenstandsbereich beschrieben wird. Das Entstehen einer Ontologie kann vom Standpunkt der natürlichen Sprachverarbeitung aus untersucht werden. In dieser Dissertation werden die Gültigkeit und der theoretische Hintergrund des Wissenserwerbs der natürlichen Sprache erörtert. Zudem werden der theoretische und der experimentelle Rahmen der NLP-getriebenen Ontologieerstellung sowie Aufgabenstellungen der Evaluation vorgestellt. Im lezten Kapitel wird unser Beitrag auf dem Gebiet des Ontologielernens zusammengefasst und Ansätze für die weitere Forschung auf diesem Gebiet gegeben.

Diese Dissertation leistet einen Beitrag zum aktuellen Stand des NLP-getriebenen Ontologielernens und -bewertens. Zunächst wird der Rahmen der automatischen Erfassung von Ontologiebausteinen umrissen; dies beinhaltet die Begrifflichkeiten des Gegenstandsbereichs und deren semantische Beziehungen. Des Weiteren wird der Ansatz von Bewertungen der pragmatischen Qualität der Ontologien auf Basis des Thesaurus vorgestellt. Abschließend wird die experimentelle Vorgehensweise der vorgeschlagenen Methodik durch deren Anwendung auf zwei unterschiedliche Gegenstandsbereiche bewertet.

In Kapitel 1 werden die Notwendigkeit der Ontologie und ihre Rolle auf interdisziplinären Gebieten diskutiert. Wie in Kapitel 2 dargestellt, kann die Ontologie unterschiedlich wahrgenommen werden, was sich jeweils nach der Sichtweise der Forschungsgebiete richtet. Es werden folglich die wesentlichen Standpunkte bzgl. der Ontologie aus den Bereichen der Philosophie, der Informatik und der Sprachwissenschaft abgeleitet. Hauptaugenmerk der Dissertation ist es, die Aufgabe der Ontologieerstellung und - bewertung vom Standpunkt der Sprachwissenschaft einerseits und der NLP andererseits näher zu untersuchen. Kapitel 3 fasst die theoretischen Voraussetzungen des *bottom-up*-Ansatzes der Ontologiebildung zusammen und liefert Argumente zu seiner Untermauerung.

Anschließend gibt Kapitel 4 einen Überblick über diejenigen Aufgabenstellungen der Extraktion von Begriffen und semantischen Beziehungen, bei denen die Techniken der NLP hinreichend gute Ergebnisse liefern. Begrifflichkeiten des Gegenstandsbereichs und ihre semantischen Beziehungen sind die Bausteine einer Ontologie. Kapitel 5 berichtet über den aktuellen Stand der Ansätze, die zur Bewertung von Ontologien herangezogen werden, und erklärt, wie NLP zum speziellen Fall der Glasbox-Bewertungsstrategie beitragen kann.

Es wird die Hybrid-Methodik für die Extraktion der Terminologie von Gegenstandsbereichen und die Bewertung gemäß *Termhood* vorgestellt, welche auf der Vorverarbeitung von linguistischen NP-Mustern und der statistischen *Termhood*-Filterung basiert. Die vorgeschlagene Methode erreicht eine 79%ige Genauigkeit und verbessert damit den älteren AUTOTERM-Ansatz (Hong et al. (2001), Haller (2006)) um 4%. Zudem gliedert die vorgeschlagene Methode die Begriffe des Gegenstandsbereichs in eine hypernym-hyponym Hierarchie.

Zur Ableitung von Beziehungen wird eine neuartige Methode vorgestellt, welche sich Anordnungen monolingualer Paraphrasen zur Extraktion von Synonymen bedient. Unser Ansatz verzichtet auf die Verwendung jeglicher Tools der Sprachverarbeitung. Die erweiterte Methode von Cordeiro at al. (2007) zeigte eine Leistung von 72 bis 89% hinsichtlich ihrer Genauigkeit, synonyme Wortpaare und synonyme MWU-Paare zu extrahieren.

Zusätzlich zur unüberwachten Erkennung von Synonymie wird ein Ansatz zum Musterabgleich von sprachwissenschaftlichen Argumentstrukturen vorgestellt, welcher den KURD-Prozess (Carl and Schmidt-Wigger (1998)) erweitert.

Die Aufgabenstellungen der Extraktion von Begriffen und von semantischen Beziehungen bilden den hauptsächlichen Beitrag zur Ontologieerstellung vom NLP- Standpunkt aus. Noch ein weiteres Gebiet, auf dem die Rollen von natürlicher Sprache und NLP neuerdings untersucht werden, ist die Bewertung der *domain ontology*. Als Beitrag dazu wird eine Methodik der Bewertung ihrer pragmatischen Eigenschaft vorgeschlagen. Die Bewertung der Gebietsabdeckung einer Ontologie mit spezialisierten Bereichsthesauri bildet einen innovativen Versuch, andere als syntaktische Eigenschaften von *domain ontologies* einzuschätzen. Beiträge zu dieser Forschung werden in Kapitel 6 vorgestellt.

Abschließend wird in Kapitel 7 gezeigt, dass die entwickelte Methodik effizient ist, und erfolgreich an zwei unterschiedlichen Forschungsbereichen angewendet und bewertet wurde.

Ein exakter Überblick über verwandte Arbeiten wird in allen Kapiteln gegeben.

Acknowledgments

Three years of intensive work have resulted in this thesis, thereby I would like to express my gratitude to all the people who have supported me during my study period in Saarbrücken.

Firstly and most importantly, I would like to express my gratitude to my *Doktorvater* Prof. Dr. Johann Haller. He has provided a wonderful environment for the research and my professional growth. His excellent experience in terminology extraction has helped to frame my research and has been the backbone of my thesis.

This work would not have either been accomplished without my secondary supervisor prof. Algirdas Avižienis whose extensive feedback has helped to improve this thesis. His optimism and endurance in important times has been most inspirational.

I would like to thank all colleagues from IAI[1] and Saarland University for creating friendly and helpful environment during my stay in Saarbrucken. I thank Oliver Čulo, Mahmoud Gindiyeh, Susanne Preuß and Jörg Schütz for their feedback at different stages of my research. I also thank Peggy Daut for smoothing the path by her undertaking of administrational duties. To the people of Saarland University I would like to mention Kerstin Kunz, Stella Neumann, Andrea Stockero, and Marc Summkeller.

I am indebted to my colleagues Cornelia Zelinsky-Wibbelt, Rūta Marcinkevičienė, Jolanta Kovalevskaitė, Adriana Pagano and Kaustubh Patil who have read through the chapters and have contributed with very valuable remarks and advice that helped to improve this thesis. I also thank Patrick Dempsey for his diligent proofreading.

I would like to thank colleagues from Porto University Pavel Brazdil, João Paulo Cordeiro and Gaël Dias for the fruitful cooperation on the topic of the relationship learning, and for their warm reception during the month of my internship.

I would also like thank all colleagues from IFOMIS[2], especially Mathias Brochhausen for the joint work on ontology evaluation and for providing me with valuable research data and feedback.

I thank all colleagues from the ReSIST project for the fruitful discussions which helped me frame the topic of the research and allowed to apply my work on the domain of computer dependability.

I also thank DAAD for the scholarship that allowed me to pursue my ambitions in academia. Thanks go to my DAAD coordinators Ludmilla Winter-Souhradová, Hans Golombek, Maria-Luise Nünning, and especially Antje Johanning who has taken keen interest in the development of the paper.

---

[1] Institut der Gesellschaft zur Förderung der Angewandten Informationsforschung an der Universität des Saarlandes, http://www.iai-sb.de/iai/
[2] The Institute for Formal Ontology and Medical Information Science, http://www.ifomis.org/

I would like to thank NGSLT School for the financial support to attend courses on various topics on computational linguistics. The courses and discussions with the people I have met there has been the basis of forming my perspective on the subject.

Finally, I would like to thank my family and all friends for their support and encouragement. Lastly, I would like to kindly thank my partner Linus Roune for his love and support. He has contributed to this thesis with his graphic design skills.

Table of Contents

List of figures

List of tables

List of abbreviations

ACGT MO – ACGT master ontology;
ACM CCS – the ACM classification system;
AI – artificial intelligence;
BNC – the British National Corpus;
COCD – Corpus of Computer Dependability;
COCR – Corpus of Cancer Research;
CPA – Corpus Pattern Analysis;
DB – database;
EU – European Union;
FCA – Formal Concept Analysis;
GL – generative lexicon;
IDF – inverse document frequency;
IE – information extraction;
IR – information retrieval;
KR – knowledge representation;
MI – mutual information;
MUC – Message Understanding Conference;
MWU – multi-word unit;
NL –natural language;
NLP – natural language processing;
NP – noun phrase;
OWL - Web Ontology Language, W3C standard;
POS – part of speech;
PP – prepositional phrase;
RDF - Resource Description Framework, W3C standard;
RE – reverse engineering;
SE – software engineering;
SVO – subject verb object;
TE – terminology extraction;
TKB – terminological knowledge base;
VP – verb phrase;
W3C – World Wide Web Consortium;
WSD – word sense disambiguation;
WSM – word space model.

1. Introduction

In this section we introduce the motivation behind ontologies and outline the objective and organization of the study.

1.1 Motivation

Science and technology aim at fostering *understanding* and supporting *communication* which is closely bound to *information processing*. The emerging vast discourse of electronic texts and Internet content have made acquisition, storage, organization and sharing of information important and eventually caused the automation of these activities.

An *ontology* is a knowledge representation structure made up of concepts and their interrelations. It usually means shared understanding delineated by some domain. Ontologies provide explicit context for data interpretation, and thus can be easily adapted to tasks of *information processing.*

Ontologies have been used in the artificial intelligence field since the 1960's (Buitelaar and Cimiano (2008)). From the wider perspective of applications, ontologies are explicit knowledge networks that are ubiquitous, interoperable and enable machine-to-machine communication. Ontologies became a standard of knowledge representation in the semantic web (Berners-Lee (1999, 2005)), where they are mediators used to exchange and share the knowledge between information systems and knowledge bases.

Ontologies are also topical in applications of natural language processing. For instance, by integrating an ontology, and thus adding the level of semantics, quite many NLP tasks can be improved. An example of using such knowledge can be the interpretation of the concept *virus* which can refer either to malicious code or to an infectious agent causing disease in living organisms. Among examples of NLP application fields are machine translation, information retrieval, question answering, sentiment analysis, text summarization, etc.

Constructing ontologies however is a laborious task, demanding years of experts' work. For instance, the CYC project was developed in ten years (Douglas (1995)). A whole lot of ontologies already have been created and published, for example the OntoSelect[3] (Buitelaar (2004)) library registers over 1500 ontologies, which provides the possibility of reuse for most applications. However, many specific domains still remain uncovered presently, e.g., computer dependability (Avižienis (2008)).

The building of an ontology can be addressed from the perspective of natural language processing when ontology components can be automatically acquired from domain specific corpora (Cimiano (2006)).

This thesis reports the contributions to the state-of-the-art of NLP-driven ontology learning and evaluation.

1.2 Objective of the Thesis

Ontology is an interdisciplinary field. For thousands of years it has been associated with philosophy (from Aristotle 350 B.C. to Sowa (2000)). Recently new trends have emerged. Ontology has put on different clothes and became an application, or rather an integral part of knowledge intensive applications, as in the field of computer science, or a network of related concepts, as in linguistics. In this thesis we will take a standpoint of linguistics and try to answer the questions:

- Is it possible to build an ontology from natural language? What evidence of knowledge is there in natural language?
- How easy is to access the knowledge contained in natural language? Can an ontology be built with the assistance of NLP?
- What are the contributions of NLP in building ontologies?
- What are the contributions of NLP in evaluating ontologies?

1.3 Outline of the Thesis

In this chapter I have presented the motivation of the research and outlined the objective of the thesis. The structure of the thesis is as follows:

- Section 2 overviews three perspectives on ontologies: philosophy, computer science and linguistics. Based on these three distinctions, the methodologies of building ontologies are analyzed. Additionally the existing classifications of ontologies are overviewed.
- Section 3 explores the validity and premises of bottom-up ontology building. Different types of the evidence of knowledge is discussed as well as complexity of knowledge discovery from text is explained. Major points of criticism on bottom-up ontology engineering is analyzed.

---

[3] OntoSelect library can be found at: http://olp.dfki.de/ontoselect/

- Section 4 presents the tasks necessary for ontology building from the perspective of NLP. First the role of the corpus as a shared knowledge medium is explained and the definition of domain corpus is presented. Next the thesis presents the term extraction task, theoretical term extractions premises, and state-of-art term extraction techniques. Further, semantic relationships are analyzed from the perspective of two ontology building related tasks: delineating concepts of an ontology and providing hierarchical and non-hierarchical structure of an ontology. Finally different semantic relationship extraction methods are presented.
- Section 5 overviews the field of state-of-art ontology evaluation. Different quality metrics of ontologies are presented, and strategies of evaluation are explained. In particular the role of NLP in ontology evaluation is emphasized.
- Section 6 presents proposed research methodology which reflects the contributions of NLP in building and evaluating a domain ontology. An ontology building methodology comprises term extraction, relationship learning, and SVO (subject-verb-object) triplet extraction. Additionally the methodology for domain thesauri-based ontology evaluation is described.
- Section 7 presents the results of applying the proposed methodology in two different application domains: computer dependability and cancer research.
- Section 8 summarizes the main contributions of the thesis and discusses the further work in the area.

2. Ontology: Three Perspectives

"Above and beyond the everyday world of appearances, there exists another, more perfect realm of pure Ideas, universals, or Forms, which are the true reals or existences: permanent, unchanging, and divine."
Plato (Cunninghan C. (2004:1))

2.1 Definition(s) of Ontology

The concept of *ontology* has it`s origins in ancient Greece. The etymology of the word has it`s roots in the Greek word : *onto* ('of beings') and *logos* ('speech', 'reason'). The oldest record of the term ontology dates back to 1606, where the Latin form *ontologia (logia = 'science')* appears in *Ogdoas Scholastica* by Jacob Lorhard (Øhrstrøm et. al. (2008), Guizzardi (2007), and Smith and Welty (2001)). The first definition of *ontologia* was presented later in 1729 in *Philosophia Prima sive Ontologia* (First Philosophy or Ontology) by Christian Wolff:

"*Ontologia seu Philosophia Prima est scientia entis in genere, seu quatenus ens est*" (Ontology or First Philosophy is the science of Being in general or as Being). Nickles et al. (2007:23)

The meaning of the term *ontology* has been influenced throughout history. The concept of *being* was already discussed by the classical Greek philosophers: Plato and Aristotle. Plato's notable contribution was a defined dichotomy between *illusion* and *reality*, i.e., between the world of appearances and reality of *being*. This has also been depicted in a recent interpretation by J. Arieti:

"The intelligibility of perfect, unchanging things, to which Plato give the name ideas or forms – like geometric shapes – suggests that alongside the physical realm there exists an abstract realm that is perfect and unchanging . [...] Everything for which there is a name has a perfect form in an eternally changeless, immaterial reality of Being. [...] the realm of Being, however, all is constant, unchanging, and universal." Arieti (2005:175)

Another contribution by Plato, of equal importance, introduced the notion of the idea *universal, i.e.,* how one thing in general can be and have many meanings in *particulars*.

For Plato *form* (universal) is a singular entity but causes plural representations of itself in particular objects (individuals).

"Individuals were often felt to be logically, epistemologically and/or ontologically inferior to universals, especially by adherents of Plato's view that FORMS, IDEAS or universals are prior to individuals." (Inwood, M. (1992:303))

Aristotle extended Plato's notion of *being* in *Metaphysics*. The perception of *being* (senses in which a thing can be said to *be*) can be separated into three different aspects: definition, order of knowledge (perception) and time.

"Now there are several senses in which a thing is said to be first; yet substance is first in every sense-(1) in definition, (2) in order of knowledge, (3) in time. For (3) of the other categories none can exist independently, but only substance. And (1) in definition also this is first; for in the definition of each term the definition of its substance must be present. And (2) we think we know each thing most fully, when we know what it is, e.g. what man is or what fire is, rather than when we know its quality, its quantity, or its place; since we know each of these predicates also, only when we know what the quantity or the quality is." Aristotle – Metaphysics (2005: 95)

The concept of *ontology* has not only evolved throughout history, but has also been transmuted when employed in areas other than philosophy. Partially due to its ubiquity but also due to the specificity of research areas and weight placed in the interest of relevance, has lead to diverse definitions of the term.

In philosophy, *ontology* is a discipline, a systematic account of existence/being. It concerns the World as it is studied by science. It is

"[…] the science of what is, of the kinds and structures of objects, properties, events, processes and relations in every area of reality." (Floridi (2004:155))

In computer science, the concept of *ontology* is a schematic representation of reality. Logics and formal representation is a basis of a conceptualization. According to Genesereth and Nilsson (1987),

"The formalization of knowledge in declarative form begins with a conceptualization. This includes the objects presumed or hypothesized to exist in the world and their interrelationships." (Genesereth and Nilsson (1987: 9))

Furthermore,

"A body of formally represented knowledge is based on a conceptualization: the objects, concepts, and other entities that are presumed to exist in some area of interest and the relationships that hold them […]. A conceptualization is an abstract, simplified view of the world that we wish to represent for some purpose." (Gruber (1993: 199))

W3C[4] gives the following definition of *ontology* and underlines the aspects that are important to ontology in the sense of '*software*': sharing, reuse, computer-usability:

"An ontology defines the terms used to describe and represent an area of knowledge. Ontologies are used by people, databases, and applications that need to share domain information (a domain is just a specific subject area or area of knowledge, like medicine, tool manufacturing, real estate, automobile repair, financial management, etc.). Ontologies include computer-usable definitions of basic concepts in the domain and the relationships among them […]. They encode knowledge in a domain and also knowledge that spans domains. In this way, they make that knowledge reusable." (W3C website: 292).

Among other well-known definitions of the concept of *ontology* in computer science are the following: Gruber (1993) calls ontology an explicit specification of a conceptualization; for

---

[4] World Wide Web Consortium; http://www.w3.org/TR/webont-req/

Uschold and Grüninger (1996) ontology is a shared understanding of a domain of interest; Guarino (1997) describes ontology in three aspects: (1) an engineering artifact, (2) a specific vocabulary used to describe a certain reality, and (3) a set of explicit assumptions with regard to the intended meaning of the vocabulary.

Although the above-mentioned definitions vary in substance and instrumentality, the generalized concept of ontology in computer science accommodates four basic components of ontology: a part of reality; concepts referring to the described part of reality; formal language expressing concepts and relationships between them; and a natural language that expresses concepts and refers to the reality they represent.

In linguistics, other aspects of *ontology* are given emphasis. Here an *ontology* is perceived as a network made up of relations among concepts deriving from linguistic materialization. As Fellbaum describes it:

> "We define an ontology as a structured inventory of basic, atomic concepts, as well as complex concepts that are derived via well-formedness rules. [...] We assume that the ontology is independent of any particular language, but that it acts as a filter on the possible lexicons of human languages. Only concepts that are sanctioned in the ontology can potentially be lexicalized. We argue that the lexicon reflects the ontology, which can be "discovered" through the patterns by which existing words are related to one another." (Fellbaum (2007:419)).

From Fellbaum's viewpoint, *ontology* is a network made up of atomic concepts. The concepts of *ontology* refer to the concepts used in a language. Therefore, naturally it is possible to study *ontology* by studying language.

Yet another viewpoint on *ontology* is presented by Nickles et al. (2007). The authors underline the importance of human language *users* and their way of understanding and interpreting conceptual contents:

> "The job of the linguist is to find convincing answers to the question: *What kinds of things do people talk as if there are?* [...] It should be clear by now that the subject matter of Language Ontology [...] should interest every linguist who subscribes to the view that linguistic signs associate perceivable forms with conceptual contents, because these conceptual contents are never isolated in human language users, but integrated into the way they conceptualize their world, their individual ontology." (Nickles et al. (2007:36))

Based on two previous definitions, we can suppose that for a linguist, *ontology* contains the world, concepts representing the world, and the language expressing the concepts. Language plays the most important role with respect to the interest that lays in language-related, language-based conceptualizations. Lenci (2008) grounds the role of language in three different ways to language-related conceptualizations:

- Ontology is derived from language. The behavior of linguistic expressions is the unique source of the conceptualizations used in an ontology.
- Ontology is used to represent the meaning of lexical items. The meanings of lexical expressions are represented as the concepts of an ontology.
- Ontology provides an explanation of grammatical generalizations. For instance, ontology can represent morphological marking, syntactic distribution, patterns of language acquisition, typological universals, etc.

2.2 Types of Ontologies

The variety of viewpoints on the definition of an ontology suggests that there won't be a single and coherent viewpoint regarding types of ontologies. In this section we give an overview of some authors' notable contributions in classifying ontologies.

In the field of computer science major classifications have been introduced by van Heijst et al. (1997), Guarino (1998), Gómez-Pérez et al. (2004) and Fensel (2004).

Van Heijst et al. (1997) proposed classifying ontologies according to their difference in specification and the ontology's purpose of usage, in other words, according to the problem that the ontology is meant to solve. Based on this assumption, authors define three types of ontologies:

- Terminological ontologies – which specify the terms used for knowledge representation.
- Information ontologies – are meant to specify the storage structure of the data, used in databases.
- Knowledge modeling ontologies – describe the conceptualization of knowledge.

Van Heijst's et al. (1997) dimension of classification has received critique from Guarino (1997) due to its binding to the symbolic level, i.e., terminologies and data bases.

"[...] there is no reason to hypothesize a distinction among ontologies on the basis of "the amount and type of structure of their conceptualization". [...] a distinction can be made among different ontologies on the basis of the degree of detail used to characterize a conceptualization." (Guarino (1997:299)).

Latter, Guarino (1998) presents his standpoint on types of ontologies. The defining feature is a level of generality of ontology:

- Top-level ontologies – describe very general concepts that are independent of the particular domain or problem. Such concepts are space, time, object, event, etc.
- Domain ontologies – describe a vocabulary related to a domain, for instance, agriculture, medicine, etc.
- Task ontologies – describe a generic task or activity, such as automatic code generation in software engineering, or selling.
- Application ontologies – describe concepts in relation to two aspects: the particular domain and the particular task. Very often, the concepts correspond to the roles performed by the domain entities during the specific task.

Gómez-Pérez, Fernandez-Lopez and Corcho (2004) classify ontologies according to the richness of their internal structure:

- Lightweight ontologies – including concepts, taxonomical structure of concepts, relationships among concepts and properties that describe concepts.
- Heavyweight ontologies – in addition to lightweight ontologies, contain axioms and constraints which disambiguate the meaning of terms (concepts) on ontologies.

Fensel (2004) takes into account generality and ontology roles in the process of building knowledge-based systems. Based on these criteria he distinguishes the following types of ontologies:

- Domain ontologies – describe the knowledge related to a particular domain.
- Metadata ontologies – provide a vocabulary for describing the content of on-line information resources (Dublin Core ontology (Weibel (1998))).
- Generic or common sense ontologies – represent general knowledge about the world, describe concepts like time, space, event, etc. (e.g., Mereology ontology: Borst et al. (1997)).
- Representational ontologies – provide representational entities without committing to any particular domain (e.g., Frame ontology: Gruber (1993)).
- Task and method ontologies – respectively provide terms specific of a particular task (e.g., diagnosis) and to a specific problem solving method.

The most systematic classification so far that takes into consideration ontologies across disciplines, their generality and objectivity (see Figure 1.) is proposed by Nickles et al. (2007).

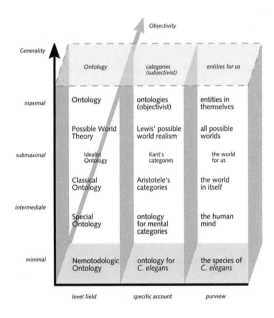

Figure 1. Example of variation dimensions and aspects of ontology (Nickles et al. 2007).

According to Nickles et al. (2007) classification, three dimensions are differentiated in the following manner:

- Specificity – generality (vertical dimension): from the categorial aspects of entities to the common properties of all entities. This dimension allows us to distinguish between philosophical notions of ontology and specific domains.
- Objectivity – subjectivity (depth dimension): the distinction between reality and the outcome of thought and reason. This dimension distinguishes between the plain existence of a thing and the subject of someone's interpretation.
- Field of study – specific account (horizontal dimension): draws a line between a field of study and the product of a field of study.

Apart from the main three dimensions Nickles et al. (2007) suggest other aspects of ontology classification which are defined as:

- Origin – specifies whether ontology has an author, or it's creation was an evolutionary process.
- Author – known, unknown, inexistent.
- User – for what purpose an ontology is created, i.e., with respect to who is going to use it: computer or human.
- Evaluation – how an ontology is evaluated: according to it's adequateness or usefulness, i.e., how well it serves a purpose.
- Representation – concepts (which granularity), relations (which kind, which granularity), properties, axioms, which formal language, reasoning, inference.

2.3 Methodologies for Building Ontologies

Different research approaches towards ontologies result in different methodologies with respect to ontology building. In this section we will briefly describe three methodologies originating from philosophy, computer science and linguistics. We will also discuss the possibility of combining methodologies originating in different disciplines.

2.3.1 Methodologies in Philosophy

In philosophy, ontology is perceived as a discipline. The methodology of modeling ontology in philosophy is top-down, in other words it is the modeling of already perceived knowledge. As Guarino notes: "first ontological analysis and then knowledge representation and reasoning" (Guarino (2008)). The schematic ontological analysis becomes an essential "ingredient" of ontology. Therefore language's role is not central in respect to it's ability to influence ontology. In Guarino (1998) mentions that every natural language "commits to some ontology".

The phenomena of reality are observed. It forms our perception and hence presentation patterns. The role of language is confined to conceptualization as the presentation of reality. Language is bound to ontology through conceptualization. Language itself is not seen as a part of perception, as it is linguistics (see Figure 2.):

> "An ontology is a logical theory accounting for the *intended meaning* of a formal vocabulary, i.e. its *ontological commitment* to a particular *conceptualization* of the world. The intended models of a logical language using such a vocabulary are constrained by its ontological commitment. An ontology indirectly reflects this commitment (and the underlying conceptualization) by approximating these intended models.
> " (Guarino 1998:5).

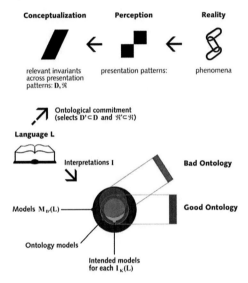

Figure 2. Relationship between conceptualization, language, ontological commitment and ontology.[5]

Guarino sees conceptualization as the result of a complex abstraction process from multiple presentation experiences. He uses R.Carnap's[6] terms *intension* and *extension* to refer to relations: ordinary relations (extensional r.) defined on a domain **D**; intensional relations are defined on a domain space <**D,W**>. Situations are states of words. Words themselves are particulars. Situations are partial states of affairs. The clear division line between vocabulary and situations explains the necessity of the ontological analysis in philosophical methodology and distinguishes it from approaches of other research disciplines, e.g., computational

---

[5] Figure adapted from Guarino (2008) tutorium slides at FOIS 2008.

[6] R. Carnap *Introduction to Semantics* (Cambridge, Massachusetts, 1942); *Meaning and Necessity* (Chicago, 1947). The meaning of any expression comprises two components: intension and extension. Intension is apprehended by the understanding of the expression. Extension is determined by empirical investigation.

ontologies[7]. According to Guarino – a philosophical ontology is a structured system of entities assumed to exists, organized by means of categories and relations. The benefits of philosophical ontology are: mutual understanding, ability to recognize disagreement, ability for general abstractions, careful explanation and justification of ontological commitment. Computational ontologies, in contrast, are meant to provide interoperability, data integrity and problem solving.

This thesis does not follow along the lines of the top-down methodology. Further reading on the subject can be found from Sowa (2000a), Burkhardt and Smith (1991), Künne (2003), Albertazzi (2007).

2.3.2 Computer Science Methodologies

In computer science *ontology* is seen as a software. Due to this perception it has inherited a handful of software engineering (SE) principles, for instance, reusability, software process, life cycle. The most popular concepts bearing SE notions adapted to ontologies are: ontology engineering, reverse engineering (denoting ontology's extraction from texts), ontology lifecycle, ontology integration, ontology reuse, etc.

From the perspective of ontology engineers, ontologies can be built either from scratch or by reusing existing ontologies. Hence this conception has left a footprint on methodologies. The core conception underlying all methodologies of ontological engineering is ontology's lifecycle, or the ontology building process. Recently the ontology building process became more standardized. An effort to describe the lifecycle of an ontology came for instance from Gómez-Pérez, A. (1995), Uschold and Grüninger (1996), and Fernandez-Lopez et al. (1997).

Fernandez-Lopez et al. (1997) has suggested a methodology comprising 5 *stages* which has to be passed in order to build an ontology: namely specification, conceptualization, formalization, implementation, and maintenance. The proposed methodology is entirely coherent with *IEEE Standard for Developing Software Life Cycle Processes*, 1074-1995. All the stages are accompanied by the tasks of knowledge acquisition, evaluation and documentation, as depicted in Figure 3.

The specification stage is intended to identify the purpose and scope of the ontology. Here the important questions like "why we are building the ontology?" and "how and who will use the ontology?" should be raised.

The conceptualization stage is intended to describe the ontology in a conceptual model assuring that the ontology meets specification requirements.

In *the formalization stage* the conceptual model is transformed into a formal model.

The implementation stage is supposed to implement the ontology according to the formal model and in a formal knowledge representation language.

---

[7] i.e., based on computer science methodologies.

The maintenance stage is for changing and updating the ontology.

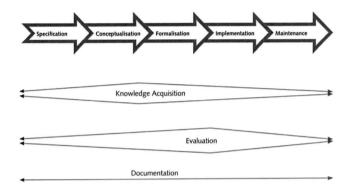

Figure 3. Activities in ontology development cycle[8].

Within the recent decade, a number of methodologies for building ontologies have been proposed. Very often, these methodologies became the best practices for successful projects when developing ontologies. Such as for instance the CYC methodology (Lenat (1995)), the Tove methodology (Fox et al. (1995)), the Enterprise ontology (Uschold et al. (1998)), and KAKTUS (Schreiber et al. (1995)). We will also briefly summarize some of the most popular methodologies.

The methodologies for **building ontology from scratch**:

The Tove methodology (Grüninger and Fox (1995)) comprises six steps:
1. Identifying the scenarios of the motivation for building an ontology;
2. Asking competency questions, i.e., questions that must be answered by the ontology. These questions are intended to evaluate the ontology and to find the restrictions imposed on the ontology;
3. Specifying the terminology;
4. Expressing the competency questions (2) by the specified terminology (3);
5. Specifying axioms by using FOL;
6. Specifying the completeness constraints.

The Enterprise ontology was built using the methodology proposed by Uschold et al. (1998). The main guidelines include:
1. Identifying the purpose of the ontology.
2. Building the ontology within three activities:

---

[8] Adapted from: AIFB activities in ontology development cycle, can be accessed at:
http://www.aifb.kit.edu/web/Ontologiemodellierung

    a. capturing the knowledge, i.e., concepts and relationships between them;
    b. formalizing the captured knowledge;
    c. integrating the formalized knowledge.
3. Evaluation of the ontology.

The Methontology (Corcho et. al. (2003)) adopted the best practices of SE. Methontology has three main phases that follow the lifecycle of an ontology:

1. Project management activities;
2. Development activities;
3. Support activities.

Theseus medico (Wennerberg et al. (2008)) is a methodology that was applied in the medical domain. The methodology follows seven phases:

1. Query Pattern Derivation, i.e., what are the typical queries domain experts are interested in?
2. Ontology Identification
3. Ontology Modularization and Pruning
4. Ontology Customization
5. Ontology Alignment
6. Reasoning-Based Ontology Enhancement
7. Testing and Deployment

The methodologies for **building ontology by reuse** can be classified by means of method: ontology *merging* and ontology *integration*.

Merging is the process of building an ontology in one subject reusing two or more different ontologies on that subject (Pinto and Martins (2001)). During the merge process source ontologies are consolidated into one resulting ontology. The main feature of the resulting ontology is that it usually has no obvious regions that can be easily identified within the source ontologies. By contrast, the *integration* process is about aggregating, combining and assembling two or more ontologies into one resulting ontology. Different regions of the source ontologies can be identified in the resulting ontology. According to Pinto and Martins (2001), integration is the process of building an ontology in one subject reusing one or more ontologies in different subjects.

KAKTUS (Bernaras et al. (1996)) is the methodology for the reuse of knowledge about technical systems during their lifecycle. The *merging* methodology specifies 3 main stages:

1. Specification of the new application, context of the application, and the components that the application tries to model.

2. Designing new ontological components based on the relevant existing top-level ontological components. Top-level ontological components are the list of terms and tasks developed during the previous phases. New components are designed to be coherent with the global model.

3. Refinement and restructuring of the ontology.

An example of an integration methodology is ONIONS (ONtologic Integration On Naive Sources) methodology (Gangemi et al. (1996)). The methodology contains six phases:
1. Building the corpus of a domain. The corpus needs to be agreed upon.
2. Taxonomic analysis of the domain.
3. The conceptual analysis of terms in order to define their constraints and definitions.
4. Multi-local source analysis. The conceptual analysis of the descriptions allows integration of local definitions with multi-local concepts and general knowledge.
5. Building an integrated ontology library. An ontology library covers all the local definitions and general knowledge.
6. Implementing the library. This step includes using the ontology for building the classifier.
This thesis does not follow along the lines of the presented methodologies. If the reader is interested in pursuing further reading on the subject then the following literature should be considered: Staab and Studer (2004), Gómez-Pérez et al. (2004), Sharman et al. (2007), Ehrig (2007), Antoniou and Harmelen (2008), and Cardoso and Lytras (2008).

2.3.3 Linguistic Methodologies

All linguistic methodologies for building ontologies share a bottom-up approach for acquiring knowledge from language. The underlying hypothesis is that language use, in particular, used words, are directly meaningful. Linguistic methodology for building ontologies has its roots in linguistics theories, which we will shortly discuss.

The early stages of relevant linguistic methodology can be traced back to generative linguists approach to analyzing the linguistic form: Mel'chuk's and Xolodovic's (1970) research on diathesis alternations, Krifka's (1999) research on dative shift, Levin's (1993) research on cognitive alternations. These approaches among others contributed to forming the idea that the behavior of lexical items in grammar is determined by their ontological status.

Levin (1993)[9] describes a methodology for the classification of English verbs. The underlying assumption is: "The syntactic behavior of verbs is semantically determined" (Levin (1993:14)). Levin suggests that the behavior of verb classes with respect to syntactic alterations is caused by the meaning of verbs. This indicates that the verb class whose members are similar with, for instance, respect to diathesis alternations should be a semantically related, coherent class.

> "[...] any class of verbs whose members pattern together with respect to diathesis alternation should be a semantically coherent class: its members should share at least some aspect of meaning." (Levin (1993:14))

When such classes are identified, according to Levin's methodology, the members of the class should be examined in order to detect the specific meaning components they share. A similar

---

[9] Levin, B. (1993) English Verb Classes and Alternations. Chicago: University of Chicago Press. 14 p.

approach named "correlation analysis" is proposed by Deane and Wheeler (1984)[10]. The authors show how semantic categories can be identified by analyzing direct correlations between syntactic patterns and patterns of semantic properties. An example illustrates how a pattern (1) can be used for examining verbs with the role of an instrument. This role is defined as being capable of occurring in subject position and becoming the AGENTIVE type of phrase. (see Example 1).

Example 1

```
[AGENT [...[with INSTRUMENT]]]

[INSTRUMENT [... [for AGENT]]]

a. I cured the sick man with the medicine.
b. The medicine cured the sick man for me.

c. I filled the sink with water.
d. *Water filled the sink for me[11].
```

The grammatical behavior of the verb *cure* in the first sentence pair (a. and b.) confirms the rule (Example 1), whereas the verb *fill* in the second sentence pair (c. and d.) does not allow such an alternation. Hence paradigmatic properties of a word can be detected by investigating syntagmatic ones.

Yet another branch of linguistics – cognitive linguistics – needs to be mentioned as it is relevant to ontology building due to the connection between the meaning and the conceptual categories. In cognitive linguistics the meaning of the word is seen as being compositional as in for instance the classical theories of Katz's (1972) semantic markers[12] and Wierzbicka's (1985,1996) semantic primes[13]. This implies top-down approach to modeling conceptual categories. Another subject of the research in cognitive linguistics is how linguistic structures relate to the meaning, resulting in the conjugation between top-down and bottom-up approaches. The most distinctive theories are: Talmy's (2000) theory on semantic typologies and universals of semantic structure[14], and construction grammar[15] Lakoff (1987), Fillmore et al. (1988), Goldberg (2003, 2006).

This thesis will not follow a cognitive linguistics approach, but concentrate on purely data-driven, usage driven methods, which are for instance, advocated by corpus linguists.

---

[10] Deane and Wheeler (1984) On the Use of Syntactic Evidence in the Analysis of Word Meaning. Papers from the Parasession on Lexical Semantics, Chicago Linguistic Society, ETATS-UNIS, p. 95-106
[11] Example taken from Deane and Wheeler (1984), p. 98.
[12] Semantic representations of senses are composed from smaller semantic units – semantic markers, e.g., *chair* contains semantic markers like *object, artifact*, etc.
[13] Word sense can be decomposed into a finite number of universal semantic primitives – semantic primes.
[14] Talmy sees language as a dual system comprising grammatical and lexical subsystems. "Basic function of grammatical form is to structure conception, while that of lexical form is to provide conceptual content." Talmy (2000:5).
[15] The patterns of construction grammar - *constructions* integrate form and meaning. The *form* in constructions is the combination of syntactic, morphological, or prosodic patterns and *meaning* includes lexical semantics, pragmatics, and discourse structure.

Prominent corpus linguists like Biber et al. (1998), Hanks (2000), and Hajicová (2008) argue that words bear meaning potentials, rather than meanings. The meaning can be constructed compositionally, by analyzing the text. Instead of being attached to a word, sense needs to be attached to patterns. Corpus linguists see the definition of sense as being data-driven. Hanks (2007) describes a pattern as an "argument structure with semantic values for the arguments"

Example 2

```
[[Human]] attend [[Event]] 16
```

Given pattern is made up of a verb and two lexical sets. It also encompasses a semantically motivated syntagmatic distinction. An example of a lexical set could be:

Example 3

```
[[Event]] = [meeting, conference, funeral, ceremony, course,
school, seminar, lecture, session, class, rally, dinner, hearing,
briefing, reception, workshop, wedding, inquest, summit, concert,
event, premiere] 17
```

It is necessary to note that the idea of a pattern is different and more extensive than the ideas of *synsets* in WordNet or *frames* in FrameNet. For example, the *synset* of the word *dictionary* comprises a set of synonyms of the word, but it does not bear the sense:

Example 4

```
Dictionary -> S: (n) dictionary, lexicon (a reference book
containing an alphabetical list of words with information about
them) 18
```

On the other hand, in FrameNet, *frames*, such as the *emotion_active* event pattern (see Table 1.) do not represent a word's syntagmatic behaviour.

Table 1. Emotion_active frame report[19]:

Core	Experiencer [Exp]	Kim WORRIED about the phone bill.
	Topic [Top]	He WORRIES a great deal about the house.
Non core	Degree [Degr]	He WORRIES a great deal about the house.
	Manner [Manr]	I FRETTED endlessly about the work that was needed to co-ordinate it all.
	Means [mea]	Although she tried to distract me over that week, I still worried about them by noticing all the little things that they left behind .
	Result [Result]	She was WORRYING herself sick about Biggles.

---

[16] Adapted from Hanks (2008).

[17] Adapted from Hanks (2008).

[18] http://wordnetweb.princeton.edu/perl/webwn?s=dictionary&sub=Search+WordNet
&o2=&o0=1&o7=&o5=&o1=1&o6=&o4=&o3=&h=

[19] http://framenet.icsi.berkeley.edu/index.php?option=com_wrapper&Itemid=118&frame
=Emotion_active&

Hanks (2004) talks about a *pattern dictionary* – an inventory of **all normal**[20] patterns of verb use, and a procedure of how to acquire these patterns: Corpus Pattern Analysis (CPA)[21]. CPA is a purely bottom-up methodology which is made up of five stages:

1) Create a sample concordance for a word. A reliable recommended set size is 250 examples of actual uses of the word.

2) Identify the typical syntagmatic patterns.

3) Assign each line of the sample to one of the patterns. Hanks highlights, that all examples must be classified and proposes a schema:

- Norms;
- Exploitations;
- Alternations;
- Names (Midnight Storm: name of a horse, not a storm);
- Mentions (to mention a word or phrase is not to use it);
- Errors (e.g. learned mistyped as leaned);
- Unassignables.

4) Take further samples if necessary. This step is an iteration through 2) and 3).

5) Store the pattern in the entry manager.

The notion of the *pattern dictionary* already comes quite close to the conception of ontology in linguistics. It is evident through *conceptualization* of the lexical set, *instances* of the lexical set, and verb playing the role of the *relation*.

More recently, linguistic methodologies for ontology construction are emerging, as for instance the methodologies proposed by Lenci's (2008), Aussenac-Gilles et al. (2000, 2005, 2008), Ottens et al. (2007), and Cimiano (2006).

Lenci (2008) underlines that for linguists, ontology consists of the World, concepts representing the World and language expressing the concepts (see Figure 4.).

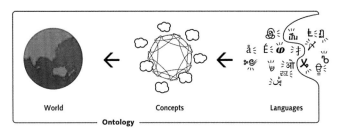

Figure 4. The ingredients of ontologies, adapted from Lenci (2008).

---

[20] Hanks differentiates between normal and exploitational use of a word, e.g., "It rains (rain)." vs. "It rains cats and dogs."

[21] Hanks (2004) and Hanks (2007) provide detailed description of CPA.

In contrast to philosophical ontology language which has a different role because linguists are interested in language-related conceptualizations.

The relation between language and ontology was nicely defined by Schalley and Zaefferer:

> "[…] to know a language means to have a special kind of ontological knowledge." Schalley and Zaefferer (2007:3-10).

Lenci (2008) underlines the importance of transition from implicit knowledge grounded in texts to explicit knowledge in structured contents such as ontologies. The gap between both can be bridged by natural language processing and statistical analysis. The NLP is used for identifying more abstract linguistic context, the statistical analysis is used for inducing and analyzing word co-occurrence patterns. The schematic use of these techniques is depicted in Figure 5. The neologism "ontolexical" learning denotes a merger of more or less standard lexical acquisition methodology applied to learning ontologies from language.

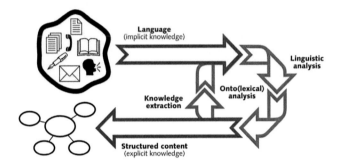

Figure 5. Onto(lexical) learning process, adapted from Lenci (2008).

In Aussenac et al. (1995) knowledge engineering is methodologically approached from a terminology perspective . The authors call the methodology *terminological processing*. The methodology is made up of four main steps: identifying terms, identifying semantic relations, identifying concepts "denominated by several terms" and identifying terms "denominating several concepts". This account assumes a strict dichotomy between lexicalization (terms) and meaning (concepts).

This dichotomy has become generally adopted in later methodologies. One example is the famous *ontology layer cake* methodology proposed by Buitelaar et al. (2005). The *ontology layer cake* methodology distinguishes between different ontological components. Namely terms, synonyms, concepts, taxonomy structure, relations, rules and axioms. See Figure 6.

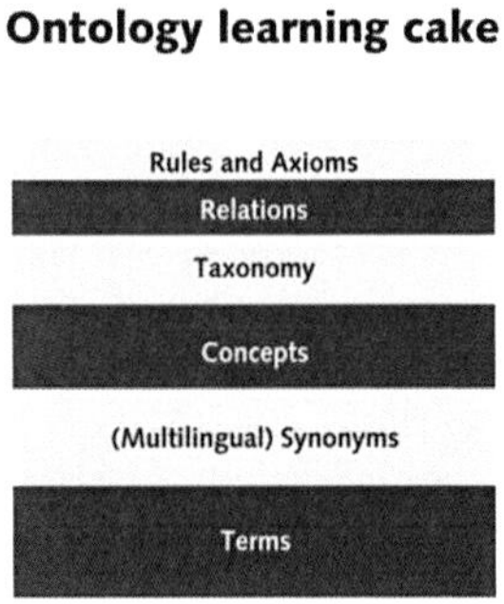

Ontology learning cake

Figure 6. Ontology Learning Layer Cake adapted from Buitelaar et al. (2005).

This thesis to a great extent follows the linguistic, bottom-up methodology for ontology building. Our approach is discussed in section 6.

2.3.4 An Attempt to Find the Best Practice

Hovy (2005) identifies five origins of methodologies: the *philosophers,* the *cognitive scientists,* the *linguists,* the *Artificial Intelligence reasoners,* which includes the *computational linguists,* and the *domain specialists.*

On the one hand the presented methodologies are similar in the way that they share some of the phases of methodologies:

- defining the purpose of the ontology, specifying who is going to use the ontology and what is the objective of the usage;
- collecting suitable knowledge resources such as thesauri, domain glossaries;
- using existing tools for ontology construction;
- selecting the criteria of ontologization;
- documenting the process.

On the other hand, they differ a lot in the purpose and the essence of ontologies to be built by using these methodologies. As described earlier the concept ontology has many interpretations in various research fields. The methodologies have likewise emerged from different research fields and therefore have inherited specific phases that are not common to other methodologies. For instance, formalization is commonly used in ontological engineering, but less familiar in linguistics, similarly, using existing glossaries makes sense in computational linguistics, but does not satisfy goals in philosophy.

As E. Hovy notes about different methodologies,

"it is tempting to consider these approaches as complementary; one could for example ask the philosophers to build the uppermost, most abstract, regions, the cognitive scientists to provide some overall ontology framework that the computationalists and domain specialists can then flesh out and refine, etc. " Hovy (2005: 6).

Although this idea seems to be quite natural, it is not that trivial in practice. We may illustrate the intricacy of this interdisciplinaryness by reference to an old Lithuanian fable about the collaboration of a bull, a swan and a cray-fish. Taken on their own these parties are unique and can perform their tasks perfectly, but once they are asked to move a wagon together, they fail because of doing it in their own specific way, i.e., flying, pulling, diving. In order to get something out of this collaboration, each group (philosophers, cognitive scientists, domain experts) need to learn about the other's approaches.

The presented ontology building methodologies have their own advantages and differ in content and scope. A question arises naturally if it is possible to integrate several of the methodologies for the purpose of an application. Such an attempt was presented by E. Hovy (2005) who proposed the methodology that can mediate between different research approaches of ontologies. The *Continual graduated refinement methodology* has 7 phases, several of them can be repeated iteratively:

1. Determining the domain, the purpose, the granularity level of the ontology to be built.
2. The reuse aspect: gathering related knowledge resources such as upper-ontologies, existing ontologies, thesauri, glossaries, tools, algorithms, etc.
3. Strictly defining the area of interest by identifying main concepts and their features. Existing upper-ontologies or taxonomies of domain can be helpful for this purpose.
4. Defining a list of terms or/and concepts.
5. Documenting the principles justifying the creation of concepts and relationships. Such as meronymy, synonymy, hypernymy-hyponymy, etc.
6. By iterating through phases 3-5, warranting the regularity of ontologization process and balance of the ontology, as well as documenting the arising issues alongside.
7. Defining the main parameters of the ontology in a unified way, so that it can later serve for evaluating the ontology.

The *Continual graduated refinement methodology* obeys the idea of the life-cycle of the ontology, as it encapsulates specification, development, evaluation and documentation phases. Additionally, it underlines the importance of expert supervision and iteration through the process in order to come up with the sound system of parameters for the ontologization. Finally it suggests using terminology and existing knowledge resources.

3. Natural Language, Natural Language Processing, and Ontology

" ...the meaning of a word is its use in the language" Wittgenstein (1953:43)
"text is a social exchange of meanings" Halliday and Hasan (1989)

We have presented different approaches to creating ontologies. Ontologies can be built: a) By human-experts – they are the most reliable knowledge source – this approach is exercised in different disciplines (Lenat (1995), Jimenez-Ruiz and Berlanga (2006), Dimitrova et al. (2008)) and is present in different methodologies (top-down approach). b) By employing computers and using other, alternative knowledge sources such as natural language (bottom-up approach), e.g. (Hahn and Schultz (2002), Maedche and Staab (2001), Shamsfard and Abdollahzadeh Barforoush (2003), Zhou (2007), Völker et al. (2008)), Hahn et al. (2002).

The question whether natural language is a source of knowledge, or is only data and something we only infer from that data, can be called knowledge. This is interfused through philosophy, psychology, and linguistics. Due to specificity of this work, we will mainly focus on aspects relative to linguistics. And the property of meaning being not a psychological phenomena but rather a social phenomena represented in text discourse. In this thesis we will advocate bottom-up approach for ontology building. Domain specific knowledge can be mined from domain specific discourse. As Teubert (2007) notes: "[...] it is only the discourse[22] that can be empirically analyzed". The domain specific discourse is a place where the meaning is present. According to Teubert, "There is no content unless it is represented" (Teubert (2007:67)).

Text resources such as technical reports, scientific papers, Wikipedia pages are depositories of specific domain knowledge[23]. This knowledge is collective knowledge as it is a result of collaboration and communication of many individuals.

---

[22] According to Teubert (2007), discourse is „the entirety of all the utterances of a discourse community" Teubert (2007:73).
[23] According to Oxford English Dictionary **knowledge** is: "1) expertise, and skills acquired by a person through experience or education; the theoretical or practical understanding of a subject, 2) what is known in a particular field or in total; facts and information or 3) awareness or familiarity gained by experience of a fact or situation." (OED 2nd edition (1989)).

Hence the concept *knowledge* has a clear reference to human expertise. Knowledge in the context of knowledge discovery – is a result of cognitive process of perception, learning and reasoning. Putnam H. (1975) differentiates between intentional and extensional[24] usage of concepts. He explains how understanding works extensionally on the basis of linguistic communication. Thus, *knowledge discovery from text* is a process of learning explicit and implicit knowledge from unstructured data (Girju (2006)).

Lately in Cimiano (2006) the paradigm of Reverse Engineering (RE)[25] was explained in the light of data mining, and adapted for ontology population from texts. The premise of RE for ontology population is that textual data is a representation of knowledge. In other words discourse is the source of knowledge. According to Teubert (2007), "[...] we experience only what is already conceptualized in the discourse" Teubert (2007:64). Ontological knowledge is transmitted into text by humans in the act of communication. Hence, it should be possible to decode the noise of communication channel and reconstruct, i.e., extract, the knowledge from text.

The purpose of this section is to overview the theoretical premises and assumptions grounding our standpoint that texts can be mined and specific knowledge items can be identified in texts (like terms and semantic relationships). Therefore natural language is an expedient source of knowledge for building domain ontologies.

3.1   Evidence of Knowledge in Text

The 20th century gave us two main perspectives on analyzing language and therefore meaning: generative transformation grammar introduced by Chomsky (1965) and usage-based, experience-based acquisition of conceptual representation (schemata) advocated by Lakoff (1987), Bybee (1985), Goldberg (2006), Langacker (1987), and others. We will not dwell on analyzing the dichotomy between rules (constraints) and their unconstrained usage in language, vs. dynamic schemata in this paper, but rather highlight the main viewpoints that can be applied practically in acquiring knowledge from texts.

The seed of linguistic structuralism was first introduced by Ferdinand de Saussure (1916). Later in 60s Chomsky (1965) presented the theory on deep structure and transformational grammar, which allowed the deconstruction of language in an innovative way. Presupposition that text is directly mapped on shallow structures related to deep structure allowed not only the interpretation of grammar, but also inspired new methods of approaching the meaning. The pioneer of generative semantics G. Lakoff (1968) included the idea of deep structure being the key of semantic interpretation. Ch. Fillmore's (1976) *frame semantics* assigned a few important

---

[24] Frege's (1892) distinction between sense and reference.
[25] According to ACM portal: http://www.acm.uiuc.edu/sigmil/RevEng/, "Reverse engineering [...] is simply the act of figuring out what software that you have no source code for does in a particular feature or function to the degree that you can either modify this code, or reproduce it in another independent work."

roles relating meaning to a word: a word specifies the frame from which meaning is viewed, and words highlight concepts.

Later together with corpus linguistics new approaches for tackling meaning emerged. Sinclair (1996) differentiates between "lexical unit" and "unit of meaning". Different to before, meaning is not confined to one word, but rather to it's context, i.e., to an extended or compound lexical item, and it is manifested in the regular patterns of its usage, i.e., meaning resides beyond the limits of lexical unit.

In next two sections we will discuss the meaning conveyed by words and by the context of words.

3.1.1 Lexical Semantics Evidence

Early understanding of the concept in linguistics was inseparable from the word. The modular approach to language analysis conveyed by generative linguists allowed the making use of different language analysis layers.

Pustejovsky, the pioneer of generative lexicon (GL) Pustejovsky (1991, 1995), argues that words denote concepts and things in the world. In 1991, he points to the fact of the typical semantic behavior of the syntactic category, such as for instance nouns behave like arguments, and verbs – like predicates. According to Pustejovsky, word's meaning is bound to deep structure and is related to the domain. Syntactic structures are coherent with semantic structures and they ground non-linguistics, conceptual interpretation of language (word).

> "The meaning of words should somehow reflect the deeper conceptual structures in the system and the domain it operates in. [...] semantics of the language should be the image of nonlinguistic conceptual organizing principles." (Pustejovsky (1995:410))

However it is important to note that those nonlinguistic conceptual organizing principles can be pinpointed only by observing the usage of the word in language, by analyzing texts.

The importance of syntactic categories is evident in the recent Wilks' (1996) research on homographs present in Longman Dictionary of Contemporary English (1978). Wilks proves that over 90% of homography can be disambiguated based only on POS markers.

More explicit association between the meaning and a word is grounded in Wierzbicka's (1972, 1989, 1996) and Goddard's (2002) theory of semantic priming. The theory of semantic priming reveals how some words explicitly express concepts. Authors distinguish two main features of semantic primes: *indefinability* and *universality*. Regarding the first, complex expressions can be paraphrased by using simpler ones. Such as

Example 5

```
"desire" -> "want".
```

However there is a set of linguistic expressions that can not be paraphrased in simpler terms. Consider for instance:

Example 6

> "part", "I", "You", "want", "feel"[26].

As for the argument of universality, Goddard (2001) shows how semantic primes embody lexical equivalents across languages. For instance:

Example 7

> "part", "dalis", "Teil"[27]

Given examples emphasize the meaning residing in the lexical unit. Hence NLP approaches are suitable for mining the knowledge from text for ontology building. To illustrate with a practical example we may cite Cimiano (2006):

> "In general, different syntactic categories are used to refer to different types of ontological entities. Proper nouns are, for example, typically used to refer to individuals. Verbs in general express beliefs, attitudes, events, actions, states or commands, whereas nouns can be regarded as referring to classes. Determiners are typically used to pick out a set of members of a certain class [...]" Cimiano (2006:35).

3.1.2 Contextual Semantic Evidence

In the previous section we showed evidence of meaning being accessible through lexical units. However meaning also resides in context. Contextual semantic evidence is popularly explained by a well-known slogan of corpus linguist J. Firth (1957): "You shall know a word by the company it keeps". The idea that the meaning of the word is in it's context comes from the studies of language use and is often found in the research field of corpus linguistics, but not necessarily here alone. A similar statement was made by a structural linguist Z.Harris (1970):

> "If we consider words or morphemes A and B to be more different in meaning than A and C, then we will often find that the [contextual] distributions of A and B are more different than the [contextual] distributions of A and C. In other words, difference in meaning correlates with difference of [contextual] distribution". (Harris and Hiz (1981:13))

That is to say, the context of the word reflects the meaning of the word, since in the contextual analysis the difference or the similarity to other words is highlighted. This argument can also be illustrated by idiomaticity principle (Sinclair (1991)). Some words are fully or partially delexicalised and therefore they share the same meaning with other words. When words have autonomous meaning their collocates reveal certain semantic aspects of that meaning.

Similarly the contextual aspect is very important in psycholinguistics: we learn the meaning of words by the way how they are used in language, we induce word's meaning from different examples of it's usage. As Miller and Charles (1991) marks,

> "[...] people learn how to use words by observing how words are used. And because words are used together in phrases and sentences, this starting assumption directs attention immediately to the importance of context". (Miller and Charles (1991:2)).

---

[26] Example taken from Wierzbicka (1989).
[27] i.e., in English, Lithuanian, German.

Moreover, Charles (2000) points to an important feature of generalization (or agregation) of the meaning due to the contextuality:

"[...] an abstraction of information is the set of natural linguistic contexts in which a word occurs". (Charles (2000:506)).

The meaning of the word in not an implicit set of contextual features, but rather a result of generalization of the contexts of the word's usage.

As a different case or an approach to contextual semantics, **statistical semantics** has to be mentioned. Statistical semantics is a relatively new study of how statistical patterns of word usage can be used to model the semantic knowledge. Turney (2006) explains the idea of this approach:

"Given a word pair X :Y with some unspecified semantic relations, can we mine a large text corpus for lexico-syntactic patterns that express the implicit relations between X and Y ?". (Turney (2006:313))

In other words, the premise is that if two words frequently appear within some pattern in a large corpus, then that pattern bears implicit relationship between those words.

Eventually the role of contextuality is of paramount importance in addressing the problem of word sense disambiguation (WSD) in NLP (Hirst (1987), Navigli (2009)). Consider senses of the word *sole* in the example:

Example 8

```
1. sole -- (the underside of footwear or a golf club)

2. sole, fillet of sole -- (lean flesh of any of several
flatfish)

3. sole -- (the underside of the foot)

4. sole -- (right-eyed flatfish; many are valued as food; most
common in warm seas especially European) 28
```

Obviously the meaning gains it's shape in the context of the sentence. For that reason, very often dictionaries like WordNet (Miller (1995), Fellbaum (1998)), or Rogets Thesaurus[29] are used for solving the WSD problem (Yarowsky (1992), Miller et al. (1993), Stevenson and Wilks (2001), Lapata and Brew (2004)). Nevertheless the usage of statistical information (Brown et al. (1991), Yarowsky (1995), Ng and Lee (1996), Riloff and Jones (1999), Pedersen (2000), Andreopoulos et al. (2008)) and corpus data distribution (Leacock et al. (1993), Dagan and Itai (1994), Diab (2000), Kaji (2003)) are equally significant.

3.2   Complexity of Knowledge Discovery from Text

"For a long time, the idea of using natural language processing tools to robustly analyze text from any domain and any genre was a fiction — it still is if you want a deep understanding of textual meaning." Daelemans and Reinberger (2004)

---

[28] WordNet 2.0 output.
[29] Can be accessed at: http://machaut.uchicago.edu/rogets

In the previous section, we have shown that text is the suitable source for mining knowledge and therefore building ontologies. However, the mining of knowledge is non-trivial, since knowledge resides in different layers of language. Namely: morphology, syntax, semantics, pragmatics and discourse. Girju (2008) accurately depicted the complexity of discovering knowledge from text – see Figure 7. Current state of the art of language analysis is semantics, i.e., this is a barrier level that computational linguistics faces today (Parseval/GEIG project (1991), Morpholympics (1994), SFCM (2009)[30], Parseval (2002), dependency parsers evaluated as a CoNLL task (2006, 2007), CIPS-ParsEval-2009, Senseval-1 (1998), Senseval-2 (2001), Senseval-3 (2004), SemEval (2007)).

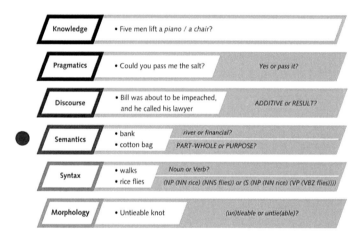

Figure 7. The complexity of discovering knowledge from text, adapted from Girju (2008).

Knowledge discovery from text is a complex task, due to **ambiguities in language**. For instance, consider examples:

Example 9

    a) The (name of the gene, or particle)

    b) Virus infection (computer science or medicine)

As we can observe from the Example 9, case (a) that already POS tagging faces ambiguities such as defining whether the word *The* is a name of the gene and therefore is a proper noun, or it is a particle. In the case (b), word *virus* semantically may refer to for instance medical domain, as *virus infection*, *viral infection*, and also it is an accepted term in within computer science – *virus infection*, *computer virus*. By incorporating information from upper layers of

---

[30] Workshop on systems and frameworks for computational morphology.

language analysis, we can normally solve language ambiguities. However, we ideally, need, to be able to process within all the layers of language analysis. Computational modeling and analysis of languages is facing difficulties with ellipsis, anaphora, metaphor, ambiguities in pragmatic and discourse levels, idioms, polysemy, etc. As Sinclair (1991) noted, it will take quite some time before computers can identify discourse functions and it's coherence.

State-of-art computational linguistics reveals the standpoint in the field of knowledge acquisition: symbolic appearance relates to meaning. The **distinction between word and meaning** was firstly illustrated in Frege's (1892) example of *morning star* and *evening star* in fact referring to the planet Venus. Later Ogden and Richards (1923)[31] revealed this observation schematically in the word-meaning triangle: symbol -> referent -> thought of reference. Dichotomy between the word (symbol) and the referent was treated as misuse of the language.

In 2007, Hanks to some extent reactivates the idea in the context of empirical Corpus Pattern Analysis (CPA) and talks about "normal" and **"abnormal" usage of language**. According to his observation, people exploit language forms not only to say new things, but also to say things in a new, unconventional way. Therefore exploitations like metaphor, ellipsis, word creation, figures of speech, etc. occur. The assumption is illustrated with verb *abate*:

```
abate/V BNC frequency: 185 in 100m.³²
```

Example 10

     1. `[[Storm]] abate [NO OBJ](11%)`

     2. `[[Flood]] abate [NO OBJ](4%)`

     3. `[[Problem | Emotion]] abate [NO OBJ] (64%)`

     4. `[[Person | Action]] abate [[Nuisance]] (19%) (Domain: Law)`

The prototypical meanings like the ones related to storm and flood are so-called *norms*, whereas in the cases like emotion and action the usage becomes *exploitations*. The interpretation of *exploitations* is possible with the help of an analogy with prototypical usage.

Yet another complication is that word **meaning is fuzzy and vague**. It can be captured only in context, since text provides an overall meaning. However even if context is able to minimize vagueness, too much precision acts contrary. As explained by Wierzbicka (1985):

> "An adequate definition of a vague concept must aim not at precision but at vagueness; it must aim at precisely that level of vagueness which characterizes the concept itself." (Wierzbicka (1985:12)).

Finally even knowing that meaning when determined by context, we cannot **clearly delineate what context**[33] **is**, or distinguish context from noise (Hanks 2007).

Nevertheless, acquiring knowledge from text with the current advances in NLP can still be very helpful for the task of building an ontology. Since it can catalyze the ontology building process through providing with specific building segments, such as for instance terms which are

---

[31] For more details see section 4.2.

[32] Example source: Hanks (2007), course slides 3:6

[33] In principal context can be classified: context of situation and linguistic context. The latter one can be divided into minimal/close context and context of paragraph and text. However for the computational purposes, it is not clear which type of context should be used, which type of context is mostly informative.

important for conceptualization, or semantic relationships – for defining ontological relationships. In sections 4 and 5 we will discuss methodological premises of ontology building and evaluation. In the following two subsections we will concentrate on challenges raised by major building blocks of ontology: multi-word units, which constitute the significant amount of domain terminology, and extraction of semantic relationships.

3.2.1 Multi-word Units in Domain Texts

Domain terms are a valuable source for defyning concepts of domain ontology. Multi-word units (MVUs) embody significant amount of domain specific terminology. It is already hard to draw conceptualizations from single word terms of the domain. Therefore complex lexical structures like MVUs cause more difficulties for conceptualization. The reason for that partly lays in MVUs' that include metaphoric expressions. Consider for instance example:

Example 11

```
Self-healing system
Fault-tolerant system
Gene expression
Lymph node
```

Traditionally the way to identify the meaning of a word had two directions: examining schemata (e.g., Lakoff (1968)) or performing deep structure analysis (e.g., Chomsky (1965)). More recently, S. Richardt (2004) proposed an interpretation of a word's meaning based on overlapping schemata and showed that domain specific language in an expert-to-expert communication shows a strong tendency towards metaphorisation:

"[...] expressions from everyday language which have been taken over to enlarge the scientific vocabulary, to denote newly invented or discovered phenomena, to fill lexical gaps. [...] familiar source domains are mapped onto target domains [...]" (S. Richardt (2004:249)).

The constituents of MVUs, in 11 Example, can be mapped on familiar source domains via the meaning of words *healing, tolerant, expression, node*. It seems that in this way non-experts get a clue of how to interpret given lexical expressions. However, from the psycholinguistic perspective, within a certain discourse, concepts are activated partly and therefore differently.[34] In domain specific texts, especially scientific articles, discourse conveys scientific knowledge. As Graefen (1997:100) points out: "scientific article is a medium of scientific knowledge". Which means that in the expert-to-expert communication, or in scientific text for that matter, discourse is influencing (or activating) the specific, domain dependent meaning. That correlates

---

[34] In 1987, Langacker explains *reference point* related variations, which are dependent on a part of concept which is activated.

with Putnam's (1975:62) argument that extension (or meaning) of expression "depends on the nature of the things", which is accessible to experts, but not to lay persons.

What differentiates scientific (or domain specific) metaphorization from non-scientific is the multitude of uses in different communicative settings (Zelinsky-Wibbelt (2000), Richardt (2004)). In other words, the deviation from convention to creativity shows that the metaphor is irrelevant and scientifically inaccurate.

3.2.2 Challenges Posed by Semantic Relationships

Semantic relationships is yet another resource of conceptual modeling. Guarino and Welty (2000) notes that properly structured taxonomies are essential in conceptual models for a few reasons: they bring order to elements, convey views (or interpretations), are critical for tasks like reuse and integration of ontologies. Guarino and Welty (2000) talks about expert established taxonomies, and warns that "improperly structured taxonomies have the opposite effect."

The debate whether mining of semantic relationships is useful for an ontology building task, reaches the disjucture of different perspectives named in section 2. However, extraction of semantic relations already proved useful in a number of knowledge intensive projects like: ACE (Automatic Content Extraction)[35], DARPA EELD (Evidence Extraction and Link Discovery)[36], ARDA-AQUAINT (Question Answering for Intelligence)[37], and Global WordNet[38]. Girju (2003) showed how linguistic processing of semantic relations can be helpful in knowledge acquisition, and establishing taxonomic structures. See Figure 8.

Q : What does the Apache helicopter consist of?

A : AH-64A Apache helicopter
    Hellfire air to surface missile
      millimeter wave seaker
    70mm Folding Fin Aerial rocket
    30mm Cannon camera
    armaments
    General Electric 1700-GE engine
    4-rail launchers
    four-bladed main rotor
    anti-tank laser guided missile
    Longbow millimetre wave fire control radar
      integrated radar frequency inferferometer
    rotating turret
    tandem cockpit
      Kevlar seats

Figure 8. An example of application of semantic relationships, adapted from Girju et al. (2008).

---

[35] http:/ /www.itl.nist.gov/ iad/894.01/ tests/ace/, and http://projects.ldc.upenn.edu/ace/tools/

[36] http:/ /w2.eff.org/Privacy/TIA/eeld.php

[37] http://www.informedia.cs.cmu.edu/aquaint/index.html

[38] http://www.globalwordnet.org/

What are the premises of discovering relationship from domain texts? According to Lenci (2008), "Semantic knowledge is grounded on conceptual representations depending on salient features of the world". For example, one type of such knowledge is semantic similarity. Perceiving similarity between two entities depends on what common features those entities share: color, shape, size, function, parts, locations, etc. This information can be implicitly encoded in linguistic structures.

What we are interested in is computer-accessible salient features of words in natural language. To name some sources of reference to such information we are looking at lexical, structural and contextual semantic processing of NL.

Nevertheless automatic discovering of semantic relationships is difficult for many reasons:

a) Semantic relationships are implicit and context dependent.

b) The acquisition of semantic relationships is knowledge intensive task. For example analysis of given phrases is not possible without knowing that *WT* and *DB* are proper names:

Example 12

```
WT patients

DB management system
```

c) Semantic relationships are encoded in various lexico-syntactic levels:

Example 13

```
Syntax          Booth assassinated Lincoln.
                Lincoln was assassinated by Booth.
                The assassination of Lincoln by Booth.
                Booth went through with the assassination of Lincoln.
Semantics       Booth assassinated Lincoln.
                Booth murdered Lincoln.
                Booth fatally shot Lincoln.[39]
```

d) Compounding process.

e) The interpretation of relationships is hard. In fact there can be many semantic relationships between the constituents of a noun pair.

f) Finally – there is no finite list of semantic relationships (e.g., Pustejovsky et al. (2003), Lauer (1995), Moldovan et al. (2004), Schalley (2004)).

3.3 Critics of Ontology Learning

"Ontology is hard. Life is short. Let's do conceptual modeling instead." B. Smith (2009)[40]

Automated ontology learning procedures, when domain texts are analyzed and terminology and semantic relationship information is provided to experts, is time saving and helpful in ontology building. Nevertheless, having in mind the current state-of-art NLP technologies, it is

---

[39] Example adapted from Girju (2008).
[40] About computational approaches for building an ontology.

unrealistic and unwanted to entirely rely on the idea of automatic ontology learning. Expert knowledge and decisions should be the central factor in the process of ontology building.

Recently B. Smith (2009) expressed critique towards automatic the idea of ontology learning. His examples of how facts often found in texts can be irrelevant to ontology building knowledge are as follows:

Example 14

    a) *Swimming* is healthy.

    Swimming has eight letters.

    b) *8* is the square root of 64.

    8 is the output on X measuring device.

We have to admit, that these examples could be harmful in domain ontology construction if two criteria are met:

1) semantic relationship patterns like:

X is Y,

X has Y

would be applied without analyzing syntactic features, i.e., *noun is adverb* can not be interpreted as an ontological *is-a* structure.

2) scientific and common-sense knowledge is mixed, i.e., common-sense, domain irrelevant sentences would occur in scientific domain corpus. However, discourse featured within one domain is usually coherent. In other words, if we analyze scientific publication from the domain of Public health, theoretically, the first sentence given in example (a) is likely to appear, but not the second sentence. Even if there is such a possibility. Firstly, words wouldn't gain distributional weight since they occur very rarely and secondly, the multitude of uses of term *swimming* would indicate vagueness and irrelevance to domain knowledge.

Here we have to underline a necessary condition of text quality and relevance to the domain. Graefen (1997) points out that scientific article is a medium of scientific knowledge. Scientific articles undergo peer-reviewing of domain experts and editing of journal proceedings. The purpose of this type of communication is expert-to-expert transferred knowledge. Therefore the message is direct and relevant to the domain. As Richardt (2004) remarks, experts of the respective domain, such as scientists, engineers, do reflect scientific knowledge which is accurate and consistent and therefore appropriate, whereas common-sense models considering domains are wrong and incomplete. We will discuss the importance of expert chosen domain representing corpus in section 4.1 further.

A good quality domain corpus does not eliminate the danger coming from language "representation" interface. The danger lays in knowledge representation through language, as Budin (1996) pinpoints, scientific communication besides it's scientific knowledge, is also made up of pre-scientific knowledge and everyday experience. Therefore there is no such thing as pure scientific communication (in text), since everyday experience is inevitable.

Richardt (2004) in her study on metaphorisation was investigating economic expert model and economic common sense models, and has observed an overlapping of these models to a "considerable degree".

Similarly Guarino (2008) warns about ontologies developed in a bottom-up way:

> "Computational ontologies, in the way they evolved, unavoidably mix together philosophical, cognitive, and linguistic aspects." Guarino (2008)

These facts underline the necessity of proper, usage-based linguistic analysis which, as dicussed in section 3.2.1, can be useful in discriminating between scientific and common-sense knowledge.

Yet another direction of critique includes bottom-up development and overall usability of ontology.

Regarding methodology, Guarino (2008) argues for "no ontology without ontological analysis". His statement is exemplified in Figure 9.

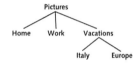

Figure 9. An example of the result of automatic knowledge classification, adapted from Guarino (2008).

Guarino (2008) highlights the importance of ontological structure and contrasts it with the classifications based on only a pre-determined criteria like syntactic features. Naturally the meaning of term together with structure of domain should be the guiding criterion.

B.Smith (2009) has introduced the principle of orthogonality, which excludes the standard *ontological engineering* methodologies and practice oriented ontologies and includes expert governed methodologies and *scientific ontologies*[41] by introducing requirements like:

- Unified way of using terminology and classification of domain objects;
- The same terms cannot mean different things in different information systems;
- Different terms cannot mean the same thing;
- Different systems have to be adjusted and possibly integrated within upper ontologies.

To a great extent, we agree with the arguments mentioned above, especially with the necessity of expert's contribution in ontology building. However, we cannot deny the existence of a different, application-based paradigm of ontologies, i.e., semantic web, a great number of information systems, and applications. In the case of these applications, the aims of computational ontologies are quite different from the aims of philosophical ontologies.

---

[41] i.e, ontologies of science, necessary created by experts, top-down approach.

Nevertheless varied perspectives do not diminish the role of NLP in providing experts with relevant knowledge that can be used in the building, evaluation and maintaining of ontologies. A few among the numerous language processing examples speak for themselves such are Mitkow (2002), Porzel and Gurevych (2003) - anaphora resolution, Girju et al. (2004) - semantic role labeling, Guo and Diab (2009) - word sense disambiguation, Finkel et al. (2008), Ng (2009) - coreference resolution, etc.

4. NLP-based Segments of Methodology for Ontology Learning

Chomsky: The verb perform cannot be used with mass word objects: one can perform a task but one cannot perform labor.
Hatcher: How do you know, if you don't use a corpus and have not studied the verb perform?
Chomsky: How do I know? Because I am a native speaker of the English language.
Harris (1993)

"Technology tamed knowledge in text because in text the experiential data (i.e., speech) is converted to symbols by humans."
Ramesh Jain (2008)

In 2005 Buitelaar et al. delineated the contours of the NLP-based methodology of ontology learning:

"Ontology development is primarily concerned with the definition of concepts and relations between them, but connected to this also knowledge about the symbols that are used to refer to them." (Buitelaar et al. (2005:4)).

This methodology is known as *ontology learning layer cake* (Figure 6. Ontology Learning Layer Cake adapted from Buitelaar et al. (2005).)[42] and represents an array of tasks for building ontologies from the perspective of NLP. Term extraction, hierarchical relation extraction, synonyms, rules and axioms – these are the phases of populating an ontology. Layers are presented according to the granularity of information complexity, starting with terms and finishing with axioms and rules. Technically NLP can assist the ontology learning process through all the layers, however not at the same performance level. The study of lower layers of the ontology 'learning cake' approach is methodologically better established compared to its higher levels, and is therefore more reliable. Normally in bottom-up NLP-based approaches of ontology learning three main stages are discussed: term extraction, synonymy detection and hypernym-hyponym detection (Hjelm (2009)).

As presented previously in section 2, domain ontologies are types of ontologies that address a specific part of reality, i.e., a domain. Domain ontologies are usable, sharable, extendable and applicable to domain applications. Sound methodology is necessary to keep domain ontologies satisfying these criteria.

---

[42] See section 2.3.3.

The thesis holds that domain ontology is a model of domain knowledge that is usable (suitable) for the application it is created for.

Ontology building is seen as a collaborative effort between computational linguists, domain experts and ontologists. Well chosen corpora and reliable NLP tools are the cornerstones of the proposed methodology (see Figure 10.).

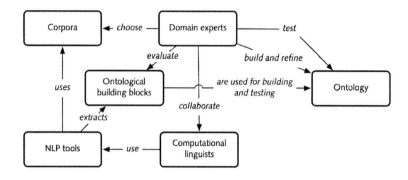

Figure 10. The schematic view of NLP-based ontology building.

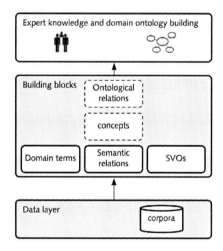

Figure 11. Architectural view of NLP-based ontology building.

This section investigates the role of NLP in building domain ontologies. Therefore the main parts of the processing sequence will be discussed. They are 1) defining domain corpus and 2) acquiring ontology building blocks: terms, hierarchical and non-hierarchical relations, SVO triplets (see Figure 11.).

4.1 Domain Corpora

The corpus of the domain is the data source from which the knowledge of the domain can be mined. Experts of the domain define the coarse features of the corpus, such as its size, the topics to be represented and the genres to be included. Moreover, the fine-grained features can be defined, for example, the choice of texts that make up the corpus of the domain. Later in ontology building process, the corpus can be used for learning word frequencies, context, occurrence patterns and to generalize this information in order to define domain concepts and relationships between them.

4.1.1 Role of a Corpus

Since the 1950s corpus-based methodologies have been established in quite a few fields of linguistics, such as language acquisition (Brown (1973), Bloom et al. (1974)), comparative linguistics (Eaton (1940), Oakes (1998))), syntax (Fries (1952), semantics (Lorge (1949)), lexicography (Lafon (1984), Church and Hanks (1989), Calzolari and Zampolli (1990), Church et al. (1991), Daille et al. (1994)), etc.

Despite the fact that corpora is being widely applied and used, there are no strict rules that define a corpus intended for language research that separate it from a collection of machine-readable texts. A corpus is seen as an electronic collection of texts, which is necessarily machine readable, the bigger – the better, and is made up of the texts that are of interest to a given research area. Lately McEnery and Wilson (2005: 29) have given a more fundamental definition of a corpus by emphasizing four main properties of a corpus:

- **Sampling and representativeness** – it is an entirely task-dependent property of a corpus. It can be supported by calculating statistical values such as, dispersion, frequency counts and ratio for each token. As Manning and Schütze noted "a sample is representative if what we find for the sample also holds for the general population." (Manning and Schütze (1999:119)). Sampling and representativeness is a task-dependent property of a corpus, therefore it is sufficient to sample topics of interest instead of considering each token in the corpus.

- **Finite state** refers to the final size of the corpus, for instance it can be one million running words, as in the Brown corpus[43], or 100 million, as in the BNC[44].

---

[43] The Brown corpus, http://icame.uib.no/brown/bcm.html

-   **Machine-readable form** – this refers to electronic texts.
-   **A standard reference** – the corpus is available to other researchers.

Representativeness as a feature of a corpus includes the property of *balance*. According to Manning and Schütze, a balanced corpus should be such that

> "[…] put together as to give each subtype of text a share of the corpus that is proportional to some predetermined criterion of importance" (Manning and Schütze (1999:120)).

Equally important is the size of a corpus:

> "[…] having more training data is normally more useful than any concerns of balance, and one should simply use all the text that is available" (Manning and Schütze (1999:120)).

In the task of ontology learning, the property of a fixed *finite state* needs to be modified. It should obey the requirement for minimum size, but at the same time should allow the corpus to be dynamically extended in order to be updated with new data.

When it comes to an application of IE, and construction of domain corpus, the above properties are necessary. In essence, a corpus of the domain should be machine readable, representative of the domain, be of sufficient size, and available for reuse.

The corpus of a domain is an arbitrary collection of unstructured language texts that are topically relevant to the domain. The proportions of text on different topics are balanced, i.e., all relevant topics are represented by about the same quantity of textual data. Corpus of the domain to some extent reflects the knowledge of the domain, as it is a collaborative input of domain experts (Graefen (1997)).

A domain corpus enables the tracking of the usage of words by their frequency and context. It also supports the process of term extraction, domain concept definition, and semantic relationship detection.

It is necessary to observe that the corpus-based approach, or the usage-based approach to language analysis is closely related to the *empiricism*[45] *paradigm* and excludes introspection of *rationalism*. It is out of the scope of this work to discuss the distinction between these foundations of linguistics.

4.1.1.1 Defining the Domain Corpus

The starting point for the information extraction task is the choice of a corpus of the domain. A corpus can contain any domain specific texts, such as scientific publications, project reports, books and manuscripts. There are several important properties that a domain corpus should have. First, we emphasise the **qualitative** property of a domain corpus. In order to safeguard against acquiring domain-irrelative data, domain-topical texts have to be used. Such data are peer-reviewed scientific articles, books and technical reports from the domain. Texts selected

---

[44] The British National Corpus, http://www.natcorp.ox.ac.uk/

[45] In section 3.1 we gave an account of usage-based evidence of knowledge that can be found in language.

by domain experts ensure that they belong to the domain register, and also ensure representativeness with respect to the diversity of the data.

Second, the **quantitative** property of domain corpus has to be taken into account. The most important feature of a corpus is that it has to be sufficient for the intended task. To perform statistical calculations, a reasonable quantity of texts is necessary. The rule of thumb is "the more the better". However, the size of around one million tokens in a corpus has proven to be sufficient in other areas of research: collocation extraction (Kjellmer (1994), Frantzi and Ananiadou (1999)), word sense identification (Gale et al. (1992), Wu and Palmer (1994), Agirre and Rigau (1996)), semantic role labelling (Gildea and Jurafsky (2002)), and knowledge acquisition (Schubert and Tong (2003)).

In section 7 the experiments on two research areas: computer dependability and cancer research is discussed. In both cases, domain corpora were built from conference articles of the respective domains. The procedure of article selection was created by experts of the domain, which was mainly formed by the following questions:

- What is the area we want to model?
- What are the main topics of the area?
- Which texts represent the main topics of the area?
- What genres of text should be chosen? Scientific articles, technical documentation, instructions, manuals, books, etc.
- How many texts are available for each of the topics in the area?

4.2 Term Extraction

The idea of extracting domain terminology from corpus was first introduced 20 years ago by Ahmad (1995), Pearson (1998), Sager (1981), Meyer (2001). A corpus as the resource transmitting the domain knowledge, played a central role. Word usage became the most important aspect of defining whether a word is a term. This corpus linguistics driven assumption that the form encodes the meaning, allowed automatic term acquisition methodologies to develop (Salton and Buckley (1988), Church and Hanks (1989), Daille et al. (1994), Mima et al. (2001), Bourigault (1992), Pantel and Lin (2001), Paulo et al. (2002), Park et al. (2002)).

Assuming that word usage is the most important aspect of a word being a term, naturally we aim to find interesting regularities in texts. These regularities are the type of information that can be acquired from the surface of textual data. In practice, we look for interesting points in a text such as word frequency and length, or some constraints such as part of speech. The term extraction is dependent on the level of the granularity of language analysis, i.e., morphological, syntactical or semantic.

Term extraction is also possible due to redundancy in the data. For example the stable or invariant occurrence of two (or more) words in a certain pattern points to a candidate term.

Statistical frequency can also be a reliable factor for weighting the candidate terms. Naturally, to identify these regular occurrences a sufficient quantity of data is required (Biber (1990, 1993)).

Nevertheless, term acquisition is not a trivial task due to the complexity of text analysis. The analysis can be carried out at different levels: word level, sentence level, document level, document collection level, etc.

Moreover, the extraction of invariant occurrences is not the final goal, but just an intermediate step. Through the symbolic appearance of a word we try to capture the object it represents, i.e., the meaning. As originally presented by Ogden and Richards (1923), the model of *semiotic triangle* (see Figure 12.) explains how symbols (linguistic) are related to the objects they represent. The symbolic appearance of word *serbentas* (en. a currant) **A** stands for the referent **C**, symbolic appearance invokes the concept **B**, concept **B** relates to the referent **C**, and referent **C** is an object.

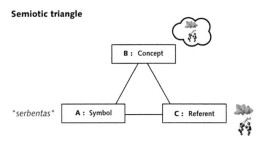

Figure 12. Semiotic triangle.

The concept of *semiotic triangle* is especially important for *ontology learning*, i.e., to cite Cimiano:

> "Ontology learning from text thus deals with uninterpreted symbols or signs for which the appropriate sense needs to be identified as some sort of reverse engineering, i.e. contrary to the direction by which these symbols are produced." (Cimiano (2006:57)).

It is important to observe the difference between a term and an ontological concept. A term ad hoc is not an ontological concept (Buitelaar et al. (2005), Daille (2003)). From the perspective of knowledge acquisition, the terms found in domain corpus are used to abstract domain concepts and relations. To underline this difference, several authors Maedche (2002), Gilles and Soergel (2005), Reymonet et al. (2007) talk about physical binding of terms to ontology in order to label the concepts of an ontology. Equivalently there is a W3C[46] OWL[47] standard, called *rdf label*[48]. According to Roche et al. (2009):

---

[46] W3C, World Wide Web Consortium, http://www.w3.org/

[47] OWL, Web Ontology language, http://www.w3.org/standards/techs/owl#w3c_all

[48] `rdfs:label` is an instance of a class that may be used to provide a human-readable version of class name.

"[…] in terminology (especially for technical domains), terms i.e. the "verbal definition of a concept" [ISO 1087[49]] need to be separated from concept names since they belong to two different semiotic systems. The first is a linguistic system while the second is conceptual." Roche et al. (2009:1-2).

Roche points to the dichotomy between the theory and the practice of terminology: "[…] the main goal of terminology is not to represent concepts in order to manipulate them (as in artificial intelligence) but to define a common vocabulary we hope is consensual." Roche et al. (2009:2). They see terms as linguistic explanations at most. This necessitates some kind of an intermediate layer. As a solution, Roche et al. (2009) have introduced the neologism *ontoterminology*,

"[…] term definitions written in natural language need to be separated from concept definitions written in a formal language. The former are viewed as linguistic explanations while the latter are considered logical specifications of concept. […] a new kind of terminology called *ontoterminology* (since the meaning of terms relies on a formal ontology) brings these two non-isomorphic systems together into a coherent, global one." (Roche et al. (2009:2)).

A term as a linguistic expression definitely helps to conceptualize, i.e., to describe ontological concepts. This is where the meaning of a term (concept in linguistics) and a concept (an ingredient of ontology) are related.

The common practice to define concepts includes acquiring domain terminology and defining semantic relationships such as synonymy, meronymy, hypernymy-hyponymy. All this information provided to domain experts is of paramount importance in the process of conceptualization. Hjelms (2009) refers to terms as building blocks of ontology. Terms are the transitional phase between textual data and conceptual knowledge.

Additionally domain terminology acquired from domain corpus that reflects the consensus knowledge of the group of experts, represents overall description of the domain. This was first noticed by Gilles et al. (1995), who pointed out major qualitative differences between terminology and the result of the process of knowledge acquisition:

"In a usual situation of knowledge acquisition, a domain model is built according to the **type of problem-solving procedures to be implemented**. The corpus of textual documents is a source of information, in which knowledge engineers draw pieces of knowledge in order to abstract domain concepts and relations, and, in a complementary way, **to identify the domain items playing the roles expected by the problem solving method**." (Gilles et al. (1995:4)).

In other words, because of the a priori binding to a particular problem-solving model, knowledge acquisition can result in incomplete, partial knowledge models. Contrary to this, extracted terminology can provide an overview of the domain, as it is not bound to one particular perspective, but rather reflects steady and uniform domain knowledge:

"In a usual situation of terminological analysis, terminologists are not guided by a specific application. For them, the textual corpus is not merely a source of information, it must be considered as a reference: the terminologists must remain as faithful as possible to a reference corpus, reflecting the consensus knowledge of a group of specialists. Terminologist building a TKB[50] will aim at developing a static description of the domain, regardless of any expert's problem-solving knowledge. " (Gilles et al. (1995:4)).

---

[49] ISO 1087-1:2000. Terminology work-Vocabulary-Part1: Theory and application. International Organization for Standardization.
[50] TKB, i.e., refers to terminological knowledge base.

Later we will return to this property of domain terminology in section 6.6.1 when describing activity and results of ontology evaluation.

4.2.1 Procedure of Term Extraction

Term extraction became a standard task of Information Extraction (IE), which is a technique used for locating and extracting specific pieces of information from texts (Appelt and Israel (1999)). There are two different approaches of how to build IE systems: knowledge engineering and machine learning.

The knowledge engineering approach is conceptually easy to design and implement. Systems which are handcrafted have the best performance (Cabre et al. (2001)), however building such a system takes months of human labor and requires linguistic and domain expertise.

Therefore the appeal of the machine learning (Mitchell (1997)) approach is that grammars do not need to be constructed by humans and thus require less "hand work". Such systems are less domain dependent. Expert annotated corpora can be used not only for training a system but for its evaluation procedure as well (Appelt and Israel (1999)).

Terminology extraction systems exist for the most widely used languages. The performance of rule based systems is rather high, often reaching precision > 95% and recall > 90% (Grishman and Sundheim (1996), MUC-7(1997)). Machine learning based systems perform almost as well, with an outstanding result between 98.5-100% recall and a precision of 95-98% achieved with NPtool[51] (Arppe (1995)).

IE systems share about the same methodological framework. It is typically a pipeline comprising tokenization, morphological and lexical processing, syntactic analysis and domain analysis (see Figure 13., part b). Tokenization, morphological and syntactic analysis form the language processing block, whereas domain analysis includes term definition, filtering and weighting of terms.

Similarly, in the field of terminology extraction, the architecture of a term acquisition system is a pipeline, where NLP tools and language resources (word lists, grammar rules, etc.) help to identify term candidates (see Figure 13., part a). As presented by Zielinski (2002):

> "Automatic term extraction is a procedure, during which a set of words and phrases (output) are filtered out from domain corpus (input) with the help of computer. Each word and phrase represents term candidate."[52] (Zielinski (2002), and Zielinski (2007) lecture material).

---

[51] NPtool: http://www2.lingsoft.fi/doc/nptool/term-extraction.html, applied domain: cosmology.

[52] Translated by author. Original text: „Automatische Termextraktion ist ein Vorgang, bei dem mit Hilfe eines Computers aus einem fachsprachlichen Textkorpus (*Input*) eine Menge von Wörtern und Phrasen (*Output*) herausgefiltert wird, von denen jede/s einzelne einen möglichen Terminus (Termkandidaten) darstellt".

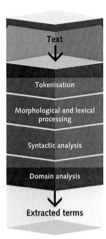

Figure 13. Term extraction process adapted from Haller (2006) (a) and general IE process schema adapted from Appelt and Israel (1999) (b).

4.2.2 Theoretical Background of Term Extraction

In this section theoretical aspects of term extraction (TE) are discussed. Information about terms can be obtained via the linguistic term model, or via statistics of word usage in text. The linguistic term model passes through several layers of analysis: morphology, syntax, and semantics. From the statistics perspective, terms can be recognized by how frequently they appear and in what context they are found.

4.2.2.1 Linguistic Term Model

The **morphological** model of terms is defined by information such as: derivation, POS tag, case, lemma, tense, form, etc. Terms can be represented by different POS: noun, e.g., "hacker", verb, e.g., "enter", adjective, e.g., "false". Automatic term acquisition includes tokenization and POS-tagging or morphological analysis (Frantzi and Ananiadou (1999), Bourigault (1992), Pantel and Lin (2001)). The morphological model of terms is necessary for resolving compounds in cases like, "ultrasound", "download", (see Example 15). Examples of morphological analysis of these words are:
Example 15

```
"<download>"

    "download" <SVO> V PRES -SG3 VFIN @+FMAINV

    "download" <SVO> V INF

    "download" <SVO> V IMP VFIN @+FMAINV

    "download" <SVO> V SUBJUNCTIVE VFIN @+FMAINV


"<hackers>"

    "hacker" <DER:er> N NOM PL


"<entered>"

    "enter" <SVO> <SV> <P/in> <P/for> V PAST VFIN @+FMAINV

    "enter" <SVO> <SV> <P/in> <P/for> PCP2 [53]
```

Examples of compound analysis[54]:

Example 16

{ori=**download**,nb=**sg**,case=**acc;nom**,s=**state**,ds=**down$load**,ss=state,ls=down$load, c=**noun**,w=1,ew=0,lu=download,ts=download,t=download,mlu=**download**}

{ori=**ultrasound**,nb=**sg**,case=**acc;nom**,s=**phen**,ds=**ultra$sound**,ss=phen,ls=ultra$so und,c=**noun**,w=1,ew=0,lu=ultrasound,ts=ultrasound,t=ultrasound,mlu=**ultrasound**}

{ori=**email**,nb=**sg**,case=**acc;nom**,s=**text**,ss=text,ds=**e-mail**,ls=e-mail,w=1,cs=n,c=**noun**,ew=0,lu=e-mail,ts=e-mail,t=e-mail,mlu=**e-mail**}

Extraction of multi-word units (MWUs), as discussed by Bourigault (1992), Mima et al. (2002), Dias (2003) relies on the **syntactic** model of terms that describes patterns like noun phrases (NPs) or prepositional phrases (PPs). For instance, some the most frequently implemented syntactic rules included in TE systems are:

Example 17

```
NP=Adj. + N (mammar carzinoma)
mammar - mammar - premodifier, adjective, noun phrase begins
carzinoma - carzinoma - nominal head, noun, noun phrase ends

NP = N + N (bit rate)
bit - bit - premodifier, noun, noun phrase begins
rate - rate - nominal head, noun, noun phrase ends [55]
```

---

[53] Output from http://www.lingsoft.fi/ demo.
[54] Output from MPRO (Maas et al. (2009)) demo, tags are explained in Appendix B3.
[55] Example processed with Connexor software demonstrates phrase analysis output. Demo available at http://www.connexor.eu/technology/machinese/demo/tagger/

Other frequently found types of syntactic patterns include N+N+N, Adj+N+N, Adj+Adj+N, V+N, etc.

The TE process can additionally benefit from **semantic** information. Maynard and Ananiadou (1999) describe the TE approach that incorporates syntactic and semantic information (the latter one was acquired from UMLS[56] meta-thesaurus) in order to calculate the importance of context to the terms and in this way to determine similarities.

An example of semantic information that can be used in term candidate acquisition is:

Example 18

```
Alcohol      s=material, edible
Transition   s=process
User         s=agent
Committee    s=collection
Isopropyl    s=material[57]
{ori=pass,nb=sg,case=acc;nom,s=loc&way,ss=loc&way,ds=pass,ls=pass
,w=1,cs=n,c=noun,ew=0,lu=pass,ts=pass,t=pass,mlu=pass}[58]
```

Semantic information like the semantic class of a word is useful in determining relationships between terms, i.e., synonyms, hypernyms, meronyms, hyponyms (Maynard et al. (2001), Piao et al. (2003)). See section 6.3.1 for more discussion on this topic.

4.2.2.2 Statistical Term Model

Statistical information can give important clues when detecting terms. First, there are general observations such as that texts have a predictable amount of vocabulary, i.e., Heaps' law, and that some words tend to occur more frequently than others, i.e., Zipf's law. Second, there are more complex observations such as Debowski (2009) who has shown that the number of frequently repeated phrases is not less than the number of facts presented in a text.

Heaps' (1) law (Heaps (1978) explains the relationship between the size of a vocabulary M and the size of a document collection T, where k and b are free parameters determined empirically.

$$M = kT^b \qquad (1)$$

According to Heaps, the most probable relationship between vocabulary size and document collection size is presentable in the log-log space. As an example (the distribution is depicted in Figure 14., part a., the vocabulary size M of the Reuters document collection (Reuters-RCV1[59]) can be calculated with the parameters b=0.49, k=44 and a collection size 1,000,020:

---

[56] i.e., Unified Medical Language System, http://www.nlm.nih.gov/research/umls/

[57] MPRO (Maas et al. (2009)) software output.

[58] MPRO demo, demonstrates semantic information delivered for the word *pass*, i.e. two semantic tags are assigned – *way* and *location*. The tags are explained in Appendix B3.

[59] Reuters document collection: http://trec.nist.gov/data/reuters/reuters.html

Example 19

$$M = 44 \times 1000020^{0,49} = 38,323^{60}$$

Zipf's law (Zipf (1945, 1949)) models a situation where the most common words t_1, t_2, ...t_n in the collection obey the collection frequency rule:

$$cf_i \propto \frac{1}{i} \qquad (2)$$

where, cf_i is a collection frequency of t_i, and i is a rank

Zipf's law means that if the most frequent term occurs cf_1 times, then the second most frequent term will be two times less frequent, the third most frequent term – three times less frequent, etc. The dependency between the frequency of a word and its rank is depicted in Figure 14., part b.

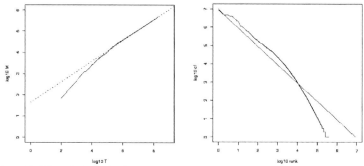

Figure 14. a) Heaps' distribution for the Reuters document collection: unique vocabulary (y axis) vs. dependency on text size (x axis); b) Zipf's distribution for the Reuters document collection: frequency of a word (y axis) vs. dependency on the rank of a word (x axis). [61]

According to the statistics of the Brown Corpus, nouns are the most frequent POS in English language. So only the **frequency of the word** gives a strong basis for the statistical detection of term candidates. A small experiment with a *Statistical Keyword analysis tool*[62] on a tiny Lithuanian text, highlights the most frequent words:

Example 20

```
ir 12 - eng. and

Mes 7 - eng. we

Reklamos 5 - eng. advertisement
```

---

[60] Example source: http://nlp.stanford.edu/IR-book/html/htmledition/heaps-law-estimating-the-number-of-terms-1.html#fig:heaps

[61] Source of images: http://nlp.stanford.edu/IR-book/html/htmledition/zipfs-law-modeling-the-distribution-of-terms-1.html

[62] Can be accessed at: http://seokeywordanalysis.com/seotools/

```
Jūsų 4 - eng. your
Agentas 3 - proper name
```

This analysis shows that single word frequency should not be the only criterion, because of the high frequency of functional words like conjunctions, e.g., "ir" ("and") and personal pronouns, e.g., "we", "your", etc. It is a common practice in statistical text analysis (χ^2 goodness of fit test, log-likelihood test, mutual information test) to take into account so called bigrams, trigrams, ..., n-grams (Church and Hanks (1989), Sinclair (1991), Stubbs (1996), Manning and Schütze (1999), Daudaravičius and Marcinkevičienė (2004), Zielinski (2002)).

Word length is yet another important criterion to identify a term. It is well supported by quantitative linguists (Altmann (1981), Grzybek and Stadlober (2002), Grzybek (2004), Köhler and Naumann (2005), Köhler and Naumann (2007)) who show that frequency distribution of words in a natural language reveals a connection between word's length and its rank, and relates to the Zipf's law in information theory. To quote a popular example of distribution observed in the Brown Corpus:

"[...], in the Brown Corpus "the" is the most frequently occurring word, and by itself accounts for nearly 7% of all word occurrences (69,971 out of slightly over 1 million). True to Zipf's Law, the second-place word "of" accounts for slightly over 3.5% of words (36,411 occurrences), followed by "and" (28,852). Only 135 vocabulary items are needed to account for half the Brown Corpus."[63]

Returning to the given frequency analysis of the Lithuanian text (see Example 20), if we only consider the frequency information in text and words that have at least four letters (rank=4), then the accuracy for spotting term candidates would be 66%!

4.2.3 Techniques of Terminology Extraction

In this section we discuss three main directions in TE techniques: rule based approaches, statistical approaches and hybrid approaches.

Rule based approaches were the first approaches for TE starting with the first TE system TERMINO (Plante and Dumas (1998)). Rule-based systems incorporate a language processing phase, i.e., morphological tagging, and they aim at detecting patterns that match with predefined term candidate rules. Rule-based approaches have been useful due to the low *silence*[64] effect. Unfortunately, high *noise*[65] level in predicting candidate terms is a major weakness of this approach.

Alternatives of the language independent approach are statistical approaches that target lexical units whose occurrence is higher than a given level in the analyzed corpus. Lexical unit co-occurrence reveals the usage of lexical units, as in one of the most applied principles – Mutual Information (MI). A general drawback of statistical approaches becomes apparent with low

---

[63] Citation source: http://en.wikipedia.org/wiki/Zipf%27s_law

[64] *Silence* is the evaluation measure used in TE, it refers to the number of terms not detected during TE process.

[65] *Noise* is the evaluation measure used in TE, noise refers to the ratio between discarded term candidates and the accepted ones.

frequency terms. However, the dependence on numeric information rather than on language specific rules makes statistical approaches convenient to use.

Hybrid approaches have proven to work best, since they can compensate both weaknesses: *noise* in rule-based approaches and *silence* in statistical approaches, thus yielding a benefit of both paradigms.

4.2.3.1 Rule-based Techniques

As already seen from the process of TE pipeline, language analysis and linguistic knowledge play a significant role, first, providing morphological interpretation of text[66], second, applying linguistic patterns in order to detect term candidates, and finally using *stop-word lists* for linguistic filtering.

In the last two decades a number of TE approaches were developed, to name but a few - Plante and Dumas (1998), Bourigault (1992), Bourigault (1994), Grefenstette (1994), Daille et al. (1994), Jacquemin (1999), Maynard and Ananiadou (2000), Oh et al. (2000), Ozdowska (2004), etc. An extensive overview of TE systems is given in Cabre et al. (2001).

The usage of linguistic patterns is the key feature distinguishing the rule-based approach. Cabre et al. (2001) name two categories of linguistic patterns: *term specific* and *language generic*. The former is term pattern oriented. Common examples could be noun + adjective, or noun + preposition + noun. The latter category refers to the syntactic layer of the language. Common examples are noun phrase (NP), prepositional phrase (PP), etc.

The TE approach presented by Plante and Dumas (1998) includes a tokenization stage and a morphological analysis stage in which lemma and morphological tags are identified. Disambiguation of morphological tags is processed with syntactic parser, and finally noun groups are identified by applying various NP patterns.

Justeson and Katz (1995) introduced the rule based approach by differentiating between terminological noun phrases and non-terminological noun phrases. The authors noticed that (particularly in technical texts) NPs denominate terms, and most frequently found NP pattern is adjective + noun (occurs in 97% of cases). Moreover, terminological NPs are likely to be two-word phrases, as an average length of terminological NPs is 1.19 word.

Next to linguistic patterns which in most cases are used for delimitation of the term, it is important to consider *stop-word* lists that are used for filtering candidate terms. Stop-word lists normally include determiners, prepositions, pronouns, general adjectives, etc., i.e., all common words that are not informative and do not help to define a term.

Other resources such as proper noun lists, or domain specific and generic thesauri can also be used in determining the suitability of a candidate term (Enguehard and Pantera (1994), Oh et al. (2000), Frank et al. (1999), Maynard and Ananiadou (1999), Medelyan and Witten (2006)).

---

[66] Note: this step includes tokenization for identifying sentence and word boundaries, morphosyntactic analysis for grammatical category identification, POS tagging for grammatical category disambiguation and lemmatization.

4.2.3.2 Statistical Techniques

Statistical techniques represent yet another way of acquiring terms. A major advantage is that TE systems based on statistical techniques do not require huge databases with term patterns constructed by humans and also do not require running through language analysis pipeline[67]. The assumption in using statistical models in TE is that words which tend to co-occur together are related. See for instance the concordance of the word *computer* taken from the Brown Corpus:[68]

Example 21

```
rd IBM punch card equipment, including an IBM 650 COMPUTER. The first step in processing was to anal
  resistance bridge, followed by a simple analogue COMPUTER which feeds a multichannel recorder. From
  is admirably suited to the powers of the digital COMPUTER. At the same time, every device that can
ve type well suited to programming on the digital COMPUTER. In finding the optimal R-stage policy fr
y complex spectra of the rare earth elements. New COMPUTER and automation techniques were applied to
iling a list of text forms as text is read by the COMPUTER. A random-storage scheme, based on the sp
ms in the text list are marked. A location in the COMPUTER store is also named for each marked form;
to the form of each occurrence. For this step the COMPUTER memory is separated into three regions: c
urse into the computer. The curve on the card the COMPUTER spat back at him couldn't be argued with,
```

Phrases like *analogue computer, digital computer, computer store* emerge due to the frequency of occurrence. Such phrases are a perfect fit as term candidates.

In section 4.2.2.2 it was briefly explained how frequency and rank information can be used to detect single word terms. Similarly, co-occurrence information is used to detect MWUs. Statistical association measures such as MI, log-likelihood, t-score, chi-squared test, dice, or Fisher's test were successfully applied for term and collocation extraction.

Mutual Information (MI) in the field of lexicography was first used by Church and Hanks (1990). For given two words w_1 and w_2, with probabilities $P(w_1)$ and $P(w_2)$, and joint probability $P(w_1,w_2)$, their mutual information $I(w_1, w_2)$ is defined as:

$$I(w_1, w_2) = \log_2 \frac{P(w_1, w_2)}{P(w_1) P(w_2)} \qquad (3)$$

A larger joint probability denotes the strength of association, i.e., positive values mean association, whereas negative values - dissociation. Consider for instance:

Example 22

```
C(computer) = 40, C(science) = 20
C(computer,science) = 20
N = 15.000.000
```

$$I(computer, science) = \log_2 \frac{\dfrac{20}{N}}{\dfrac{40}{N} \cdot \dfrac{20}{N}} \approx 6.57$$

---

[67] Note. Here we are referring to the term extraction schema presented by Zielinski (2002).
[68] Source: http://conc.lextutor.ca/concordancers/wwwassocwords.pl

The disadvantage of the MI measure is overestimation of the strength of association for low frequency co-occurences. In Church et al. (1991) the *t-score* measure was introduced:

$$t - score = \frac{P(w_1, w_2) - P(w_1, w_3)}{\sqrt{\sigma^2 P(w_1, w_2) + \sigma^2 P(w_1, w_3)}} \qquad (4)$$

$P(w_1, w_2)$ is the probability of word w_1 occuring with w_2, $P(w_1, w_3)$ is the probability of word w_1 occuring with w_3, σ^2 is the variance. Table 2., shows the analysis of the *t-score* measure of two words *strong* and *powerful* co-ocuring with other words[69].

Table 2. An example of t-score application.

t-score	Strong (w2)	powerful (w3)	w1
11.94	175	2	Support
9.97	106	0	Defense
-5.37	3	31	Minority
-4.91	0	24	Post
9.76	102	0	Economy

Evert and Krenn (2001) pointed out that the *t-score* is more suitable for the collocation detection than term extraction.

Pearson's *chi-squared test* in lexicography is modeled upon the 2x2 contingency table:

	x	y	
w	a	b	a+b
¬ w	c	d	c+d
	a+c	b+d	a+b+c+d=N

Pearson's test shows statistical independence for word w in texts X and Y. Occurrences of w in text X (a+c words) and in text Y (b+d words) are expected frequencies f_e. The frequencies f_o are observed frequencies. Then the chi-squared test measures how far observed values are from expected values:

$$\chi^2 = \sum \frac{(f_o - f_e)^2}{f_e} \qquad (5)$$

A drawback of the *chi-squared test* is that it works poorly with rare co-occurrences (Kilgarriff (1997), Dunning (1993)).

An improved model of previously mentioned *chi-squared test* is the *log-likelihood* ratio test that was proposed by Dunning (1993):

$$Log - likelihood = 2\sum f_o \log \frac{f_o}{f_e} \qquad (6)$$

Other widely applied models for association detection are Fisher's exact test (Pedersen (1996)), and Dice coefficient (Smadja (1993)). Novel TE approaches include Cen et al. (2008) term detection that uses *Hidden Markov Model*, Aires et al. (2008) that uses the *Suffix Array*

---

[69] Table adapted from Church et al. (1991).

method[70] for MWUs detection, and Fahmi et al. (2007) that incorporate known terms in order to asses the termhood of extracted terms.

To conclude, it was shown how statistical models meant for calculating association can be used for TE. However, one general drawback of these approaches is overestimation of the association value for low frequency co-occurrences. It is important to note that statistical models work well for very large corpora that have high frequencies of co-occurrences.

Next section discusses how the strengths of rule based and statistically based techniques can be exploited by hybrid TE models.

4.2.3.3 Hybrid Techniques

There are two main underlying reasons for using hybrid techniques for TE. The first is approach limitations of statistical and rule based models, and the second is data insufficiency. Statistically based systems produce too much silence, and linguistically based systems produce too much noise. Combining both so far appears to be the best solution in terms of quality measures (Daille (1994), Ananiadou (1994), Cabre et al. (2001), Haller (2006), Grigonytė and Haller (2008)). Data insufficiency means: the lack in quantity of texts, the noise in data and insufficient frequencies of tokens. Here a language generic model combined with statistical filtering can improve extraction of domain terms.

Frantzi et al. (2000) used the hybrid approach combining POS tagging, morphosyntactic patterns and stop-word list for candidate term detection together with a statistical *c-value* filter for termhood assessment. The authors have used the following linguistic filters:

Example 23

    Noun+Noun

    (AdjjNoun)+Noun

    ((AdjjNoun)+j((AdjjNoun)*(NounPrep)?)(AdjjNoun)*)Noun[71]

Given that a is a candidate string, $f(a)$ is a frequency of occurrence in the corpus, T_a is a set of term candidates containing string a; $f(b)$ is the frequency of the candidate term b that contains a; and $N(T_a)$ is a number of candidate terms, then:

$$C - value(a) = \begin{cases} \log_2 |a| \cdot f(a) & a \text{ is not nested} \\ \log_2 |a|(f(a) - \dfrac{1}{N(T_a)}\sum_{b \in T_a} f(b)) & otherwise \end{cases} \quad (7)$$

A useful observation on the termhood of a term is that the higher is the number of longer terms in which the observed string appears nested[72], the more likely it is an independent term. Consider for instance candidate terms like:

---

[70] Manber and Myers (1990) Suffix arrays: a new method for on-line string searches.

[71] *, + and ? should be interpreted as RegEx symbols.

Example 24

```
malignant rhabdoid tumour
renal rhabdoid tumour
congenital rhabdoid tumour
metastatic rhabdoid tumour
cutaneous rhabdoid tumour
paravertebral rhabdoid tumour
pediatric rhabdoid tumour
cerebellar rhabdoid tumour
multifocal rhabdoid tumour
```

Here *rhabdoid tumour* is nested in longer term candidates, and very likely *rhabdoid tumour* is a term on its own.

The proposed approach was evaluated on the medical domain corpus (COCR) and showed that the statistical model improves the precision score for recognizing nested term candidates up to 20-38%.

The *c-value* is often used in the combined measure called *NC-value* that takes context into account. Given that a is the candidate term, C_a is the set of context words for a, b is a word from C_a, $f_a(b)$ is the frequency of b, *weight(b)* is the weight[73] of b.

$$NC-value(a) = 0.8 \cdot C-value(a) + 0.2 \cdot \sum_{b \in C_a} f_a(b)weight(b) \qquad (8)$$

Maynard and Ananiadou (1999) made use of *NC-value* by extending it with semantic information from the UMLS thesaurus. Their *CF value* additionally uses a similarity weight *sim(d,a)* of the term d occurring with the term a, which is acquired from given (semantic) resource, such as a thesaurus.

$$CF(a) = \sum_{b \in C_a} f_a(b) \cdot weight(b) + \sum_{d \in T_a} f_a(d) \cdot sim(d,a) \qquad (9)$$

Maynard and Ananiadou see context as a key to understanding termhood. Koeva (2007) uses context word lemmas in WSM[74] in order to cluster *candidate terms* into terms or non-terms. Termhood assessment is improved by taking into account not only the association measure but also contextual data.

---

[72] Nested terms, according to Franzti et al. (2000) are " [...] those that appear within other longer terms, and may or may not appear by themselves in the corpus." An example can be *real time expert system*, as *expert system* may occur on it's own.

[73] In Frantzi et al. (2000) weight measure is calculated as a number of terms the word occur with divided by the number of all terms.

[74] *Word space model* is explained in section 4.3.2.3.

4.3   Relationship Extraction

Semantic relationships are building blocks, that can be used in a wide variety of tasks such as concept formation, hierarchy establishment, and defining non-hierarchical relationships. According to Casado et al. (2005)

> "In most of the cases, ontologies are structured as hierarchies of concepts, by means of the relation called hyponymy (*is-a*, class inclusion or subsumption) and its inverse hyperonymy, which arranges the concepts from the most general to the most specific one." (Casado et al. (2005:380)).

This section discusses the role of semantic relationships in building ontologies and the techniques used for automatically acquiring semantic relationships.

4.3.1   Semantic Relationships for Ontology Building

Ontological relationships are components of the ontology. They show how different parts of ontology, like classes, individuals and properties are interconnected. Two major groups of relationships: hierarchical and non-hierarchical, are presented in the web W3C portal. Hierarchical or taxonomical relationships (see Figure 15.) show the connections between classes and individuals or classes and subclasses.

Example 25

```
1)<owl:Class rdf:ID="Winery"/>

2)<owl:Class rdf:ID="FootballTeam">

<owl:sameAs rdf:resource="http://sports.org/US#SoccerTeam"/>

</owl:Class>

3)C1 rdfs:subClassOf C2
```

Next to taxonomical relationships between classes, subclasses, and individuals, there exist non-hierarchical relations (see Figure 16.) between instances of two classes called *properties*[75]:

Example 26

```
<owl:ObjectProperty rdf:about='http://www..../1.0#ageOf'>

<owl:ObjectProperty rdf:about='http://www..../1.0#beginningOf'>

<owl:ObjectProperty rdf:about='http://www..../1.0#birthOf'>

<owl:ObjectProperty rdf:about='http://www..../1.0#bloodPressureOf'>

<owl:ObjectProperty rdf:about='http://www.../1.0#breadthOf'>

<owl:ObjectProperty rdf:about='http://www.../1.0#brotherOf'>
```

---

[75] In OWL "Properties let us assert general facts about the members of classes and specific facts about individuals", There are two types of properties: *datatype properties*, relations between instances of classes and RDF literals and XML Schema datatypes; and *object properties*, relations between instances of two classes; source: http://www.w3.org/TR/2004/REC-owl-guide-20040210/#BasicDefinitions

```
<owl:ObjectProperty rdf:about='http://www…./1.0#causedBy'/>
<owl:ObjectProperty rdf:about='http://www…./1.0#causes'/>
<owl:ObjectProperty rdf:about='http://www…/1.0#characterizedBy'/>
<owl:ObjectProperty rdf:about='http://www…./1.0#characterizes'>
<owl:ObjectProperty
rdf:about='http://www…./1.0#CommonToxicityCriteriaGradeOf'/>[76]
<owl:ObjectProperty rdf:ID="hasChild">
<owl:inverseOf rdf:resource="#hasParent"/>
</owl:ObjectProperty>
```

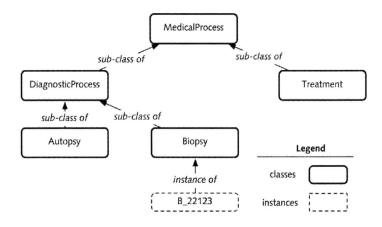

Figure 15. An example of hierarchical relationships in the ACTG MO ontology snippet.

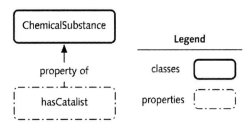

Figure 16. An example of non-hierarchical relationship in ACTG MO ontology snippet.

---

[76] Source: BFO ontology, "http://ontology.buffalo.edu/bfo/"

Semantic relationships benefit the process of ontology building in three different ways: 1) concept definition, 2) establishing hierarchical ontological relationships, and 3) non-hierarchical ontological relationships.

Terminology of the domain can give a general overview of the domain by highlighting all terms used in the domain. Thus terminology is of paramount importance in defining the borders of the domain. Moreover, terms have a conceptual (referential) meaning (as shown in section 4.2). However, when formalizing the knowledge, the terms can not be directly interpreted as concepts of the ontology. Consider for instance the terminology snippet:

Example 27

```
state
| architectural state
| design state
| distinct state
| dominant state
| implementation state
```

The direct assumption that the term *state* is a class, and the above given 5 examples of different *states* are subclasses or instances is not correct (see Figure 17.).

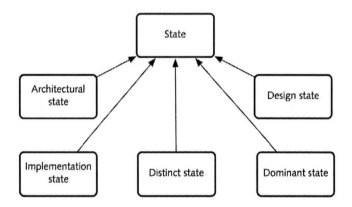

Figure 17. An example of terminological subsumption.

However knowing that:

```
design state
architectural state
implementation state
```

are meronyms of the term *software development process*, and that

```
distinct state
dominant state
```

are near synonymous expressions, already helps us to take a benefit of related terminology and use it for the definition of the concept. Similar to the notion of how synonyms and co-hyponyms of a term can help to define the concept, Cimiano (2006) used clusters of terms to define concepts. Semantic relationships that can help to define concepts are: hypernym-hyponym, holonymy-meronymy, synonymy, near synonymy, antonymy, co-hyponomy.

In *formal concept analysis* (FCA) a set of all possible attributes of an object and a set of all objects sharing the given attributes are used to derive a mathematical description of the concept. As illustrated in Figure 18., objects, attributes and relationships form a concept (Rudolph (2006), Rudolph et al. (2008)).

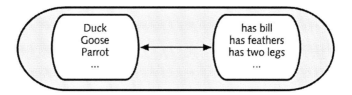

Figure 18. Forman Concept Analysis, adapted from Rudolph and Völker (2008).

Working from the NLP perspective, we modify this approach and relate to the object as a term, and the list of the object's semantic relationships is the set of all possible attributes, see Figure 19.

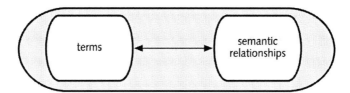

Figure 19. NLP-based concept formation.

In other words, we aim to discover semantic relationships that can show dependencies between domain terms.

Another application of semantic relationships is to establish hierarchical and non-hierarchical ontological relationships[77].

The parallel between semantic relationships which can be mined from text and ontological relationships is depicted by the *ConceptNet Relation Ontology*[78], that assumes that syntactic patterns can be directly used for generating ontological relationships (see Table 3.).

Table 3. Linguistic patterns that are interpreted as ontological relationships.[79]

Linguistic pattern	Ontological relationship
`NP is a part of NP`	`PartOf`
`NP is a kind of NP`	`IsA`
`NP is made of NP`	`MadeOf`
`NP is used for VP`	`UsedFor`
`NP can VP`	`CapableOf`
`An example of NP is NP`	`InstanceOf`
`NP is AP`	`PropertyOf`
`The effect of VP is NP|VP`	`EffectOf`

Example 28 shows, how from the sentence (a) we can mine the ontological relationship (b):
Example 28

```
a) An example of message is incoming message.

b) InstanceOf (incoming_message, message)
```

It is important to mention that Schwarz and Smith (2008) suggest the schema that defines ontological relations by analyzing logical properties[80] and by differentiating the level of granularity. For instance the subsumption relationship (is-a relationship) can be established between:
Example 29

```
<universal,universal> e.g., (OrganismalProcess, disease)

<instance, universal> e.g., (cancer, disease)

<instance, instance> e.g., (cancer, mammarcarcinoma)
```

According to the proposed schema, relationships like "`bloodPressureOf`", are only valid in some particular domains and therefore do not meet the criteria of ontological relationships. This thesis deals with acquiring semantic relationships and using them as building blocks of domain ontology, thus both ontological and domain dependent relationships are of interest.

This thesis considers two sets of semantic relationships: hierarchical[81], such as hypernym-hyponym, holonymy-meronymy; and non-hierarchical, such as synonymy, near synonymy,

---

[77] Non-hierarchical relations mark *attribute type* of relationships in ontologies, whereas hierarchical relationships mark *taxonomical* relationships.

[78] Liu and Singh (2004), "ConceptNet - A Practical Commonsense Reasoning Tool-Kit. BT Technology Journal, Springer.

[79] Source: Gabor Melli's research KB: http://www.gabormelli.com/RKB/

[80] Like reflexivity, symmetry, transitivity, e.g., part-of relationship is asymmetric and transitive (Guarino (2008)).

[81] Not to be mixed with hierarchical ontological relationship.

antonymy, co-hyponomy, and association. In the following subsections we present definitions of semantic relationships.

4.3.1.1 Synonymy and Near Synonymy

According to Cambridge online dictionary, synonym is defined as "a word or phrase which has the same or nearly the same meaning as another word or phrase in the same language".[82] Consider for instance:

Example 30

```
{adverse effect, adverse impact}
{incoming message, new message}
{frequency control, frequency tuning}
```

Synonymy is probably one of the most studied semantic relationships in NLP. Early methodologies for synonymy detection were described by Michiels and Nöel (1982), Tsurumaru et al. (1986), Grefenstette (1994). Recent work on synonymy extraction includes Edmonds (1999), Wu and Zhou (2003), Dyvik (2004), Muller et al. (2006), van der Plas and Tiedemann (2006), Ohshima and Tanaka (2009), Wei et al. (2009), and many others.

Synonymous pairs of domain terms show variation in terminology and are important for concept formation.

4.3.1.2 Antonymy

An antonym is a non-hierarchical relationship. An antonym is a word whose meaning is opposite to the meaning of another word. Two antonyms of the word 'light' are 'dark' and 'heavy'.[83] Discovering antonyms helps to spot related terms and assists to define concepts. For instance consider:

Example 31

```
{lowest bit, highest bit}
{incoming throughput, outgoing throughput}
```

Main contributions to the topic of antonym detection are Lin et al. (2003), and Turney (2008).

---

[82] http://dictionary.cambridge.org/define.asp?key=80855&dict=CALD&topic=terminology-and-vocabulary
[83] http://dictionary.cambridge.org/define.asp?dict=CALD&key=3330

4.3.1.3 Co-hyponymy

Another important non-hierarchical relationship is co-hyponymy. Co-hyponyms are words or phrases that share the same hypernym. Terminology organized in co-hyponym groups is particularly useful for defining domain concepts. Consider for instance co-hyponyms of the hypernym *message*:

Example 32

```
incremental message
full message
diagnostic message
digital message
excessive message
hint message
minimal message
point-to-point message
unexpected message
update message
```

Research on discovering groups of co-hyponyms is presented by Gamallo et al. (2002), Davidov and Rappoport (2008), Lendvai (2009).

4.3.1.4 Holonymy – Meronymy

Holonymy-meronymy (or part-whole) relationship describes the relationship between a term denoting the whole and a term denoting a part-of. If Y is a holonym and X is a meromym, then:

```
X is a part of Y
X is a member of Y
Y contains X
```

Examples of holonym-meronym pairs are:

Example 33

```
{message, attachment}
{message, message header}
```

Part-whole relationships are hierarchical relationships. In ontologies they refer to *isPartOf* or *has* relationships. Main contributions in acquiring holonym-meronym relationships are presented by Roberts (2005), Girju et al. (2003, 2007), Ritter et al. (2008), Maynard and Peters (2009).

4.3.1.5 Hypernymy – Hyponymy

Hypernymy-hyponymy relationship characterizes the relation between a class and its subclass, or between a class and an instance. It is the most common type of hierarchical relationship found in ontologies and is expressed by *ISA* relation. If X is hypernym and Y is hyponym, then hypernym-hyponym relationship implies:

```
Y is kind of X
Y is subordinate to X
Y is narrower than X
X is broader than Y
X is generic of Y
Y is specific of X
```

Examples of hypernym-hyponym relationship:
Example 34

```
{message, incoming message}
{tumor, Wilms tumor}
```

A number of authors have contributed to the topic of hypernym-hyponym relationship detection. To name a few: Hearst (1992), Caraballo (1999), Phillips and Riloff (2002), Pekar and Staab (2002) Dyvik (2004), Cimiano et al. (2005), Snow et al. (2006), Dias et al. (2008) Pantel and Pennacchiotti (2006), Vela and Declerck (2009), etc.

4.3.1.6 Association

Association relationships are implicit and cannot be clearly defined. This type of relationship, "covers associations between terms that are neither equivalent nor hierarchical, yet the terms are semantically or conceptually associated to such an extent that the link between them should be made explicit in the controlled vocabulary"[84]. In ontologies the relationships of semantic association can applied to express explicit non-hierarchical relationships like: *worksIn, livesIn, causes*, etc. Examples of association relationships are:
Example 35

```
{physician, hospital}
{researcher, university}
{chemotherapy, survival}
```

---

[84] Citation source: http://www.slis.kent.edu/~mzeng/Z3919/44association.htm

Recent approaches to determining association relationships include Steyvers and Griffiths (2007) and Turney (2008).

***

The roles of the semantic relationships and their applications are summarized in Table 4.

Table 4. The role of semantic relationships in building ontology.

Semantic relationship	Example	Concept analysis	Hierarchy establishment	Non hierarchical relations
Synonymy, near synonymy, antonymy	tumour, tumor, carcinoma	+		+
Holonymy-meronymy	Hand – finger	+	+	+
Co-hyponymy	intensive chemotherapy systemic chemotherapy primary chemotherapy aggressive chemotherapy cytotoxic chemotherapy	+		+
Hypernym-hyponym	patient – child	+	+	
Association	chemotherapy – survival	+		+

4.3.2 Methods of Relationship Extraction

The idea of discovering semantic relationships through a linguistic analysis of corpus dates back to at least 1958, when the idea of building data bases through linguistic analysis and using these data bases for document retrieval was discussed by Harris Z.[85].

Later the task of acquiring semantic relationships became a standard IE task. The process became standardized, and Grüninger and Fox (1995) described the task of relationship extractions as containing two major steps, namely collecting the patterns for a given relationship and identifying instances of these patterns in text.

The methodology of discovering semantic relationships can be divided into two major strategies: *distributional similarity* and *semantic relatedness*. Budanitsky and Hirst (2006) draw a clear line between two:

> "Three differences between semantic relatedness and distributional similarity are immediately apparent. First, while semantic relatedness is inherently a relation on concepts, [...] distributional similarity is a (corpus-dependent) relation on words. [...] Second, whereas semantic relatedness is symmetric, distributional similarity is a potentially asymmetrical relationship. [...] Third, lexical semantic relatedness depends on a pre-defined lexicographic or other knowledge resource, whereas distributional similarity is relative to a corpus. " (Budanitsky and Hirst (2006:30)).

---

[85] Z. Harris (1958) "Linguistic Analysis for Information Retrieval", Int. Conf. on Scientific Information, Washington, D.C. *Linguistic Transformations for Information Retrieval.*

In addition to distributional similarity-based approaches and semantic relatedness-based approaches, we will discuss classical pattern-based approaches.

4.3.2.1 Pattern-based Approaches

The pioneer of pattern based approaches, Hearst (1992) introduced *lexico-syntactic patterns*. Specific patterns like "x and other y" or "x such as y" were used for hypernym-hyponym detection. Latter the idea was extended and adapted by other researchers, including Roark and Charniak (1998), Hearst (1998), Cimiano et al. (2004), Pantel and Pennacchiotti (2006). Examples of the lexico-syntactic patterns are:

Example 36

```
x also called y
x such as y
x especially y1, y2... yn-1 and yn
x1,x2,... xn and other y
x consist of y
x is made of y
x is a member of y
```

Patterns can be of different generality. Maynard and Peters (2009) describe contextual synonymy patterns. An example of a such a generic pattern is:

Example 37

```
... name (name) ...
```
[86]

Similarly, Sasano and Kurohashi (2008) investigate parenthesis expressions with the constraint that allows only those synonymic pairs for which the frequency of pattern A(B) is as high as the frequency of pattern B(A).

In general, manual pattern definition is time consuming and requires linguistic skills. Usually, systems based on lexico-syntactic patterns exhibit very high *precision*, but lower *recall*. This is due to the fact that these patterns are rare. However, recent work by Ohshima and Tanaka (2009) on large Web data corpus reported 70-80% precision.

In the IE field a different approach is applied: so-called generic pattern models are employed in order to acquire the semantic relationships. Instead of using specific lexico syntactic patterns Yangarber (2003), Stevenson and Greenwood (2005) use *predicate-argument model*, which is often referred to as SVO[87]. The output of a parsed text is analyzed for extracting SVO tuples, that normally contains one verb per sentence. However, SVO models have the drawback that

---

[86] An example of a pattern is *argemone (prickly-poppy)*.
[87] In English, it is the pattern of subject-verb-object.

they can only model the information represented in SVO constructions, and exclude other linguistic constructions such as nominalisations or prepositional phrases (Stevenson and Greenwood (2006)).

Sudo et al. (2001) describe *chain pattern model*, which is a partial SVO model. The difference is that chain patterns are built for every path in the dependency tree of the sentence including the verb and all other nodes. Inevitably the link between arguments of the verb is missing. Nevertheless chain patterns take into account nominalizations and prepositional phrases, unlike the SVO model. Later Sudo et al. (2003) extend the chain pattern model by proposing *subtree model* where any set of nodes (larger than 1 and connected to one another) of the parse tree are subtree patterns.

Yet another modification of the chain model - *linked chains model* by Greenwood et al. (2005) generates even higher number of patterns as it links together the combinations of chains via the same verb.

For an illustration of four different pattern models see the sentence (Example 38) and its dependency tree (see Figure 20.) and generated patterns (see Table 5.).

Example 38

```
This report examines cosmesis as a function of age.
```

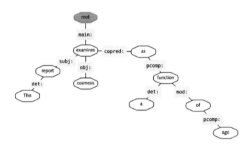

Figure 20. The dependency parse tree obtained from Connexor parser.

Table 5. Some of example patterns generated by using SVO, chain, subtree and linked chain models.

SVO	Chain	subtree	linked chain
1) Subj: the report + verb: examines + obj: cosmesis	1) V: examines + subj: this report 2) V: examines + subj: report 3) V: examines + obj: cosmesis 4) V: examines + prepp: as a function 5) V: examines + prepp: as function ...	1) subj: report + v: examines 2) subj: this report + v: examines 3) subj: report + v: examines + obj: cosmesis 4) obj: cosmesis + v: examines + prepp: as function ...	1) V: examines + subj: this report + obj: cosmesis 2) V: examines + subj: report + prepp: as function 3) V: examines + obj: cosmesis + prepp: as function ...

Stevenson and Greenwood (2006) give an evaluation of these pattern models on the MUC6[88] corpus and conclude that the SVO model covers the smallest part of relationships, especially in domain specific corpus[89]. According to authors, "this is because the items of interest[90] are commonly described in ways which the SVO model is unable to represent."

4.3.2.2 Semantic Relatedness-based Approaches

Relationships are encoded in linguistic knowledge sources such as dictionaries (*Longman Dictionary of Contemporary English* (LDOCE) (Procter (1978)), thesauri (Roget's thesaurus (Roget (1852)) and wordnets (WordNet (Miller (1990), Fellbaum (1998)). An example snippet of the hyponym taxonomy in WordNet is shown in Figure 21.

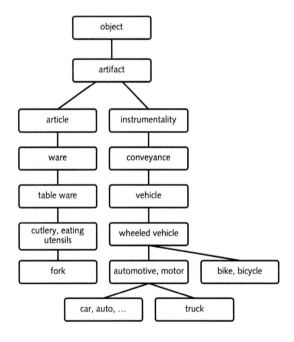

Figure 21. An example of hyponym taxonomy in Wordnet[91]

---

[88] Message Understanding Conference in 1995.
[89] Biomedical corpus used in LLL-05 challenge task (N´edellec (2005)).
[90] Note: in domain specific corpus.
[91] Image source: http://www.codeproject.com/KB/string/semanticsimilaritywordnet.aspx?msg=3300718

The simplest way of calculating the measures of the relatedness is using the gloss information. The assumption is that if the glosses of two terms overlap, terms are related. The higher overlap means a stronger relation. See Figure 22.

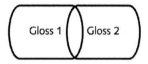

Figure 22. The overlap of two glosses.

The Lesk (1986) measure evaluates the overlap of the words of two concepts:

$$\operatorname{Re}l(c_1,c_2) = \left| gloss(c_1) \right| \cap \left| gloss(c_2) \right| \qquad (10)$$

Similarly Gurevych (2005) uses so called *pseudo glosses* by forming the gloss from concepts that are in close relation. For given example of *truck* and *fork* glosses are:
Example 39

```
Fork (cutlery, eating utensil, table, table ware)

Truck (automotive, motor, wheeled vehicle, vehicle)
```

Thus the relation between two pseudo glosses would be:

$$\operatorname{Re}l(c_1,c_2) = \left| Pgloss(c_1) \right| \cap \left| Pgloss(c_2) \right| {}^{92} \qquad (11)$$

Yet another branch of approaches that are based on the structure of linguistic resources is represented by the similarity measure often referred to as *WordNet based-similarity*. It is based on the assumption that, the shorter the path l is between nodes representing concepts, the higher is the relatedness. For instance:
Example 40

```
{car, truck}

{car, fork}
```

In the given Example 39, based on the Figure 21., *car* is more related to *truck* than to *fork*, because the path between car and truck is shorter than between car and fork.
Rada et al. (1989) have introduced the measure of semantic relatedness based on counting the edges between two nodes of concepts c_1 and c_2:

$$\operatorname{Re}l(c_1,c_2) = l(c_1,c_2) \qquad (12)$$

---

[92] For the given example Rel (truck, fork)=0.

Leacock and Chodorow (1998) have extended the above (number) measure by adding a normalization feature, based on the depth of the graph:

$$\operatorname{Re}l(c_1,c_2) = -\log\frac{l(c_1,c_2)}{2\cdot d} \qquad (13)$$

where d is the longest path in the taxonomy.

The methods of Rada et al. (1989), Rada and Bicknell (1989), Lee et al. (1993), and Leacock and Chodorow (1998) have a major weakness because the distances of the links in the taxonomy are not the same. Resnik (1995) illustrated this situation with the example taken from the Collins COBUILD Dictionary (Sinclair (1987)): the distance between superordinate terms e.g., *safety valve is-a valve* is considered to be smaller than the semantic distance between *knitting machine is-a machine*. Also path-only information is not sufficient since the upper concepts in taxonomies are more abstract than lower ones.

Considering later notions, Wu and Palmer (1994) proposed using common ancestor (CS) and its path length to root (n):

$$\operatorname{Re}l = \frac{2\cdot n}{n1+n2} \qquad (14)$$

where n1 and n2 are $l(c1,R)$ and $l(c2,R)$, see Figure 23.

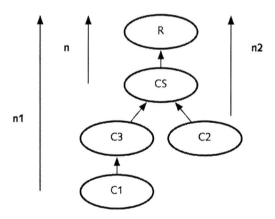

Figure 23. Wu and Palmer (1994) method for measuring semantic similarity.

However, relying on the path length alone does not maximize the benefit of using linguistic resources like WordNet or Roget's thesaurus. Resnik (1995, 1999) proposed the so-called *information content*[93] measure which is calculated as the probability of finding concept c in a corpus:

$$IC(c) = -\log p(c) \qquad (15)$$

The similarity measure is calculated as the information content of the path length of *lowest common subsumer* (lcs)[94] defined by the distance n:

$$\mathrm{Re}l(c_1, c_2) = IC(lcs(c_1, c_2)) \qquad (16)$$

The similarity measure can also be used for detecting the relationship between word senses, and thus for resolving polysemy. For the given *word senses* w_1 and w_2:

$$wsim_\alpha(w_1, w_2) = \sum \alpha(c_i)[-\log p(c_i)] \qquad (17)$$

c_i is the set of concepts related to w_1 and w_2 in any sense of either word, and α is a weighting function over concepts such that its sum equals 1.
Consider an example of the part of WordNet[95] in Figure 24.

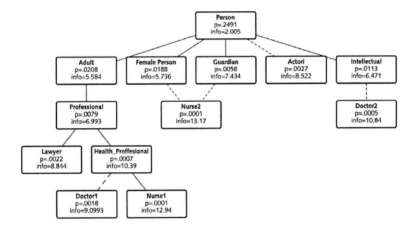

Figure 24. **An example of calculating similarity measure in WordNet, adapted from Resnik (1999).**

Resnik's similarity measure highlights related concepts, i.e., *medical doctor* and *medical nurse* are more related than, for instance, *medical doctor* and *nanny* (see example)[96]:

---

[93] In Information theory, Ross (2002) proposes to define the information content of a concept *c* as negative the log likelihood, *-log p(c)*.
[94] Compares to common ancestor (CS) in Figure 23.
[95] Adapted from Resnik (1999:98).
[96] Adapted from Resnik (1999:99).

c₁ (description)	c₂ (description)	Subsumer	sim(c₁,c₂)
Doctor1 (medical)	Nurse1 (medical)	Health_professional	8.88
Doctor1 (medical)	Nurse2 (nanny)	Person	2.00
Doctor2 (Ph.D.)	Nurse1 (medical)	Person	2.00
Doctor2 (Ph.D.)	Nurse2 (nanny)	Person	2.00

The discussed relatedness models are suitable when structured lexical resources like thesauri or wordnets are available. For specific domains, other approaches need to be considered, since general language thesauri and wordnets do not contain specific domain terms. To compute whether terms are related, one can use a domain corpus. The following section will introduce the set of approaches that take into account distributional similarity.

4.3.2.3 Approaches Based on the Word Space Model

Distributional similarity for capturing semantic relatedness relies on the hypothesis that semantically similar or related words share similar contexts. Rubenstein and Goodenough (1965) showed that, words which are similar in meaning occur in similar contexts. Later Schütze and Pedersen (1997) extended the statement saying that "words with similar meanings will occur with similar neighbors if enough text material is available." Sahlgren (2006) accurately illustrates the geometric metaphor of meaning:

> "Meanings are locations in a semantic space, and semantic similarity is proximity between the locations."
> (Sahlgren (2006:27)).

Here the semantic space is literally a two-dimensional geometrical space, which allows us to portray each word based on distributional properties that are co-occurrences with other words.

The word space model (WSM) (Schütze (1993)), is a paradigm borrowed from the field of information retrieval (IR) (Salton et al. (1975)) called vector space model[97]. WSM has been successfully applied for concept categorization (Pantel (2003), Sahlgren (2006)) and relationship extraction (Cimiano and Wenderoth (2005), Pantel and Pennacchiotti (2006), Turney (2006), Pado and Lapata (2007), Pantel and Pennacchiotti (2008), Baroni and Lenci (2009)).

Words can be modeled as WSM by describing their features (for instance, the frequency of co-occurrence with other words, or probability distribution).

Baroni (2008) use WSM to represent semantic model of tuples:

Example 41

```
arg1 link arg2 weight
```

---

[97] According to Wikipedia: vector space model is an algebraic model for representing text documents (and any objects, in general) as vectors of identifiers (of fixed length).

Tuples are acquired with lexico-syntactic patterns from the output of a dependency parser. Weighting is calculated as any preferable relatedness measure[98]. An example of the set of tuples is:

Example 42

banana	for	eating	23.9
kill	obj	man	25.9
banana	is	yellow	25.7
yellow	is-1	banana	22.2
dog	subj-1	bark	32.3[99]

For instance similarity between concepts can be modeled as matrix of co-occurences:

Example 43

	subj-1 walk	subj-1 run	subj-1 bark	obj-1 pet	Has Owner
Dog	6	2	3	1	5
Lion	3	6	0	1	0
Car	0	2	0	0	3
Light	0	0	0	0	0

where each concept is represented in the lines, features – in the columns, and cells stand for the value of the features (for instance, co-occurrence frequency as illustrated in Example 42). Let us consider two concepts c_1 *(dog)* and c_2 *(lion)*, and two vectors $v_1(2, 6)$ and $v_2(6, 3)$ presenting the co-occurrence count with other arguments in tuples (see Figure 25., a):

	subj-1 run	subj-1 walk
Dog	2	6
Lion	6	3

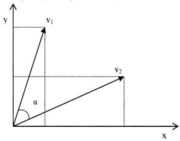

Figure 25. a) the co-occurrence matrix of concepts dog and lion; b) the relatedness of the concepts in two-dimensional space.

Then the relatedness of two concepts can be expressed in a two dimensional space (see Figure 25., b) as cosine value[100] between two vectors:

---

[98] e.g., co-occurrence frequency, MI, entropy, etc.
[99] Adapted from Baroni (2008) slides, p 38., *is-1*, and *subj-1* indicate inversed arguments.

$$\cos(\alpha) = \frac{v_1 \cdot v_2}{|v_1\| v_2|} \qquad (18)$$

Similar approach is used by Patwardhan and Pedersen (2006) for measuring the similarity between two word glosses:

$$\mathrm{Re}l(c_1, c_2) = \frac{glossVector(c_1) \cdot glossVector(c_2)}{|glossVector(c_1)\| glossVector(c_2)|} \qquad (19)$$

The relatedness of two concepts c_1 and c_2 is the cosine value between two gloss vectors $glossVector(c_1)$ and $glossVector(c_2)$.

Other word space vector related researches for word relatedness induction include Wilks et al. (1990), Qiu and Frei (1993), Pereira et al. (1993), Niwa and Nitta (1994), Schütze (1993), Lin (1998), Dorrow and Widdows (2003), Hagiwara et al. (2005), Gabrilovich and Markovitch (2007), Davidov and Rappoport (2008).

The WSM allows the use of methods based on machine learning for various tasks including semantic relationship learning. Machine learning represents the data-driven set of approaches. These methods vary in the level of supervision: from unsupervised, semi-supervised to supervised.

The example of the first type of method is clustering that is an unsupervised technique for learning groups of related items in a given set. WSM is directly applied in clustering as data representation model (see Figure 26.).

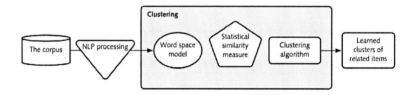

Figure 26. The components of clustering.

The clusters learned by a clustering method strongly rely on the definition of an appropriate statistical similarity measure that computes the similarity between data points (Rada et al. (1989)). A number of similarity measures between two vectors can be used, e.g., Hamming distance, Jaccard index, Dice coefficient, Sørensen similarity index, Damerau – Levenshtein distance, etc. (Pang-Ning Tan, Michael Steinbach and Vipin Kumar (2006)).

Waterman (1996) analyzes *string edit distance*[101] as a metric of similarity between two sentences:

---

[100] Instead of cosine value, a number of other statistical measures can be used: Pearson's correlation, Jacquard's coefficient, MI, Log-likelihood, etc.
[101] Also known as Levenshtein edit distance (Levenshtein (1966)).

Example 44

> The path that is the path.
>
> The way that is not the way.

The matrix of minimum number of operations that are needed to transform one word into another by deletion, and insertion operations is produced (see Table 6.) by following edit distance rule:

$$D(A_i, B_j) = \min \begin{cases} D(A_i, B_{j-1}) + D_{insert}(b_j) \\ D(A_{i-1}, B_j) + D_{insert}(a_i) \\ D(A_{i-1}, B_{j-1}) + D_{substitute}(a_i, b_j) \end{cases} \quad (20)$$

Table 6. Waterman (1996:135), Transformation matrix for vectors A and B, defined by edit distance D(Ai,Bj).

B↓ , A→		the	path	That	is	the	Path
	0	1	2	3	4	5	6
The	1	0	1	2	3	4	5
Way	2	1	2	3	4	5	6
That	3	2	3	2	3	4	5
Is	4	3	4	3	2	3	4
Not	5	4	5	4	3	4	4
The	6	5	6	5	4	3	4
Way	7	6	7	6	5	4	5

In his study, Waterman (1996) introduces the idea that

> *"Word classes* could be defined inductively on this tree of context types by classifying words according to the sets of context types in which they have appeared. The hierarchy of context types and word classes encodes the specificity of the relation to the category".

The research of Faure and Nedellec (1999) implement the idea of clusters of semantically related words based on syntactic evidence. Conceptual clustering uses instantiation frames[102] for the representation of concepts. Faure and Nedellec (1999) give an example of frames (Example 44) which are combined into synthetic frames (Example 45):

Example 45

> <to travel> <subject: father> <by: car>
>
> <to travel> <subject: neighbor> <by: train>
>
> <to drive> <subject: friend> <object: car>
>
> <to drive> <subject: colleague> <object: motor-bike>
>
> <to drive> <subject: friend> <object: motor-bike>

---

[102] The subcategorization frame is: <verb> <preposition | syntactical role: head word>*
An example of the instantiated subcategorization frame for the sentence "My father travels by car." is: <to travel> <subject: father> <by: car>. Stop-words and adjectives are excluded from the frame (Faure and Nedellec (1999)).

Example 46

```
<to travel> <subject: [father(1), neighbor(1)]> <by: [car(1),
train(1))]>

<to drive> <subject: [friend(2), colleague(1)]> <object: [car(1),
motor-bike(2)]
```

Distance dist (C_1, C_2) between two synthetic frames (x) is defined as the proportion of common heads in synthetic frames, where card (C_1) and card (C_2) are number of different head words common to both synthetic frames C_1 and C_2. ΣFC_1 is the sum of the frequencies of the head word of C_1 also occurring in C_2. word$_{iC1}$ corresponds to the i-th word in synthetic frame C_1. Ncomm – shows the number of common headwords for both synthetic frames.

$$dist(C_1, C_2) = 1 - \frac{\sum FC_1 \cdot \frac{N_{comm}}{card(C_1)} + \sum FC_2 \cdot \frac{N_{comm}}{card(C_2)}}{\sum_{i=1}^{card(C_1)} f(word_{iC_1}) + \sum_{i=1}^{card(C_2)} f(word_{iC_2})} \quad (21)$$

The clustering algorithm agglomerates synthetic frames into a cluster if the distance measure is lower than the given threshold. This approach was used for inducing verb hierarchies. The corpus of around 90000 sentences on the topic of cooking recipes was analyzed; 1000 synthetic verb frames were constructed; 249 clusters of 4 levels were learned with the similarity threshold of 43%.

Other authors who have applied unsupervised learning for evaluating contextual word similarity are Dagan et al. (1993), Pereira et al. (1993) Dagan et al. (1994), Grefenstette (1994), Lee and Pereira (1999), Lin (1998), Stevenson and Joanis (2003), mining relationships - McDonalds et al. (2005), Yan et al. (2009).

Supervised learning for semantic relationship detection requires annotated training corpus, which is typically obtained by manual tagging. The principle of relation classifiers[103] is to find a similar case in the training corpus for which class (or label) is known. Based on that, the new case is assigned to the same class. Girju et al. (2006) describe supervised learning approach for part-whole relationship learning. The authors use the following training corpus annotation schema:

Example 47

```
1. Positive examples <X hierarchy#sense, Y hierarchy#sense, Yes>

2. Negative examples <X hierarchy#sense, Y hierarchy#sense, No>

3. Ambiguous examples <X hierarchy#sense, Y hierarchy#sense,
Yes/No>104
```

Sense refers to WordNet sense number. Examples of training pairs (Example 47) and training pairs with semantic classes (Example 48) are:

---

[103] In this case – instance based classifiers.
[104] Example source: Girju et al. (2006:100).

Example 48

```
<aria#1, opera#1, yes>

<apartment#1, woman#1, no>

<hand#1,woman#1, yes>
```

Example 49

```
<leg#2, entity#1, bee#1, entity#1, Yes>
```

Before the generalization of rules, all patterns were clustered into 3 groups: genitive cluster, noun compound cluster and prepositional cluster. By applying the C4.5 *decision tree learning* (Quinlan (1993)), following rules were induced (see Table 7.) from the training patterns.

Table 7. Examples of learned part-whole rules, adapted from Girju et al. (2006:111).

Semantic class – part of	Semantic class – whole	Prec-ision	Freq-uency	Example – part of	Example – whole
communication#2	musical composition#1	50	7	lyric#1	ballad#1
written communication#1	creation#2	50	7	zip code#1	address#6
covering#2	instrumentality#3	96.50	10	roof#	car#1
way#6	structure#1	90.66	10	stairway#1	building#1
opening#10	artifact#1	84.30	10	window#2	bus#1
covering#2	structure#1	82.22	10	roof#1	building#1
artifact#1	covering#2	67.09	10	top#11	roof#1

The authors have reported an overall average precision of 80.95% and recall of 75.91%. Similar research is presented for the causality relationship[105] extraction by Girju (2003); who reported precision of 73.91% and recall of 88.69%.

Supervised learning systems can be applied to even more complicated tasks, such as relationship learning. For instance the WHISK system (Sonderland (1999)) uses user annotated, semi-structured texts[106] for event[107] learning. Evaluated on the MUC-6 Management succession task the system achieves 61% recall and 48.5% precision (Sonderland (1999)).

For more research related to supervised learning techniques for acquiring semantic relationships consider Freitag and McCallum (1999), Finkelstein-Landau and Morin (1999), McCallum and Jensen (2003), Gildea and Jurafsky (2002), Zhang (2008).

In contrast to supervised learning, semi-supervised learning techniques make use of both labeled and unlabeled data for training (Abney (2008)). Semi-supervised learning is seen as an alternative to reduce the cost of annotations required for training. The idea is to discover the similarity between annotated items and unannotated ones, by adding labeled data during iterations. An example of semi-supervised approach can be illustrated by Thelen and Riloff (2002) system Basilisk which is able to induce lexicons of certain semantic categories. The

---

[105] An example of causal pattern <NP1 verb NP2>, where typical causal verbs are: *produce, contribute (to), develop, begin, generate*, etc.

[106] An example of such texts are newspaper advertisements, medical records.

[107] Event is made up of entitie(s) and relation(s). An example of event is: PERSON works for ORGANIZATION.

system uses an unannotated text corpus and a few manually defined *seed words* for each semantic category as input. Before the bootstrapping process, an extraction pattern learner generates patterns for each noun phrase in the corpus. The bootstrapping process initializes with a subset of the extraction patterns. Basilisk measures each candidate word by gathering all patterns that extract it, and measuring how similar those contexts are with words that belong to the semantic category. The five best candidate words are added to the lexicon, and the process continues the iteration. Basilisk system achieves 79,5% accuracy for identifying the semantic category "humans" and 53,2% of accuracy for the identifying semantic category "locations".

Other semi-supervised research approaches are presented in Lapata (2002), Goertzel et al. (2006).

Machine learning algorithms vary in their ability to generalize over large sets of patterns. Patterns that were not detected by the algorithm earlier are likely to be misinterpreted. As T.Segaran (2007) notes, humans have a vast amount of cultural knowledge and experience that helps them to base the decisions about information. Whereas, machine learning methods can only generalize on the basis of the data that has already been created (Segaran (2007)).

R. Yangarber (2003) hints yet at another problem of unsupervised algorithms: when to stop learning. A possible stopping criterion could be human manual reviewing patterns, or special thresholds, i.e., the number of iterations to run, can be set. This is not an issue when the training is made automatic[108].

As far as WSM is concerned, it is important to stress that systems have to be trained for every new task, since WSM only express how strong the relation is between the words, but not the particular type of relation itself.

4.3.2.4 Hybrid Approaches

More recently approaches combining various methods have been proposed. Ruiz-Casado et al. (2005) use WordNet and Wikipedia entries to derive semantic relationships. Wikipedia hyperlinked words represent potential relationships. Firstly each hyperlinked word is matched with the corresponding WordNet *synset*. If for two hyperlinked words corresponding linked *synsets* can be found in WordNet, then the pattern is marked. Extracted patterns are compared and generalized[109]. New generalized patterns are used to find relationships that are not present

---

[108] *The Counter-training* technique for unsupervised pattern acquisition, introduced by R. Yangarber (2003). The idea is to run several identical learners at the same time, and let them compete with one another. The learner stops once, when trying to attempt learning from the text, which was previously used by the other learner. This way competing learners divide data into smaller territories. The counter-training technique brings an improvement in performance: for MUC-6 "Management succession" scenario where mono learner yields about 80% recall at 70% precision, counter-training technique yields higher then around 85% recall at 85% precision.

[109] The example from the Wikipedia: entry – *Adverb* contains the sentence "*Adverb is a part of speech.*"; the generalized pattern is: ENTRY is/VBZ part/NN of/IN TARGET.

in WordNet. Ruiz-Casado reported that 303 holonymy-meronymy relationships not present in WordNet were found. Examples of generalized holonymy-meronymy patterns are:
Example 50

```
(1) */* ENTRY/NNP is/VBZ */* a|the/DT */* Lakes|Republic
|canal|capital|city|coast|country|northeast|province|
region|southwest|state|west/NN in|of/IN TARGET

(2) ENTRY/NNP is/VBZ a|an|the/DT */* in|of/IN the/DT TARGET

(3) */* Things|city|member|north|part|planets|state/NNS in|of/IN
the/DT TARGET
```

For extraction of semantic relationships different strategies apply: linguistic patterns work well for hypernym-hyponym, holonym-meronym relationships; semantic relatedness and distributional similarity measures are effective for synonymy, antonymy, association and co-hyponymy detection. The unique attempt of unifying relationship extraction methodology to be suitable for all types of relationship extraction is proposed by Turney (2008). Turney treats 4 different tasks for recognizing analogy, synonymy, antonymy and association as a problem of classifying word pairs. *PairClass*[110] method is based on a standard supervised machine learning approach - *support vector machine* (SVM) (Vapnik (1995), Platt (1999), Witten and Frank, 2001), with feature vectors as frequencies of patterns calculated from a large corpus. First, the corpus is morphologically preprocessed and searched for phrases like:
Example 51

```
[0 to 1 words] X [0 to 3 words] Y [0 to 1 words]
```

Second, phrases are converted into patterns like:
Example 52

```
"the mason cut the stone with"

"the X cut * Y with",

"* X * the Y *"[111]
```

Each of the patterns represents the feature in the feature vector of the given pair. Finally, the SVM learning algorithm is applied. Table 8., illustrates example pairs and class labels used for training the system.
Turney (2008) reported following accuracies achieved by PairClass: synonymy – 76,2%, analogy – 52,1%, synonymy and antonymy – 75%, association – 77,1%.

---

[110] *PairClass* algorithm is a sequential minimal optimization (SMO) support vector machine (SVM) with a radial basis function (RBF) kernel (Platt, 1998), as implemented inWeka (Waikato Environment for Knowledge Analysis) Witten and Frank (1999).

[111] Example source: Turney (2008). Given word pairs are encoded as X and Y whereas the rest of the phrase is replaced with an asterisk or left unmodified. For a phrase with n words, $2^{(n-2)}$ patterns are gained.

Table 8. Examples of word pairs and class labels used for training, adopted from Turney (2008).

Class label	Word pair
Artisan:material	carpenter:wood
	mason:stone
	potter:clay
	glassblower:glass
Entity:carrier	traffic:street
	water:riverbed
	packets:network
	gossip:grapevine
Synonym	galling:irksome
	yield:bend
	naive:callow
	advise:suggest
Antonym	dissimilarity:resemblance
	commend:denounce
	expose:camouflage
	unveil:veil
Similar	table:bed
	music:art
	hair:fur
	house:cabin
Associated	cradle:baby
	mug:beer
	camel:hump
	cheese:mouse
Similar_and_associated	ale:beer
	uncle:aunt

5. NLP and Ontology Evaluation

Evaluation of ontologies is becoming a key interest in ontology-driven computing. The spread of ontological engineering over the last years fostered the development of a multitude of ontologies. On the one hand, it is good to see that ontologies are becoming more and more a common solution for interoperability problems. On the other hand, the vast number of artefacts leaves potential engineers interested in utilizing ontologies with the problem of identifying the quality of resources available for their concerns. Yet, the development of shared standards to evaluate ontologies seems to be rather slow. This is partly due to reason of difficulty in determining what elements of quality to evaluate (Burton-Jones et al. (2005)).

Lenci (2008) distinguishes three levels of ontological adequacy: observational, descriptive and explanatory. These levels can be seen as the grade system for the evaluation of ontology. Observational adequacy is reached if ontology is logically consistent and sound. Consider for instance the example of conceptual relationships:

Example 53

```
IncomingMessage IS_A Message (correct)

Message IS_A IncomingMessage (incorrect!)
```

Descriptive adequacy is reached when the ontological concepts are interpreted unambiguously:

Example 54

```
BANK1: INSTITUTION

BANK2: LOCATION¹¹²
```

Explanatory adequacy is reached when

> "the ontology provides an explanation about crosslinguistic semantic generalizations, about how concepts
> are acquired, created, etc., and is consistent with cognitive evidence" (Lenci (2008:22)).

Lenci (2008) marks that different purpose ontologies aim at different level of adequacy, for instance, application ontologies mainly are concerned with "a complete and consistent characterization of a certain domain knowledge", whereas language-related ontologies "must reach explanatory adequacy"[113].

---

[112] Example source: Lenci (2008:22).

[113] Lenci (2008) cites two sources proving that language-related ontologies have reached only the descriptive adequacy level: (1) "We believe that human language can be meaningfully mapped to a formal ontology for use in computational understanding of natural language expressions. We have created a formal ontology in a first order

Burton-Jones et al. (2005) present the semiotic metrics[114] framework (see Figure 27.) for assessing the quality of generic, domain and application ontologies.

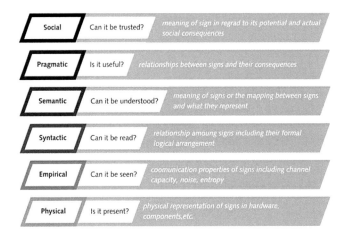

Figure 27. Burton-Jones (2005:89) semiotic framework for the assessment of the quality of ontology.

Physical, empirical and syntactic attributes can be evaluated through checking the logical soundness of the ontology. These properties mostly relate to ontology language and define the degree of right use of the language, or proportion of ontology language features used in ontology. Since physical, empirical and syntactic attributes of ontology have to do with formal analysis of ontology, they will not be analyzed in this theses. Interested readers are suggested to acquaint themselves with (Guarino and Welty (2000), Kanellopoulos (2009), Gómez-Pérez (2004), Lozano-Tello and Gómez-Pérez (2004), Welty (2006), Völker et al. (2008), Staab et al. (2004), Cimiano (2006).

However *semantic* and *pragmatic* properties of quality of ontologies can be automated by the means of NLP. First we need to explain the concept of *semantic* and *pragmatic*[115] properties of quality relevant to NLP.

---

logical language called the Suggested Upper Merged Ontology (SUMO) [...] We have created an index linking all [...] synsets from WordNet to terms in SUMO" (Pease (2007:103)).

(2) "WordNet showed that hyponymy, meronymy, synonymy, antonymy, and a small number of lexical entailment relations are indeed sufficient for organizing the lexicon of English, and WordNets have since been built successfully for a growing number of other languages. Among the most importnat findings of the WordNet experiment are that [...] there are no words that cannot easily be integrated into the network, i.e., all words can be linked to others by means of at least one semantic relation" (Fellbaum (2007:421)).

[114] Semiotic metrics (Stamper et al. (2000)) evaluates syntactic, semantic, pragmatic, and social qualities of ontologies.

[115] Note: semantic and pragmatic quality not to be mixed with the branches of linguistics.

As explained in Burton-Jones et al. (2005) the property of *semantic quality* called *interpretability*[116] has a clear reference to the lexical resources. According to Burton-Jones et al. (2005):

"Semantic quality evaluates the meaning of terms in the ontology library. [...] Preferably the knowledge provided by the ontology can map into meaningful real world concepts [...] This is achieved by checking that the words used by the ontology exists in another independent semantic source, such as a domain-specific lexical database, or a comprehensive, generic lexical database such as WordNet." (Burton-Jones et al. (2005:91)).

The property of interpretability is related to ontology user experience, i.e., how the user will interpret the meaning of ontological concepts. Regarding NLP perspective it clearly refers to WSD and linguistically guided process of concept formation which is described in section 4.3.1.

Similar observation about user related properties of quality is presented by Chimienti et al. (2009). The authors distinguish four different perspectives of evaluating ontology building methodologies: *engineer perspective, process perspective, innovation and learning perspective*[117] and *ontology user perspective*. The later one contains *social quality*[118] of ontology and *pragmatic quality* of ontology. *Pragmatic quality* shows the usefulness of the ontology "regardless of its (ontology's) syntax and semantic" (Chimienti et al. (2009)). The pragmatic quality includes the property of *fidelity*, which objective is to measure

"whether claims an ontology makes are true in the target domain. It is measured by the ration of number of terms due their description to existing trustable references and the total number of terms." (Chimienti et al. (2009:144)).

In other words, pragmatic quality of ontology measures to what extent ontological concepts relate to the source of reference, for instance to domain terminology as presented in Grigonytė et al. (2010).

5.1 Ontology Evaluation Methodologies

Different quality measures of ontologies necessitate diverse evaluation strategies. It is widely accepted that there is a central distinction traditionally[119] drawn between two different evaluation strategies namely "glass box" or "component" evaluation and "black box" or "task based" evaluation. This distinction does apply to evaluation processes regarding ontologies and

---

[116] According to Burton-Jones et al. (2005) there are three properties of semantic quality: interpretability (the meaning of term in the ontology), consistency (term has to have consistent meaning in the ontology) and clarity (the context of term has to be clear).

[117] These three perspectives are related to ontology building, and evaluate various physical and abstract factors like time needed to engineer the ontology, competency of creators of the ontology, amount of properties, concepts and relations used in the ontology, the usage of supporting tools for building ontology, etc.

[118] Social quality measures if ontology is linked with other ontologies (authority property), and how many times it was accessed (history property). In addition Ontology User Satisfaction Overall Score (OUSOS) is measured by the means of semantic quality described by Burton-Jones (2005).

[119] Term borrowed from Software engineering, i.e. *white box testing, black box testing*. Sommerville (2007) *Software Engineering*. Pearson Addison Wesley.

ontology-driven systems as well (Hartmann et al. (2005), Gangemi et al. (2006), Dellschaft and Staab (2008)). The two strategies must be seen as complementary each providing testing for different kinds of qualities.

Gangemi et al. (2006) provides a key source with respect to ontology evaluation describing four different methodologies in that field. Yet, when it comes to evaluating the usability of the methods themselves the authors are merely checking whether or not a methodology is actually in use, regardless of the outcome it produces.

5.1.1 Black Box Strategy

Black box evaluation measures the performance of an ontology-driven application and is typically carried out using the same interfaces that the end-users are going to employ (Hartmann et al. (2005)). Dellschaft and Staab (2008) notes that extrinsic evaluation, i.e., task-based evaluation is the most suitable for assessing the functional dimension of ontology. Gangemi et al. (2006) gives user-friendliness and agreement of domain experts as quintessential measurements to be done in black box evaluations. Other more recent approaches on methods of task-based evaluation include Gilbert and Williams (2008), Suomela and Kekalainen (2006) and Yu et al. (2009).

Naturally, black box evaluation can be done by end-users. Noy (2004) propagates consumer's viewpoint, by suggesting specific user experiences as a) summaries of ontologies, b) collaborative exchange of opinions, and c) accessing special, user-oriented views of the ontologies.

> "We need not only a system for evaluating ontologies objectively from some generic viewpoint [...], but also practical way for ontology consumers to discover and evaluate ontologies." (Noy (2004:8)).

To finalize, black box strategy, is user-experience and task-oriented, thus cannot be directly pursued by means of NLP. In this thesis we will mainly concentrate on the evaluation of the *content* of the ontology approached by glass box strategy.

5.1.2 Glass Box Strategy

Glass box evaluation strategy is used for those evaluation methods which aim at a direct evaluation of the ontology or its engineering as such. It covers aspects like consistency of inference, redundancy, domain coverage, and everything that has to do with logical and structural virtues of the artefact at hand, plus an assessment of the modules of which the ontology at hand is build from (Gangemi et al. (2006)).

Hartmann et al. (2005) stress that glass box evaluating should start in the preparation phase for creating an ontology (type 1) and it should accompany the entire development process (type 2) and should continue after the release of the ontology (type 3). Typically, type 1 and type 2 evaluations are done by the ontology engineer developing the artefact in question, whereas type

3 consists of activities typical for ontology experts outside the project (Hartmann et al. (2005)). Notably, there are no end-users involved in those activities.

Finally the ontology is hard to evaluate as a whole therefore normally components of ontology are evaluated instead. Brank et al. (2005) names possible levels of evaluating components of ontologies:

- **Structure, architecture and design level** refers to manual evaluation of the ontology, aiming at assessing the organization of ontology and its suitability for further development;
- **Context and application level** refers to application and user-experience evaluation, and thus is a level of ontology that can be best addressed by black box evaluation;
- **Syntactic level** evaluation concentrates on the quality with respect to ontology language. Gómez-Pérez (1995) describes the parameters like loops between definitions, and documentation availability.
- **Taxonomical hierarchy and non-taxonomic relations level** is oriented in assessing the quality of relations as components of the ontology. Major efforts include the research by Maedche and Staab (2002), Guarino and Welty (2002), Brewster et al. (2004), Spyns and Hogben (2005), Hicks and Herold (2009).
- **Lexical or concept level** evaluation aims at assessing quantitative feature of quality referring how concepts of the ontology are related to other resources of data relevant to the domain, e.g., other ontologies, domain corpus, vocabularies. Different approaches are presented by Maedche and Staab (2002), Brewster et al. (2004), Daelemans and Reinberger (2004), Gangemi et al. (2006).

From the perspective of glass box (or component) evaluation there exists three major methodologies of evaluation: namely gold standard evaluation, criteria-based and data-driven. All three methodologies are discussed in the following subsections. Of particular interest is data-driven evaluation approaches as the evaluation is processed by using NLP techniques.

5.1.2.1 Gold Standard Approach

Dellschaft and Staab (2008) present an approach for evaluating ontologies by comparing the previously created gold standard ontology with the learned ontology. Basically in this way the algorithm of ontology learning is being evaluated. Gold standard ontology either 1) can be designed particularly for the task of evaluation by human experts, or 2) an existing ontology can be taken. The similarity between ontology and gold standard is measured in *lexical* and *taxonomical levels* by means of precision and recall.

If computed ontology is O_C and reference ontology – O_R, then *lexical precision* (22) and *lexical recall* (23) are calculated:

$$LP(O_c, O_R) = \frac{|C_C \cap C_R|}{|C_C|} \qquad (22)$$

$$LR(O_c, O_R) = \frac{|C_C \cap C_R|}{|C_R|} \qquad (23)$$

where C_R and C_C are concept sets of reference and computed ontologies.

Similarly the values of *taxonomic precision* and *recall* are acquired. Two measures are combined: local measure evaluates the position of two concepts; and global measure evaluates whole structure of taxonomies (Dellschaft and Staab (2008)). The whole structure of taxonomy is evaluated by the sum of semantic cotopies, i.e., the extracts containing a concept and the path from the concept to the root of ontology.

5.1.2.2 Criteria-based Approach

The term of *criteria-based approach* is used in Dellschaft and Staab (2008) to illustrate a wide range of evaluation techniques that concentrate on how well ontology represents certain criteria. According to Brewster et al. (2004) the notions of *precision* and *recall* can not be directly applied for the whole ontology evaluation therefore decomposing an ontology evaluation task into components is a straightforward way for approaching the problem. Criteria range can vary from components of ontology till complex philosophical properties, as addressed in Guarino and Welty (2004). Criteria-based evaluation approaches are performed manually. However recently Völker at al. (2005) has presented an approach for automating the process.

As example of criteria-based approach is Guarino's (2004) paper, where he analyzes the evaluation of the *content* of ontology.

Guarino (2004) proposes to concentrate on evaluating conceptualizations:

"ontologies are only approximate specifications of conceptualizations. So it seems appropriate to evaluate them [...]" (Guarino (2004:6)).

The object of evaluation – the conceptualization – is formalized:

$$C = <D, W, R> \qquad (24)$$

Where C is conceptualization, D is a set of relevant entities in a domain which is finite, W is a set of possible states, and R is a set of conceptual relations.

The evaluation is approached by means of *precision* (26) and *coverage* (25), see Figure 28.

$$C = \frac{|I_K \cap O_K|}{|I_K|} \qquad (25) \quad [120]$$

$$P = \frac{|I_K \cap O_K|}{|O_K|} \qquad (26)$$

---

[120] I_K – the set of the intended models in the domain **D**, O_K – the set of the ontology axioms.

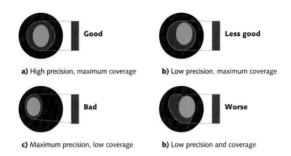

Figure 28. Guarino (2004): "A comparison of different ontologies with respect to coverage and precision".

Other criteria based approaches are presented by Guarino (1998), Gómez-Pérez (1999), Hovy (2001), Sabou et al. (2006).

5.1.2.3 Data-driven Approach

The biggest drawback of the gold standard approach is the amount of effort and time required for building a reference ontology. Criteria-based approaches are labor intensive too. A way to overcome the problem is to automate the evaluation and orientate it towards the data. Daelemans and Reinberger (2004) argue that the evaluation of ontologies should be guided not towards syntax, as it is in gold standard or criteria based approaches, but rather towards semantics of ontologies. This way it is possible to assure that ontology represents "consensual conceptualization and not just one person's ideas".

Gangemi et al. (2006) propose to evaluate ontology on the basis of the corpus. For that two conditions have to be valid: firstly classes and relation of the ontology has to be lexicalized, i.e., expressed in natural language; secondly a substantial amount of text covering the content of the ontology has to be available. The evaluation is done by identifying the frequency of ontological elements in the corpus. The relative frequency of a class c[121] is the proportion of mentions of ontology instances which are equal to c and is calculated as following:

$$P(c) = \frac{count(c)}{\sum_i count(c_i)} \qquad (27)$$

---

[121] The same applies for calculating the relative frequency of relations.

The low frequency measure is interpreted as the class is under represented in the ontology. Besides new senses of instances can be discovered as words are polysemous, e.g., 'Washington' is both a person and a location (Gangemi et al. (2006)).

Daelemans and Reinberger (2004) describe the scenario of an ontology evaluation carried out through corpus based evaluation of concepts and relationships. Differently as in Gangemi et al. (2006) here corpus is syntactically analyzed and all the occurrences of terms of the domain[122] are extracted from the corpus. By using pattern matching technique relationships are detected and used as contextual data for the clustering of terms. According to the authors clusters can be interpreted as the evaluation of the extension of concepts.

Brewster et al. (2004) proposes a more elaborated *ontology-corpus* evaluation approach. Similarly as in Daelemans and Reinberger (2004) clusters of terms are learned from the domain corpus. Then authors process with expanding the representation of lexical realizations by adding two levels of hypernyms taken from WordNet to each term in the cluster. Finally sets of clusters are mapped to the ontology. The evaluation measure called *structural fit* expresses the conditional probability of the best fit ontology O*, given the ontology O and a corpus C:

$$O^* = \arg\max_O P(O \mid C) = \arg\max_O \frac{P(C \mid O)P(O)}{P(C)} \quad (28)$$

Recently Hicks and Herold (2009) proposed data-driven approach for evaluating meta-properties of ontologies like rigidity[123]. The method is based upon the assumption that certain linguistic expressions are used that express ontological meta-properties.

"Thus, one can deduce a concept's meta-properties from the usage of the concept's lexical representation (LR) in natural language" Hicks and Herold (2009:7).

The example of rigid and non-rigid patterns:

Example 55

```
Y would make a good X

Y is no longer (-/a/an) X¹²⁴
```

The method is made up of the following steps: firstly hand crafted patterns are issued as queries for the search engines and results are being collected. Then based on the results feature vectors for each lexical representation of concept are built. Finally classification of feature vectors to the appropriate rigidity tag is performed. For the evaluation of the rigidity property of the ontology, non-rigid patterns are used. Lexical realizations of concepts are checked whether the non-rigid pattern apply to them.

---

[122] Terms of the domain can be determined manually or by means of automatic terminology acquisition.

[123] Rigidity was presented in OntoClean (Guarino and Welty (2002)) methodology for evaluating ontological taxonomies, it is a meta-property of ontologies. According to Hicks and Herold (2009:6): "The notion of rigidity relies on the philosophical notion of essence. An essential concept is one that necessarily holds for all of its instances. For example, being an animal is essential to being a cat since it is impossible for a cat to not be an animal."

[124] X can be a single word, multiword unit or a complex syntactic phrase.

***

An ontology is subject to continuous change. Therefore, its evaluation should be flexible in assessing changes in the domain. This aspect can be addressed by simply extending the corpora of the domain by adding new genres or types of texts.

Different ontology evaluation strategies are able to asses different semiotic levels of ontologies (see Table 9). Ideally evaluation strategies must be seen as complementary each providing testing for different kinds of qualities.

Table 9. Strategies for ontology evaluation and their coverage of semiotic properties of ontologies.

The evaluation strategy		Semiotic level of evaluation					
		physical	Empiric	syntactic	semantic	pragmatic	social
Manual		+	+	+	+		
Task oriented	Black-box					+	+
Component oriented	Gold standard		+	+			
	Component	+	+	+	+		
	Data-Driven				+	+	

6. Proposed Research Methodology

In this section the NLP driven methodology for the tasks of ontology learning and ontology evaluation is discussed. The research was also reported in: Čulo et al. (2008), Grigonytė et al. (2008), Grigonytė and Haller (2008), Grigonytė et al. (2009), Grigonytė et al. (2010), Grigonytė et al. (2010a).

6.1 Overview of the Experimental Domains

Two different domains are investigated in this thesis: *cancer research* and *computer dependability*. Following sections introduce these research domains and their objectives[125].

6.1.1 The ACGT Project

Advancing Clinico-Genomic Trials on Cancer (ACGT)[126] is an EU-funded Integrated Project. ACGT develops a bio-medical infrastructure supporting seamless mediation services for sharing clinical and genomic expertise. Such interactions will allow joint clinico-genomic trials and aid the finding of quicker and efficient routes when identifying patients' individual characteristics that make one treatment more appropriate than another. The semantic integration of the data will be provided by a mediator which is based on the ACGT Master Ontology (ACGT MO)[127].

The ACGT integrated project aims to address the obstacles created by the flood of multilevel datasets (from the molecular, to the organ, to the individual level), and the lack of a common infrastructure for clinical research institutions and the creators of molecular data. As a result of this situation, very few cross-site studies and multi-centric clinical trials are performed, and in most cases it is not possible to seamlessly integrate multi-level data. Moreover, clinical researchers and molecular biologists often find it hard to take advantage of each other's expertise due to the absence of a cooperative environment which enables the sharing of data, resources, or tools for comparing results and experiments, and of a uniform platform supporting the seamless integration and analysis of disease-related data at all levels Buetow (2005). ACGT

---

[125] Erlier versions of sections 6.2.1. and 6.2.2. was published in Grigonytė et al. (2010) and in Grigonytė et al. (2009).
[126] http://www.eu-acgt.org/
[127] Project description source: http://www.ifomis.org/wiki/ACGT

is endeavouring is to overcome these obstacles by setting up a semantic grid infrastructure in support of multi-centric, post-genomic clinical trials (Tsiknakis et al. (2008)).

The system which the project aims for will facilitate the horizontal transfer of laboratory findings data to the clinical management and treatment of patients' database systems. This goal can only be achieved if state-of-the-art semantic technologies are part of the IT environment. In order to meet this goal, the ACGT project needed an ontology to be utilized in the context of the selected Local-As-View (LAV) database integration strategy (Cali (2004)). In such integration strategy the ontology plays the role of a global schema, to which all local schemata are mapped, solving the different data heterogeneities present in the integrated sources. To this end, the ontology is needed to cover both, a unified terminology and an independent schema construct meanings. The ACGT project achieves the integration of heterogeneous biomedical databases through a grid service oriented semantic mediation software layer that makes use of the ACGT-MO[128] (Tsiknakis (2006)). However, before building a new terminology resource the state-of-the-art of semantic representations of cancer research and management was assessed to prevent unnecessary developments.

The ACGT Semantic Mediation Layer (ACGT-SM) is made up of a set of tools and resources that collaborate in the processes of Database Integration and Semantic Mediation (Figure 29.).

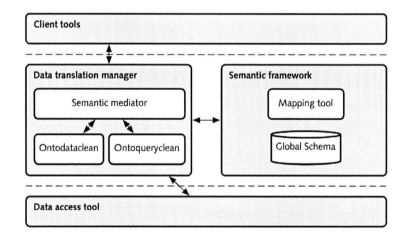

Figure 29. ACGT Semantic Mediator Layer architecture.

The ACGT-SM offers two main services, namely 1) launching a query and receiving results, and 2) browsing repository schema. The latter shows a subset of the ACGT-SM underlying

---

[128] http://www.ifomis.org/acgt/1.0

RDF schema. This subset is built taking into consideration a user's needs.

This software system has been tested with clinical relational and image databases Luis et al. (2007), obtaining promising results. The user query tool has been developed by the consortium, aiding non-technical users in the processes of building and launching SPARQL queries.

6.1.2 The ReSIST Project

ReSIST is an Network of Excellence that addresses the strategic objective "Towards a global dependability and security framework" of the EU Work Programme, and responds to the stated "need for resilience, self-healing, dynamic content and volatile environments".[129]

One of the goals of the ReSIST project is to create a structured representation of the concepts underlying the contents of the large and very rapidly increasing set of documents that represent knowledge in the technical domain of *resilience.*

The purpose of the representation, in the form of a thesaurus and an ontology, is to be able to use natural language processing tools to perform computer-aided identification and classification of existing documents concerned with resilience that have been generated from the time when the correctness of the results of computations became a concern of the first computer users in the 1940's until the present, and to classify new documents as they are generated.

Dependability has naturally concerned most disciplines of informatics (computer science and engineering) since the early days. As a consequence, significantly different terminologies were developed by different communities to describe the same aspects of dependability. The terminologies became entrenched through usage at annual conferences, in books, journals, research reports, standards, industrial handbooks and manuals, patents, etc.

As an example we have the concepts of *resilience, dependability, trustworthiness, survivability, high confidence, high assurance, robustness, self-healing*, etc., whose definitions appear to be identical or to overlap extensively. In many cases the definitions themselves have multiple versions that depend on a given author's preference.

An example of a long-term effort to create a framework of dependability concepts is the effort within the Technical Committee on Dependable Computing and Fault Tolerance of the IEEE Computer Society and the IFIP Working Group 10.4 that began with a special session at FTCS-12 in 1982. Since then it has resulted in a series of papers, a six-language book in 1992 (Laprie (1992)), and in 2004 the paper "Basic Concepts and Taxonomy of Dependable and Secure Computing" (Avižienis et al. (2004)).

The use of several synonyms or near-synonyms that lack well-defined distinctions is a source of continuing confusion that leads to re-inventions and plagiarism, impairs the transfer of research results to practical use and blocks the recognition of related documents.

The orderly progress of dependability research and its practical applications requires that past work as well as new results should be classified on the basis of a single ontology and thus made

---

[129] Project presentation source: http://www.resist-noe.org/overview/presentation.html

accessible to the entire profession. The complementary solution is to augment the human effort by the use of automatic natural language processing tools for the task of computer-aided building of a consensus ontology.

A dependability ontology is an integral part of an ontology for all of informatics, or (in North American terminology) of computer science and engineering. Such an ontology does not exist at present. The only existing and widely used taxonomy that could be used to build it is the ACM Computing Classification System (CCS)[130]. The CCS was created in 1988 and was last revised in 1998.

6.2 Domain Corpora

In this section two domain corpora, 1) on cancer research and 2) on computer dependability are presented.

6.2.1 Corpus of Cancer Research

With regard to the ACGT project, the Corpus of Cancer Research (COCR) is the collection of 3334 domain specific abstracts of scientific publications. In general, the domain of the ACGT MO is cancer research and management. Due to the focus of the project the ACGT MO ontology is concentrated on three types of cancer: mammary carcinoma, nephroblastoma (Wilms' tumour) and rhabdoid tumour. The corpus of cancer research (COCR) contains 3334 domain specific abstracts of scientific publications extracted from the PubMed[131] on three types of cancer:

>   (1) the mammary carcinoma register (COCR1) made of 1500 abstracts,
>   (2) the nephroblastoma register (COCR2) made of 1500 abstracts, and
>   (3) the rhabdoid tumor register (COCR3) made of 334 abstracts.

The small number of abstracts on rhabdoid tumour reflects Pubmed's publication situation on the topic. A high number of publications dealing specifically with this tumour does not exist. The summary of the COCR corpus is given in Table 10.; distribution of three corpus registers token-wise is depicted in Figure 30.

Table 10. The COCR corpus.

	COCR1 (mammary carcinoma)	COCR2 (nephroblastoma)	COCR2 (rhabdoid tumour)	COCR (all registers)
Tokens	336745	227477	46215	610437
Sentences	15195	10575	2321	28091

---

[130] http://www.acm.org/about/class/
[131] http://www.ncbi.nlm.nih.gov/pubmed/

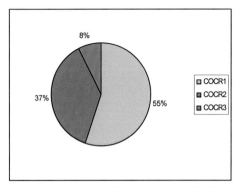

Figure 30. The Corpus of Cancer Research (COCR).

The example of a COCR abstract can be viewed in Appendix A1.

6.2.2 Corpus on Computer Dependability

The Corpus Of Computer Dependability Research (COCD) is the collection of 4854 domain specific abstracts of scientific publications. The domain of computer dependability is presented by research papers presented at:

1) the 29 annual International Symposia on Fault-Tolerant Computing (1971-1999),
2) and at their successors, the 10 International Conferences on Dependable Systems and Networks (2000-2009).

The Corpus Of Computer Dependability Research (COCD) is a collection of 4854 abstracts on computer dependability extracted from the IEEE (http://ieee.rkbexplorer.com/) repository. An example of an abstract can be viewed in Appendix A2.

The summary of the COCD corpus is given in Table 11.; The COCD corpus is a unique document collection since it captures the development of the entire domain of the computer dependability in almost 40 years spanning from 1971, when the first domain specific conference started, till the present day.

Table 11. The COCD corpus.

	COCD
Tokens	412265
Sentences	18974

6.3   Term Extraction

From NLP perspective, there are three approaches for terminology extraction: linguistic, statistic and hybrid. Terminology extraction systems based on linguistic approaches have a higher than 70% coverage in term extraction (see Bennet et al. (1999), Bourigault et al. (2001)). Statistical term extraction approaches, when given a big annotated training corpus, can perform almost as well, but these methods do not always guarantee the integrity of the term (Frantzi and Ananiadou (1999), Chen et al. (2006)). Practice, however, shows that linguistic approaches (i.e., rule based) outperform statistical ones with regard to precision, but by combining both linguistic and statistical approaches in various stages of term extraction, we get better results (Schiller (1996), Bourigault et al. (2001)).

Most of hybrid term extraction procedures share the same step where term candidates are captured. The important question which remains is how to distinguish between domain specific terms and general NPs. Nagakawa (2001) notes, that in order to extract domain specific terms from term candidates, a ranking of term candidates according to their termhood is necessary. Usually, a term's informational value (termhood) is captured by statistical methods (IDF, MI, log likelihood, entropy, etc.).

The proposed hybrid approach for terminology extraction is based on and extends AUTOTERM described by Haller (2006), Hong et al. (2001). The new method combines linguistic pattern matching and statistical termhood assessment techniques. The following section introduces the methodology.

6.3.1   Term Extraction Methodology

The methodology for automatic term extraction is made up of following steps: linguistic processing, statistical termhood evaluation, and term hierarchy building. Linguistic processing includes morphological analysis of the domain text, syntactic parsing, rule-based NP detection, stop-word filtering, and term variant detection. The termhood is evaluated by statistical IDF measure and by contrasting with general language corpus. All the steps are automated. The Architecture of TE pipeline is illustrated in Figure 31.

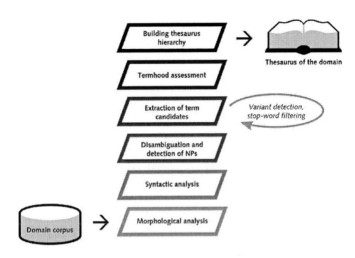

Figure 31. The pipeline architecture of TE.

6.3.1.1 Morphological Analysis

The linguistic processing starts with morphological analysis of unstructured language texts. An example of domain text is given in Appendices A1 and A2. We have used the rule based MPRO system (Maas et al. (2009)) which has linguistic data sets for English and German. The MRPO system delivers a tag set for each analyzed token. Consider for instance the output of analysis of unambiguous word *mechanism* and ambiguous word *secret*:

Example 56

```
mechanism

{ori=mechanisms,wnra=3373,wnrr=11,snr=155,pctr=yes,last=no,pctl=n
o,offset=20938,lw=no,gra=small,nb=plu,case=nom;acc,s=ismus,ds=mec
hanic~ism,ls=mechanic,w=1,c=noun,ew=0,lu=mechanism,ts=mechanism,t
=mechanism,ehead={case=nom;acc,nb=plu},mlu=mechanism}


secret

{ori=secret,wnra=3390,wnrr=28,snr=155,osaw=$iaibl$sm,pctr=no,last
=no,pctl=yes,offset=21058,lw=no,gra=small,ds=secret,ls=secret,w=1
,cs=a,deg=base,c=adj,s=nil,ew=0,lu=secret,ts=secret,t=secret,ehea
d={case=nom;acc,nb=sg;plu},saw=&b,mlu=secret}
```

```
{ori=secret,wnra=3390,wnrr=28,snr=155,osaw=$iaibl$sm,pctr=no,last
=no,pctl=yes,offset=21058,lw=no,gra=small,nb=sg,case=nom;acc,s=wi
ssen,ds=secret,ls=secret,w=1,cs=n,c=noun,ew=0,lu=secret,ts=secret
,t=secret,ehead={case=nom;acc,nb=sg},saw=&b,mlu=secret}[132]
```

The tag set includes information such as the word order in a sentence, lemma, number, part of speech, derivation, semantic class, etc. An example of an MPRO-annotated sentence is given in Appendix B1.

6.3.1.2 Syntactic Analysis

Morphological disambiguation and syntactic parsing is the following step of linguistic processing. We have used the KURD software (Carl and Schmidt-Wigger (1998)) based on finite-state technology formalism. An example of KURD output for phrase *stringent scalability requirement*:

Example 57

```
{ori=stringent,lu=stringent,mlu=stringent,snr=38,wnra=1044,wnrr=7
,offset=6295,saw=&b,osaw=$iaibl$sm,ew=0,lw=no,last=no,pctr=no,pct
l=no,c=adj,sc=adj,vtyp=nil,ehead={nb=plu;sg,per=3,case=acc;nom},n
b=plu;sg,case=acc;nom,per=3,deg=base,gra=small,error=nil,partner=
nil,dtype=nil,atype=pre;pro,advtype=nil,adjval=nil,w=1,cs=a,ds=st
ringent,ts=stringent,t=stringent,ls=stringent,s=nil,chunked=strin
gent#scalability#requirement,phr={i=111224,c=np,sc=no,b=7,e=9,of=
6,sure=yes,multi=nil,f=obj},ephr={nb=sg,case=acc;nom,per=3,s=atio
n},cl={c=hs,sc=hs,b=1,e=10,sure=yes},markcoord=nil,np_cand=a,mark
clause=111776,markphr=np,aatype=pre;pred;pro,style=np,bstyle=np}
```

```
,{ori=scalability,lu=scalability,mlu=scalability,snr=38,wnra=1045
,wnrr=8,offset=6307,saw=&b,osaw=$iaibl$sm,ew=0,lw=no,last=no,pctr
=no,pctl=no,c=noun,sc=nil,vtyp=nil,ehead={nb=sg,per=3,case=acc;no
m},nb=sg,case=acc;nom,per=3,gra=small,error=nil,partner=nil,dtype
=nil,ptype=nil,atype=nil,advtype=nil,subjtype=nil,w=1,ds=scale~ab
le~ity,ts=scalability,t=scalability,ls=scale,s=quality,chunked=st
ringent#scalability#requirement,headnoun=no,sem=quality,fc=yes,vt
ype=nil,ntype=nil,phr={i=111224,c=np,sc=no,b=7,e=9,of=6,sure=yes,
multi=nil,f=obj},ephr={nb=sg,case=acc;nom,per=3,s=ation},cl={c=hs
,sc=hs,b=1,e=10,sure=yes},markcoord=nil,np_cand=n,markclause=1117
76,markphr=np,ncand=yes,style=np}
```

```
,{ori=requirement,lu=requirement,mlu=requirement,snr=38,wnra=1046
,wnrr=9,offset=6319,ew=0,lw=yes,last=no,pctr=yes,pctl=no,c=noun,s
c=nil,vtyp=nil,ehead={nb=sg,per=3,case=acc;nom},nb=sg,case=acc;no
m,per=3,gra=small,error=nil,partner=nil,dtype=nil,ptype=nil,atype
=nil,advtype=nil,subjtype=nil,w=1,ds=require~ment,ts=requirement,
t=requirement,ls=require,s=ation,chunked=stringent#scalability#re
```

---

[132] The tags of the MRPO software are explained in Appendix B3.

```
quirement,headnoun=yes,sem=ation,fc=yes,vtype=nil,ntype=nil,phr={
i=111224,c=np,sc=no,b=7,e=9,of=6,sure=yes,multi=nil,f=obj},ephr={
nb=sg,case=acc;nom,per=3,s=ation},cl={c=hs,sc=hs,b=1,e=10,sure=ye
s},markcoord=nil,np_cand=n,markclause=111776,markphr=np,lwcl=yes,
ncand=yes,style=np,estyle=np}¹³³
```

Tags like `markphr`, or `subjcand` indicate the phrase. In analyzed phrase *stringent scalability requirement* the head word is marked by tag `chunked`:

Example 58

```
stringent    chunked=stringent#scalability#requirement,headnoun=no

scalability  chunked=stringent#scalability#requirement,headnoun=no

requirement  chunked=stringent#scalability#requirement,headnoun=
yes
```

An example of an KURD-annotated sentence is given in Appendix B2.

6.3.1.3 Noun Phrase Detection

Syntactic analysis is followed by the tagging of acronyms, proper names, possible single word terms and noun phrases. Rules for marking NPs:

Example 59

```
(1) det + N + N, e.g., the birth rate

Aa{c=det},

*Aa{c=noun}a{headnoun=no},

Aa{c=noun}a{headnoun=yes},

:Ar{np=ok}.
```

```
(2) det + adj_ing + (N) + N, e.g., (an) incoming message

Na{c=det},

*Aa{c=adj}a{subjcand=_}a{vtyp=ing},

*a{c=noun}e{headnoun=no},

Aa{c=noun,headnoun=yes},

:Ar{np=ok}.
```

```
(3) N-adj + N, e.g., fault-tolerant sytem

*Aa{c=noun}e{headnoun=no},
```

---

¹³³ The tags of the KURD software are explained in Appendix B3.

```
^a{sc=hyphen},
Aa{c=adj},
Aa{c=noun}a{headnoun=yes}e{nb=_NB}
:Ar{np=ok}.¹³⁴
```

6.3.1.4 Variant Detection and Stop-word Filtering

The final phase of linguistic processing includes variant detection and stop-word filtering. The variant detection is solved by detailed morphological analysis, i.e words that have the same morphemes[135] can be easily detected and a decision which form to use can be taken. Consider for instance:

Example 60

```
ds=mechanic~ism,ls=mechanic
ds=gossip~ing,ls=gossip
ds=techno~ique,ls=techno
ds=communicate~ion,ls=communicate
```

The stop-word filtering is a standard best practice technique in TE. Applying the stop-word list assures that only terminologically relevant NPs will be extracted. Usually stop-word lists include stop-words as for instance:

Example 61

```
less
never
next
```

Stop-word lists definitely help to reduce noise in the extracted candidate terms. The drawback of a stop-word list is that the list has to be designed for each domain that is going to be extracted. For this reason the generic stop-word list has been used. In this thesis we have relied more on statistical term candidate filtering.

6.3.1.5 Statistical Filtering of Term Candidates

The linguistic processing phase delivers the list of term candidates. Consider for instance an example text snippet:

---

[134] '*' stands for one or more, ':' indicates the tag result, 'a' – stands for and, 'e' – stands for or, '^' marks symbol, 'A' – indicates item, 'Na' – indicates optional item.
[135] In MPRO software the derivation tag 'ds' and original form tag 'ls' are encoded.

Example 62

```
Circuit techniques are used to make sections of the design robust
to non-delay faults. The combination of these is an asynchronous
defect-tolerant circuit where a large class of faults are
tolerated, and the remaining faults can be both detected easily
and isolated to a small region of the design.
```

The term candidate list for the given text is:

```
circuit techniques

non-delay faults

combination

asynchronous defect-tolerant circuit

large class

fault

remaining fault

small region

design
```

However, candidate terms like *combination, large class, remaining fault* and *small region* are not specific enough to be terms of the domain. One solution could be extending the stop-word list with adjectives *remaining, small, large,* and noun *combination.* The other is a statistical evaluation of the term candidate.

The first term candidate filtering technique is the measure of Inverse Document Frequency (IDF) which shows the importance of the candidate term in the domain corpus. IDF value for the term is obtained by dividing the number of all documents by the number of documents containing the term:

$$idf(t) = \log\left(\frac{|D|}{\{d : t \in d\}}\right) \qquad (29)$$

IDF value ensures that two requirements are met: first, a term cannot be too general, i.e., a term occurring in a document has to be a reliable indicator for what topic the article is about; and second, a term cannot be too specialized, i.e., terms that only occur once and about whose status we therefore cannot be sure. However, the statistical measures of IDF are reliable when the data set is large enough. For both domain corpora we have encountered a large number of terms that occur only once or twice.

Yet another filtering technique which deals with the domain specificity of a term is to contrast two different data sets, i.e., domain specific corpus and general corpus, to measure the difference of how the words are used in both corpora. In this thesis we have used the BNC[136] corpus as the general language corpus. The frequencies of term candidates and their constituent words calculated with respect to the BNC corpus. The high frequency of word or phrase indicates that it is general. Consider for instance the occurrence counts of words and phrases in the BNC corpus and the COCD corpus is presented in Table 12.

Table 12. The occurrence counts of words and phrases in the BNC corpus and in the COCD corpus.

Token or phrase	# in BNC	# in COCD	cf	BNC_IDF
Era	289327	1	0,0000035	18,14234
Way	240019	7	0,0000292	15,06543
System	60342	141	0,0023367	8,741324
Voting	2372	1	0,0004216	11,21189
voting system	87	1	0,0114943	6,442943

If we consider very rare candidate terms extracted from the COCD corpus like *voting*, *voting system* and *era* it is clear that statistical evaluation can be reliable only by contrasting it with the general language corpus. In the BNC corpus the word *era* has a high occurrence count; therefore it is clearly too general to be considered as a domain term. The same applies to the word *voting*. However the phrase *voting system* is met only 87 times in the BNC corpus, thus proving to be more domain specific[137].

The contrastive frequency *cf* of a term *t* is its occurrence count in the domain corpus divided by its occurrence count in the general corpus:

$$cf = \frac{N_{DOM}}{N_{GEN}} \qquad (30)$$

Similar to IDF (29), we calculate the contrastive value (gc_idf) for a term *t*, dividing the number of term *t* occurrence in general language corpus by the number of documents in domain specific corpus containing the term:

$$gc\_idf(t) = \log\left(\frac{|N_{GEN}|}{\{d_{DOM} : t \in d_{DOM}\}}\right) \qquad (31)$$

For the statistical values the thresholds have to be defined. With the threshold value $\delta \leq 9.5$, only two candidate terms from the Table 12., would be proposed as domain terms. i.e., *system* and *voting system*.

---

[136] http://www.natcorp.ox.ac.uk/, the British National Corpus is a 100 million word collection of samples of written and spoken language from a wide range of sources, designed to represent a wide cross-section of current British English.

[137] Here we are aware that *voting system* can have entirely different meaning in the BNC than in the COCD corpus. The final decision of approving the term has to be done by experts of the domain. Nevertheless the comparison of COCD corpus occurrence counts to BNC corpus occurrence counts definitely helps to determine non-domain terms and thus can be automated.

6.3.1.6 Hierarchical Organization of Domain Terms

Finally the extracted term list is structurally organized. The morphological information of NP heads[138] is used to propose hypernyms. To create a hierarchy from general to more special terms we have used a simple method: non-compound terms together with head-words are considered as higher hierarchy nodes; in addition, for each term t_x with n compound parts, we check if a term t_y consisting only of the n-1 rightmost term parts exsist; if so, the term t_x becomes a subterm of t_y. A pseudo code for establishing term hierarchy is as follows:

```
(32)

1. read all terms

1.1. arrange (all term, by number of tokens)

(read all extracted terms)


2.    for each term

2.1.  if headWord is unique

2.1.1. then uniqueHeadWord := treeRoot

(find all unique terms and head words that can be nodes of
hierarchy)


3.    for each term

3.1.  if (headWord equals uniqueHeadWord)

3.1.1. then branchPosition := insertIntoTree (term,
uniqueHeadWord)

3.2. if term is unique

3.2.1 then iterate insertIntoTree (term, branchPosition)

(arrange all candidate terms into hierarchy based on head words)


4. return tree
```

As the result all terms are arranged by hypernym-co-hyponyms structure. An example of the constructed hierarchy is:

Example 63

```
fault

| bridge fault

| design fault
```

---

[138] NP head here is the right most constituent of the NP, necessarily noun.

```
|| latent design fault
|| residual design fault
| physical fault
| redundant fault
| stuck-open fault
```

The discussed hybrid methodology for domain term extraction[139] and term hierarchy construction (Avižienis et al. (2007), Čulo et al. (2007), Grigonytė et al. (2008), Grigonytė and Haller (2008), Avižienis et al. (2009)) is applied on two different domains. The results are described in section 7.

6.4   Relationship Learning

In the previous section we have shown how domain specific terms can be organized by hypernym-hyponym and co-hyponym relationship groups. This approach is linguistically oriented, since syntactic rules are used to determine the headword of the phrase. The headwords of phrases and single terms were treated as hypernyms, and multi-word unit terms were assumed to be hyponyms.

As presented in section 4.3.2, relationship learning can be oriented towards two main strategies: semantic relatedness and distributional similarity. The first one includes using lexical resources like WordNet. However, for specific domains WordNet is not always the best resource to rely upon. According to the statistics reported by Roark and Charniak (1998) 3 out of every 5 terms generated by their semantic lexicon learner are not present in WordNet. Thelen and Riloff (2002) point out a similar drawback of WordNet, which is a general semantic dictionary and therefore lacks specialized vocabulary and jargon that is needed for specific domains (Thelen and Riloff (2002)).

These limitations can be overcome when corpus-based relationship learning strategy is based on distributional similarity.

The proposed approach for relationship learning is based on and extends the method proposed by Cordeiro et al. (2007) and Cordeiro et al. (2009). We propose an unsupervised and language-independent methodology based on paraphrase alignment which does not depend on linguistic processing, or manual definition of patterns or training sets, and outperforms other unsupervised distributional similarity-based approaches. The following section introduces the methodology.

---

[139] Also see Appendices C1, C2, C3, C4.

6.4.1 Methodology of Relationship Learning

In this section we discuss the approach originally designed for synonym and near synonym learning. Semantically similar words can be captured on the basis of textual context as thoroughly explained by Evert (2005). However the drawback of distributional similarity approach is that words need to appear in the particular context for a substantial number of times. To overcome this bottleneck we propose to align paraphrases from domain corpora and discover words that probably can be interchanged[140] within the aligned context, called *paraphrase twist* patterns.

Similarly, the role of paraphrasing is explored by Van der Plas and Tiedemann (2006):

> "People use multiple ways to express the same idea. These alternative ways of conveying the same information in different ways are referred to by the term *paraphrase* and in the case of single words sharing the same meaning we speak of *synonyms*." (Van der Plas and Tiedemann (2006: 866)).

The process of the extraction of semantically similar word pairs or phrase pairs is illustrated in Figure 32.

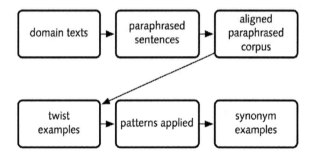

Figure 32. The process scheme for synonymy extraction.

The processing pipeline starts with unstructured domain texts. All the sentences are compared and if similarities are detected, then the alignments are established. For instance, consider sentences like:

Example 64

```
Wilms' tumor is the most common renal tumor in children.

Wilms' tumor is the most common renal malignancy of childhood.
```

---

[140] Words are synonyms or near synonyms.

These two sentences share a significant number of words, in the same order, therefore the differing parts of the sentences are potential candidates for alignment. In order to detect potential synonyms that appear in similar contexts we have applied the method proposed by (Cordeiro et al. (2007, 2009)) for monolingual domain corpus paraphrasing. Their paraphrase alignment technique uses an adapted *Sumo metric* which calculates *strength* and relies on two properties:

First, the method penalizes equal or almost equal sentences[141] that overlap substantially, for instance:

Example 65

        Hello request was sent.

        A hello request was sent.

Second, the method takes into account pairs that have a high degree of lexical reordering, and therefore a different syntactic structure is taken into consideration. The proposed approach uses *Sumo-metric* (Cordeiro et al. (2007)) which outperforms simple *N-gram overlap, edit-distance* and *BLEU metric* to calculate the semantic similarity. When the paraphrases are detected and similar sentences are aligned, a type of aligned sentence segments – *twists* are explored. By using *twist* pattern, synonymous single words or multi-word unit pairs are extracted. Some of extracted pairs appear to be not synonymic, but have another semantic relationship. Experimental results are discussed in section 7.

The steps of the proposed approach are presented in the following subsections.

6.4.1.1 Paraphrase Identification

(Barzilay and Lee (2003)) and (Dolan et al. (2004)) have proposed unsupervised method for automatic paraphrase identification and extraction. However, these unsupervised methodologies show a major drawback by extracting quasi-exact or even exact match pairs of sentences, since they rely on classical string similarity measures. This problem has been recently overcome by Cordeiro et al. (2007). The authors have proposed the *Sumo-metric* that is specially designed for identification   of asymmetrical entailed pair in corpora. *Sumo-metric* was tested on the Microsoft Paraphrase Research Corpus (Dolan et al. (2004)) and showed better performance than previously established metrics.

Sumo-metric states that for a given sentence pair, that have x and y words in each sentence and λ lexical exclusive links[142] (see Figure 33.) between them, its lexical connection strength S (S_a, S_b) is computed as defined in equations (33) and (34).

---

[141] Almost equal sentences leave no "space" for finding synonymous words or phrases, yet they are frequent in the corpus.
[142] Exclusive links are word overlaps between two sentences.

$$S(S_a, S_b) = \begin{cases} S(x, y, \lambda) & \text{if} & S(x, y, \lambda) < 1.0 \\ 0 & \text{if} & \lambda = 0 \\ e^{-k*S(x,y,\lambda)} & \text{otherwise} \end{cases} \qquad (33)$$

where k is an arbitrary chosen parameter

$$S(x, y, \lambda) = \alpha \log_2\left(\frac{x}{\lambda}\right) + \beta \log_2\left(\frac{y}{\lambda}\right) \qquad (34)$$

with $\alpha, \beta \in [0,1]$ and $\alpha + \beta = 1$ [143]

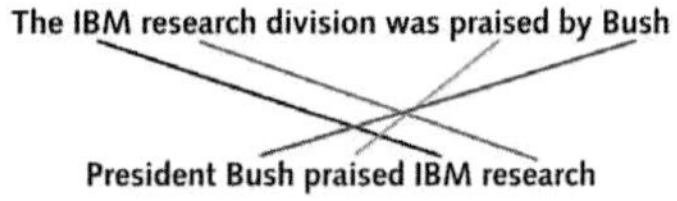

The IBM research division was praised by Bush

President Bush praised IBM research

Figure 33. Exclusive lexical links between sentences[144].

The adaptation for sumo-metric function is implemented by computing a different λ value. Instead of counting the number of lexical links among sentences, each link is weighted differently, according to the length of word being connected, hence connections of longer words will result in a larger λ value. For example in Figure 33., instead of

λ = 4,

the adapted λ value is

λ = 3+8+7+4 = 22.[145]

This adjustment was done aiming at to extract relationships between already known (see sections 6.3 and 7.1) terms. Multi-word units then are treated as longer words, for example molecular_laboratory and renal_cancer. The original λ value would have been underweight in such links whenever they hold.

A small set of three extracted paraphrases obtained from the *computer dependability* domain is shown below:

Example 66

(1)

The rest of this paper is organized as follows.

The remainder of this paper is structured as follows.

---

[143] Both parameters are chosen arbitrary.
[144] Example is taken from Cordeiro et al. (2007).
[145] 3,8,7,4 are legth of words that form exclusive lexical links.

```
(2)

Section 5 gives an overview of related work.

Section 5 discusses related work.

(3)

An embedded system gateway is the device that manages the flow of…

A gateway is a system entity that manages the flow…
```

6.4.1.2 Paraphrase Word Alignments

Paraphrases are interesting linguistic phenomena revealing equivalent ways of writing. They can be explored through powerful computational tools in order to induce sentence transformation regularities, for example for sentence rewriting, or even sentence simplification (Cordeiro et al. (2007)), which can be viewed as a particular or simplified type of rewriting.

Paraphrases can also be applied to find semantically similar words and phrases. For that, word alignments need to be established between the paraphrase sentences. These alignments reveal dissimilar parts which are possibly equivalent in the given context of two sentences. The methodology presented by (Cordeiro et al. (2007)) uses two algorithms for paraphrase inter-sentence word alignment, namely the *optimal global* and *optimal local alignment* algorithms, also known as the *Smith-Waterman* (Smith and Waterman (1981)) and *Needleman-Wunsch* (Needleman and Wunsch (1970)) algorithms used for DNA sequence alignment in *Bioinformatics*. Furthermore, we suggest an adaptation and consequent improvement of these alignment algorithms, which prioritizes the alignment of specific domain terms (single words and m*ulti-word units* (MWUs)).

Illustrative examples of term alignment between paraphrase sentences are shown below. Each paraphrase sentence pair is one of the three examples shown earlier. Due to visual purposes we represent each word by just using first two characters:

Example 67

```
Alignment Example (1):

TH __ RT OF TH PP IS __ OR AS FO

TH RD __ OF TH PP IS ST __ AS FO


Alignment Example (2):

ST 5 __ GV AN OV OF RD WK

ST 5 DS __ __ __ __ RD WK


Alignment Example (3):
```

```
A  E  S  G  I  _  _  _  T  D  T  M  T  F  O

A  _  _  G  I  A  S  E  _  _  T  M  T  F  O
```

These alignments are made with the *global aligner*, which is an algorithm that uses dynamic programming to compute the optimal *global alignment* between the two sentences. The algorithm is based on an alignment function which exploits the alignment likelihood between two alphabet symbols. For DNA sequence alignments this function is defined through what is known as a *mutation matrix*, but in our problem the words are themselves our symbols, hence we have employed the word mutation function defined by Cordeiro et al. (2007) that is named *costAlign*[146]:

$$costAlign(Sa_i, Sb_j) = -\frac{edist(Sa_i, Sb_j)}{\varepsilon + \max seq(Sa_i, Sb_j)} \qquad (35)$$

This function is a kind of *edit distance* (Levenstein (1966)), normalized by the length of the *maximum common sequence* ($\max seq(Sa_i, Sb_j)$) among the two words being considered.

Cordeiro et al. (2007) proposed the *gapScoring* function (see equations 35 and 36) which in this research is modified to prioritize the alignment of specific domain terms between two sentences. If a single word term or MWU term is met then the *gapScoring* function assigns much higher value for the sentence alignment:

(36)

$$gapScoring(Sa_i, Sb_j) = \begin{cases} -1 & if((Sa_i = \_) \wedge (Sb_j \neq \_)) \vee ((Sa_i \neq \_) \wedge (Sb_j = \_))) \\ 10 & SingleMatch \\ 50 & PhrasalMatch \\ costAlign(Sa_i, Sb_j) & Mismatch \end{cases}$$

```
Note: the '_' symbol in the equation (36) marks words that are not
aligned in sentences a or b.
```

To obtain a *local alignment* we start with the highest value in the matrix $H(i; j)$[147]. Then, go backwards to one of the positions $H(i - 1; j)$, $H(i; j - 1)$ or $H(i - 1; j - 1)$, depending on the *gapScoring* function value. The process continues until we reach a matrix cell with zero value, or the value in position $H(0; 0)$. This process is repeated recursively for the highest values in the matrix so that other local alignments can be found. Once a *local alignment* has been found, we reconstruct the alignment as follows: starting with the last value, we reach $H(i; j)$ using the previously calculated path. A diagonal jump implies there is an alignment (either a match or a

---

[146] the *edist* is the *edit distance* (Levenstein (1966)).
[147] Matrix $H(i;j)$ represents two sentences, with i and j tokens.

mismatch), a top-down jump implies there is a deletion and a left-right jump implies there is an insertion (Cordeiro et al. (2007)).

Therefore we have decided to incorporate this knowledge inside the alignment process, particularly inside our specific *costAlign* function, which gives more weight to the alignment of domain key terms as a consequence. Examples of paraphrase alignments are:

Example 68

```
The rest of this paper ---------------- is organized as follows.
The rest of the  ----- research article is organized as follows.


Wilms' tumor is the most common renal tumor ---------- in children.
Wilms' tumor is the most common renal ----- malignancy of childhood.
```

The examples of obtained paraphrase alignments is given in Appendix D1.

6.4.1.3 Synonymy Discovery Patterns

For the discovery of synonymy a specific generic pattern in the aligned paraphrase sentences has to be extracted, which highlights semantically similar terms. Due to the "topological" property of such patterns, we refer to them as *paraphrase twists*, or just *twists*, like two parallel lines that have been twisted and now share something in common, as schematized in the Figure 34.

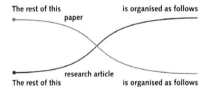

Figure 34. A paraphrase twist schematically represented.

The simplest aligned segment pattern for a *twist* is:

Example 69

```
... wordL wordx _____ wordR ...
... wordL _____ wordy wordR ...
```

where between common left and right contexts we have a word or a word sequence from one sentence, aligned with a gap, and another sequence, from the other sentence, also aligned with a gap. In the previous pattern we have "wordL" and "wordR" for left and right contexts, respectively and "wordx" and "wordy" the gap aligned words from each sentence.

The assumption is that in a *paraphrase twist* the larger the aligned contexts are, the more likely it is for the middle gap which is unaligned to be equivalent or synonymic. Note that in the *twist* shown in Figure 34., each context has a significant size, with four words in each side, and the middle sentence segments are in fact equivalent expressions. Also, for the three examples of paraphrases and their respective alignments, one can clearly identify the existence of synonymic expressions:

Example 70

```
"paper" ⇔ "research article"
"rest" ⇔ "remainder"
"organized" ⇔ "structured"
"gives an overview of" ⇔ "discusses"
"the device" ⇔ "a system entity"
```

The discussed paraphrase extraction methodology for relationship learning has been applied to the two different domains. The results are described in section 7. Examples of acquired relationship pairs are given in Appendix D2.

6.5   Subject-Verb-Object Triplet Extraction

Specific lexico-syntactic patterns are widely applied for hypernym-hyponym, holonym-meronym and synonym detection (Finkelstein-Landau and Morin (1999), Maedche and Staab (2003), Vela and Declerck (2009)). However, different patterns need to be defined for each semantic relationship. A unified way is to look for a more general pattern – argument structure also called SVO. Linguistic pattern based approach of extracting argument structures captures a variety of relationships. Consider the sentences for instance:

Example 71

```
In some sense, faults in control signals in asynchronous logic
would be analogous to faults in data as well as clock lines in a
clocked system.

Faulty asynchronous circuits can behave quite differently than
faulty synchronous circuits.

Asynchronous circuits consist of many state-holding nodes
(dynamic nodes with keepers) and handshaking signals.

This study is a retrospective review.

The primary end point was clinical response by palpation.

Patients developed febrile neutropenia.
```

SVO triplets are linguistic structures that normally capture two terms and their relation expressed by a verb.

Example 72

```
{term, relation, term}
```

The data marked by argument structure (SVO) allows the identification of concepts and their relations (Buitelaar et al. (2005)). Daraselia et al. (2004) uses SVOs to identify thematic (verb and noun complements) roles and attributive (prepositional phrases, coordinating and subordinating clauses, and conjunctional phrases) roles of concepts; Bendaoud et al. (2008) – to build concept lattices and model ontologies.

Our next contribution is to extend MPRO (Maas et al. (2009)) and KURD (Carl and Schmidt-Wigger (1998)) programs to mark argument structures in the analyzed sentences. Extracted SVO triplets provide linguistic information about terms by expressing their properties and interrelations.

6.5.1 Extraction Methodology of SVO Triplets

We have used the MPRO system (Maas et al. (2009)) for morphological analysis of the text, and the KURD system (Carl and Schmidt-Wigger (1998)) for syntactic analysis. Our contribution extended the rule set for marking SVO triplets. For instance consider the rule which marks **NP+VP+NP** group:

Example 73

```
mark_svo =
 +Aa{phr={c=np}}e{flaga=subj},
 +Ba{grup={c=vg}}e{flaga=verb},
 +Ca{phr={c=np}}e{flaga=obj}
  :Ar{flaga=subj},
   Br{flaga=verb},
   Cr{flaga=obj}.
```

The pattern based example identification usually has a high noise level and thus yields some irrelevant examples. For instance, the rule in the previous example can mark SVOs like:

Example 74

```
{subj = that, verb = recognized, obj = an epitope}
{subj = the overall survival rate, verb = was, obj = fifty
percent}
```

The straightforward way is to use filter rules. The following example is the rule which filters SVOs containing NPs made of person names:

Example 75

```
filter_pers =
Aa{sc=pers,per=1}
 :Ag{flaga~=subj}.
```

Examples of extracted SVOs are:

Example 76

```
{subj = Gender, verb = is, obj = the only significant prognostic
variable}
{subj = Older age, verb = is, obj = an adverse prognostic factor}
```

These examples are still very specific, and need to be pruned to a basic linguistic form. Each constituent of a SVO is analyzed separately. First, we start with checking which SVOs contain already extracted terms[148]. An example could be the following SVO:

Example 77

```
{subj = All children, verb = received, obj = whole lung radiation
therapy}
```

Where phrases `all children` and `whole lung radiation` are marked like *subject* and *object*. However, the extracted term list contains only terms `children` and `lung radiation`. Therefore we prune the analyzed SVO to the following form:

Example 78

```
{subj = children, verb = received, obj = lung radiation therapy}
```

Next step is to analyze the *verb* constituent in SVO. At this point we are using two criteria: 1) if the *verb* constituent is represented by a single verb, the basic form of the verb is taken; 2) if the *verb* constituent is represented by verbal expressions, then the auxiliary verb is discarded and only the main verb is taken, e.g., `is inducing → induces`.

For instance, the MPRO procedure marks the tense of an analyzed verb, therefore past tense in a SVO can be reformulated to the plain verb form in a SVO triplet. Examples of reformulated SVO triplets are:

Example 79

```
is (gender, prognostic variable)
is (older age, adverse prognostic factor)
receives (children, lung radiation therapy)
```

The results of SVO triplet extraction is discussed in section 7.3.

---

[148] Term extraction procedure is discussed in section 6.3.

6.6   Ontology Evaluation Based on Domain Thesauri

In section 5. we have presented different semiotic levels of ontology assessment and discussed two main strategies for ontology evaluation. NLP-driven approaches have already proven to be effective for ontology evaluation as in Brewster et al. (2004), Patel et al. (2003), Hicks and Herold (2009). These researches take into consideration the following levels of ontology evaluation: lexical vocabulary, taxonomic hierarchy, and non-taxonomic relations of ontologies. The contribution of the thesis described in this section includes a new semiotic level of the quality of an ontology – the pragmatic level. The pragmatic quality of the ontology denotes its usefulness "regardless of its syntax and semantics" (Chimienti et al. (2009)).

The major aspect that can be evaluated with the glass box approach is the completeness of domain coverage of the ontology. Domain coverage takes into consideration two aspects of ontologies:

-   An ontology represents entities from a specific domain. By evaluating domain coverage it is possible to check whether the ontology makes a correct distinction for its domain. In our approach it is ensured by experts choosing the suitable class of text of the domain, i.e., scientific publications, reports, specific domain documents like clinical trials, from which the thesaurus of the domain is built. Moreover, in this way it is assured that ontology represents the view of the entire domain, instead of an individual perspective.
-   An ontology is subject to continuous change. Therefore, its evaluation should be flexible in assessing changes in the domain. This aspect can be addressed by simply extending the class of the domain texts. For instance, by adding new scientific publications into the domain corpus.

We use domain specific class of texts and NLP techniques to acquire a domain specific terminology and arrange it into a domain thesaurus (see sections 7.1 and 7.4).

We assume that terms used in the domain texts reflect the concepts of the domain present in the domain ontology. Therefore mapping between domain thesaurus terms and lexicalized ontology concepts assesses two key ideas:

-   How well the ontology represents the domain?
-   What parts of the ontology refer to the explicitly available domain knowledge, and what remain unmapped?

These two questions must not govern ontology evaluation entirely, but can assist either the experts evaluating domain ontologies or the users evaluating task-driven usability of ontologies.

6.6.1 Methodology for Evaluation of Domain Coverage

Gilles et al. (1995) explain the importance of terminological analysis by stressing that:
- the corpus is a reference, reflecting the consensus knowledge of a group of specialists,
- the terminology is to be built so that it remains as faithful as possible to the reference corpus,
- terminology must reflect a static description of the entire domain, regardless of any expert's knowledge.

Based on this idea we propose a strategy for evaluating the coverage of an ontology which is based upon combining techniques of corpus linguistics and terminology extraction. We use a corpus of the domain as the source reflecting the knowledge of the domain. Domain terminology which is automatically acquired is used to evaluate the completeness and coverage of the domain with respect to lexicalized forms of concepts that are present in the ontology. The proposed approach is intended for evaluating of manually built domain ontologies. The experiments of evaluating ACGT MO ontology are described in section 7.4.

Pursuing this strategy we need to be aware of the essential differences between a thesaurus and an ontology. The thesaurus contains terms and gives specific relationships between them, whereas an ontology is a representational artifact that consists of the universals or classes, to which terms refer to, and the relationships between those entities (Smith et al. (2006)). Thus, the relations between the entities in the ontology are those between the universals and classes represented by the ontology. The relation between *term* and the representation of an *entity* in an ontology as shown in Figure 35.

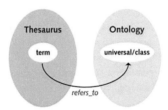

Figure 35. Relation between *term* in a thesaurus and *entity* in an ontology.

The starting point of this approach is collecting a corpus of the domain and extracting the terminology of the domain[149]. A corpus can contain any domain specific texts, namely, scientific publications, project reports, books, medical notes, etc. The most important feature of the corpus is that it has to be balanced for the task it will be used for. This issue is addressed by

---

[149] These steps are described in sections 6.2.1 and 7.1.

ensuring that the texts of corpus are diverse and corresponding to the domain; also by gathering a reasonable quantity of texts.

The judgement about the completeness of the ontology is done by acquiring a list of terms, arranging them into the thesaurus of the domain and identifying which terms map to the ontology at hand.

In order to acquire a list of terms that are **actively used** in the domain and are **specific** for the domain, we have applied Grigonytė and Haller (2008) and Avižienis et al. (2009) methodology for terminology extraction. An example of a terminology snippet is:

Example 80

```
tumour
| Wilms tumour
| | bilateral Wilms tumour
| | unilateral Wilms tumour
| | necrotic Wilms tumour
| rhabdoid tumour
| | malignant rhabdoid tumour
| | renal rhabdoid tumour
| | congenital rhabdoid tumour
```

The evaluation strategy is to check whether terms of the domain terminology list are present in the domain ontology. In order to expedite the evaluation process, mappings between ontology concepts and thesaurus terms are established. Figure 36., shows a term *metastasis* taken from an automatically acquired domain thesaurus and how it relates to an ACTG MO ontology snippet.

The main strategy for establishing mappings mainly concerns two targets: first, finding out what ontological entities are reflected in the extracted term list, and second, to indicate what sections of terms are not reflected in the ontology. For instance, in Figure 36., we show how a part of domain terminology compares to a snippet of ACGT MO ontology. A mapping between terminology's *metastasis* and ontology's *metastasis* can be established. In doing this we are always aware of the fact that the terminology provides consensual terms, whereas the ontology consists of the representation of entities whose names are chosen more or less arbitrarily[150].

We need to be aware that if it turns out that a domain specific, highly used term has no referent in the ACGT MO, the ontology can be extended with other types of *metastasis* represented in the terminology list.

Another important aspect of the process is to notice synonymous relationships between the ontology's entities and terms. For instance, *LungMetastasis* and *pulmonary metastasis* are synonymous. *LungMetastasis* is an arbitrary name created by an ontologist and is not present in

---

[150] In fact, there are quite a few ontologists who advocate the use of numbers as class names. However, the use of natural language terms as class names makes the ontology more easily accessible for users.

the domain corpus. *Pulmonary metastasis* is a frequent term in the domain texts (found 69 times), but it is not present in ontology.

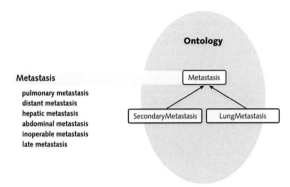

Figure 36. The concept "Metastasis": a part of the domain terminology list and a part of ontology.

The decision of which one is to be used in the ontology is entirely dependent on domain experts. However, the glass box evaluation technique can be helpful in pointing out terms used in 'real life', thus facilitating interaction between domain experts on the one hand and ontologists or the ontology on the other.

Take for instance this ontology snippet concerning *mammary carcinoma*:

Example 81

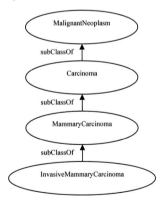

Example 82

```
<owl:Class rdf:about='http://www.ifomis.org/acgt/1.0#Carcinoma'>
     <rdfs:subClassOf>
          <owl:Class rdf:about='http://www.ifomis.org/acgt/1.0#MalignNeoplasm'/>
     </rdfs:subClassOf>
</owl:Class>
```

```
<owl:Class rdf:about='http://www.ifomis.org/acgt/1.0#MammaryCarcinoma'>
    <rdfs:subClassOf>
        <owl:Class rdf:about='http://www.ifomis.org/acgt/1.0#Carcinoma'/>
    </rdfs:subClassOf>
</owl:Class>
<owl:Class rdf:about='http://www.ifomis.org/acgt/1.0#InvasiveMammaryCarcinoma'>
    <rdfs:subClassOf>
        <owl:Class rdf:about='http://www.ifomis.org/acgt/1.0#MammaryCarcinoma'/>
    </rdfs:subClassOf>
</owl:Class>
```

Table 13. An example of the ACGT MO snippet and domain thesaurus snippet.

ACGT MO snippet	Domain thesaurus snippet
Carcinoma	Carcinoma
| MammaryCarcinoma	| Lobular Carcinoma
| | InvasiveMammaryCarcinoma	| Invasive Carcinoma
| | ColloidCarcinoma	| Breast Carcinoma
| | InflammatoryCarcinoma	| | Invasive Breast Carcinoma
| | InvasiveDuctalCarcinoma	| | Early Breast Carcinoma
| | | ComedoCarcinoma	| | Primary Breast Carcinoma
| | | MixedCarcinoma	| | Medullary Breast Carcinoma
| | | SchirrousCarcinoma	| | Metastatic Breast Carcinoma
| | InvasiveLobularCarcinoma	| | Lobular Breast Carcinoma
| | MedullaryCarcinoma	| | Operable Breast Carcinoma
| | TubularCarcinoma	| | Papillary Breast Carcinoma
| | NonInvasiveMammaryCarcinoma	| | Triple Breast Carcinoma
| | DCIS	| | Inflammatory Breast Carcinoma
| | LCIS	| | Occult Breast Carcinoma
| | PagetNippleTumor	| | Palpable Breast Carcinoma
	| | Sporadic Breast Carcinoma
	| | Invasive Ductal Breast Carcinoma
	| | Pure Mucinous Breast Carcinoma
	| Ductal Carcinoma
	| | Invasive Ductal Carcinoma
	| | Pure Ductal Carcinoma
	| | Infiltrate Ductal Carcinoma
	| | Noninvasive Ductal Carcinoma
	| | Unilateral Ductal Carcinoma
	| | Invasive Breast Ductal Carcinoma
	| Metastatic Carcinoma
	| Mammary Carcinoma
	| Infiltrating Carcinoma
	| Medullary Carcinoma
	| Recurrent Carcinoma
	| Tubular Carcinoma
	| Inflammatory Carcinoma
	| Intralymphatic Carcinoma
	| Pure Intralymphatic Carcinoma
	| Noninvasive Carcinoma
	| Extensive Intraductal Carcinoma
	| Pure Mucinous Carcinoma
	| Invasive Duct Carcinoma
	| Medullary Type Carcinoma

We use a simple measure to evaluate the lexical overlap α between reference thesaurus B and domain ontology A by calculating which thesaurus terms map into lexicalized ontology classes:

$$\alpha = \frac{A \cap B}{|A|} \qquad (37)$$

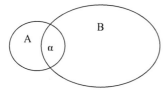

Experiments on evaluating the ACGT MO ontology are described in section 7.4.

7. Experimental Results

7.1 Experimental Results of Term Extraction

The methodology of extracting terms and arranging them into hypernym-hyponym hierarchies has been presented in section 6.3. We ran experiments on two different domains described in section 6.1. Table 14., summarizes the main term extraction results:

Table 14. Term extraction results.

DOMAIN	Cancer research (COCR)	Computer Dependability (COCD)
Tokens in domain corpora	610437	412265
Baseline: terms extracted with AUTOTERM	**8102**	**6781**
Extracted candidate terms	15599	9012
Domain terms acquired after linguistic and statistical filtering	**13663**	**7074**
Domain terms found in the BNC corpus	5086	3008
Manual evaluation of 10% of acquired terminology by means of precision	79%	67%

We have used the AUTOTERM (Hong et al. (2001), Haller (2006)) software as a baseline for evaluating domain terminology extraction. The proposed method outperforms AUTOTERM by 4% in accuracy as reported in Hong et al. (2001). In comparison to the baseline method our proposed approach extracts more terms (see Figure 37., part a and b). This is because the proposed approach takes into account all NPs found in domain corpora, therefore the number of candidate terms is very large. Thus the term learning curve is steeper than with the baseline method.

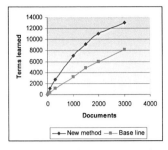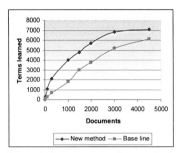

Figure 37. Comparison between AUTOTERM (baseline) method and the proposed approach: a) acquiring terms from the Cancer Research texts, b) acquiring terms from the Computer Dependability texts.

Acquired NPs are made up of single words, multi-word units, acronyms, and proper names. For the domain of Cancer Research 15599 candidate terms were extracted. For the domain of Computer Dependability 9012 candidate terms were extracted. After applying linguistic stop-word filtering and statistical filtering, term lists were pruned down to 13663 for the Cancer Research domain and to 7074 for the Computer Dependability domain.

Finally hierarchies of terms, based on their vertical hypernym-hyponym relationship, which distinguishes between specific and more abstract terms were built.

The Cancer Research terminology contains 13663 terms that are divided into 4 hierarchical levels. 86% - the majority of terms fall into the second level of hierarchy (see Figure 38.). 13,9% of terms are hypernyms and belong to the first level of terminology hierarchy. Third and fourth level terms are very rare.

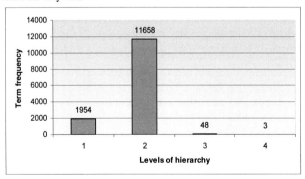

Figure 38. Term hierarchy levels of Cancer Research terminology.

An example of the Cancer Research terminology snippets:

Cancer research (COCR), (frequency, IDF value, and a term)		
20	5,12	Resection
73	3,82	| Surgical_Resection
16	5,34	| Complete_Resection
7	6,17	| Partial_Resection
4	6,72	| Tumour_Resection
2	7,42	| | Complete_Tumour_Resection
1	8,11	| | Bilateral_Tumour_Resection
1	8,11	| | Incomplete_Tumour_Resection
1	8,11	| | Intraspinal_Tumour_Resection
1	8,11	| | Retroperitoneal_Tumour_Resection
3	7,01	| Hepatic_Resection
2	7,42	| Atypical_Resection
...		
14	5,47	Growth
9	5,91	| Renal_Growth
6	6,32	| Fetal_Growth
5	6,5	| Compensatory_Growth
4	6,72	| Spinal_Growth
4	6,72	| Tumour_Growth
2	7,42	| | Aggressive_Tumour_Growth
1	8,11	| | Progressive_Tumour_Growth
1	8,11	| | Rhabdoid_Tumour_Growth
1	8,11	| | Lentivirus_Vector_Delay_Tumour_Growth
3	7,01	| Cell_Growth
2	7,42	| | Responsive_Cell_Growth
1	8,11	| | Epithelial_Cell_Growth
1	8,11	| | Uncontrolled_Cell_Growth
3	7,01	| Renoprival_Growth
2	7,42	| Neoplastic_Growth
2	7,42	| Somatic_Growth

The majority of terms in Carcer Research domain are two word phrases, or three word phrases. Term length distribution is illustrated in Figure 39. An example of the longest term – an eight word phrase is:

Example 83

    Postmenopausal_Oestrogen_And_Progesterone_Receptor_Breast_Cancer_
    Patient

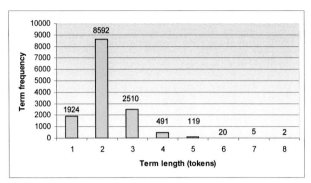

Figure 39. Term length distribution in Cancer Research terminology.

The frequency distributions of single word, two-word, three-word and four-word terms are illustrated in Figure 40. The most frequent terms are two-word, three-word terms and single word terms. However the majority of terms are rare and occur only a few times.

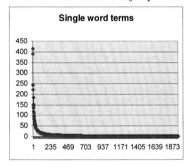

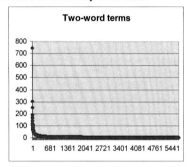

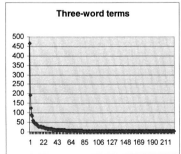

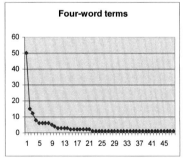

Figure 40. Frequency distributions of single word, two-word, three-word and four-word terms of Cancer Research domain.

As illustrated in Figure 40., terms where the length is two or three words are the most frequent in the domain of Cancer Research. We have also checked which of the Cancer Research domain terms occur in the BNC corpus. Out of 13663 terms only 5086 were detected. Their hierarchy levels and term length distributions are illustrated in Figure 41., and Figure 42. Obviously, single word terms occur frequently in general language corpus, i.e., 1724 out of 1924. Whereas with two-word terms only 3 out of 8 can be found in general language corpus. Three-word terms and four-word terms of the Cancer Research domain almost never occur in general language corpus.

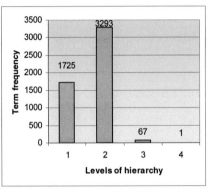

Figure 41. Hierarchy distribution of BNC word phrases equivalent to the terms of Cancer Research domain.

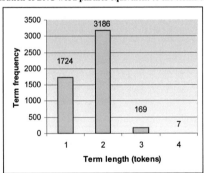

Figure 42. The distribution of BNC term length of word phrases equivalent to the terms of Cancer Research domain.

An example of word phrases and their frequencies from the BNC corpus (on the left) that were found to be equivalent to the terms of Cancer Research domain (on the right):

Example 84

```
165     irradiation              | 14    5,47    Irradiation
6       | mediastinal irradiation | 35    4,56    | Abdominal_Irradiation
5       | pelvic irradiation      | 11    5,71    | Pulmonary_Irradiation
2       | body irradiation        | 9     5,91    | Postoperative_Irradiation
2       | thoracic irradiation    | 4     6,72    | Breast_Irradiation
1       | direct irradiation      | 59    4,03    | | Partial_Breast_Irradiation
                                  | 3     7,01    | | Tangential_Breast_Irradiation
                                  | 2     7,42    | | Postoperative_Breast_Irradiation
                                  | 1     8,11    | | Definitive_Breast_Irradiation
                                  | 3     7,01    | Cranial_Irradiation
                                  | 3     7,01    | Craniospinal_Irradiation
                                  | 3     7,01    | Renal_Irradiation
                                  | 2     7,42    | Cardiac_Irradiation
                                  | 2     7,42    | Local_Irradiation
                                  | 2     7,42    | Thoracic_Irradiation
                                  | 1     8,11    | Imc_Irradiation
                                  | 1     8,11    | Body_Irradiation
                                  | 1     8,11    | Direct_Irradiation
                                  | 1     8,11    | Dose_Irradiation
                                  | 1     8,11    | Incidental_Irradiation
                                  | 1     8,11    | Inhomogeneous_Irradiation
                                  | 1     8,11    | Locoregional_Irradiation
                                  | 1     8,11    | Mediastinal_Irradiation
                                  | 1     8,11    | Nodal_Irradiation
                                  | 1     8,11    | Ovarian_Irradiation
                                  | 1     8,11    | Pelvic_Irradiation
                                  | 1     8,11    | Renal_Bed_Irradiation
                                  | 1     8,11    | Focal_Boost_Irradiation
                                  | 1     8,11    | Craniospinal_Axis_Irradiation
                                  | 1     8,11    | Supraclavicular_Fossa_Irradiation
                                  | 1     8,11    | Postoperative_Chest_Wall_Irradiation
                                  | 1     8,11    | Regional_Node_Irradiation
                                  | 1     8,11    | External_Beam_Irradiation
```

Finally, a manual evaluation on 10% of extracted terminology was performed by experts of the domain. A standard measure of *precision* was used[151]:

$$precision = \frac{tp}{tp + fp} \qquad (38)$$

where *tp* stands for true positives, i.e., extracted terms of the domain that were annotated to be domain terms; *fp* stands for false positives, i.e., extracted terms that were annotated as non-term terms.

The *precision* of term extraction in Cancer Research domain was 79%.

An example of the snippet of the acquired terminology of Computer Dependability domain:

---

[151] *Precision* and *recall* measures are standard measures used to evaluate the quality of term acquisition. In this experiment the *recall* measure was not evaluated, because no data on domain terminology was available in order to judge about the cases of *false negatives*, i.e., terms that are not acquired but remain undetected in the corpus of the domain.

Example 85

```
         Computer Dependability (COCD)

    83    2.88   fault
    19    4.35   | byzantine fault
    17    4.46   | permanent fault
    11    4.90   | intermittent fault
    10    4.99   | stuck-open fault
     8    5.22   | transient fault
     6    5.50   | detectable fault
     5    5.69   | arbitrary fault
     5    5.69   | multiple fault
     5    5.69   | operational fault
     5    5.69   | physical fault
     5    5.69   | redundant fault
     5    5.69   | software fault
     2    6.60   | algorithm-based fault
     1    7.30   | artificial fault
     1    7.30   | bridge fault
     1    7.30   | clock fault
     1    7.30   | concurrent fault
     1    7.30   | design fault
     1    7.30   | | latent design fault
     1    7.30   | | residual design fault
     1    7.30   | logical fault
     1    7.30   | memory fault
     1    7.30   | | permanent memory fault
     1    7.30   | modular fault
     1    7.30   | repairable fault
     1    7.30   | silent fault
```

The Computer Dependability terminology contains 7074 terms that are divided into 3 hierarchical levels. More than a half, i.e., 64% of terms fall into the second level of hierarchy (see Figure 43.). 32% of terms are hypernyms and belong to the first level of terminology hierarchy. Third level terms are very rare.

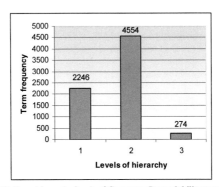

Figure 43. Term hierarchy levels of Computer Dependability terminology.

The majority of terms in Computer Dependability domain are two-word phrases, and three-word phrases. Term length distribution is illustrated in Figure 44.

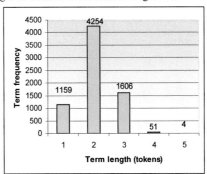

Figure 44. Term length distribution in Computer Dependability terminology.

The frequency distributions of single word, two-word, three-word and four-word terms are illustrated in Figure 45. Similarly to Cancer Research domain, the most frequent terms are single word terms and two-word terms. The majority of terms are rare and occur only a few times.

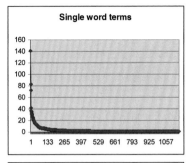
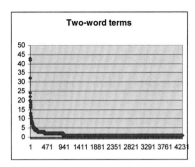
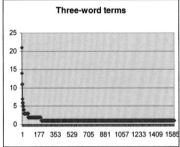
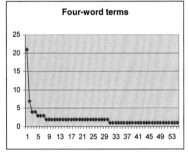

Figure 45. Frequency distributions of single word, two-word, three-word and four-word terms of Computer Dependability domain.

As illustrated in Figure 45., most frequent in the domain of Computer Dependability are terms of two words length. The same test as in Cancer Research domain was performed to check which of the Computer Dependability domain terms occur in the BNC corpus. Out of 7074 terms only 3008 were detected. Their hierarchy levels and term length distributions are illustrated in Figure 46., and Figure 47. Almost all of the single word terms of the Computer Dependability domain were as well found in the BNC corpus, i.e., 1045 out of 1159. Approximately half of two-word terms were found in the BNC corpus, i.e., 1916 out of 4254. Three-word terms almost do not occur in the BNC corpus corpus.

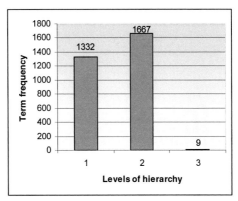

Figure 46. Hierarchy distribution of BNC word phrases equivalent to the terms of Computer Dependability domain.

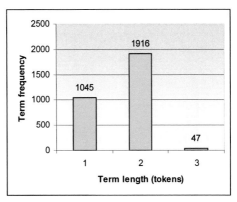

Figure 47. The distribution of BNC term length of word phrases equivalent to the terms of Computer Dependability domain.

An example of equivalent word phrases in comparison to the terms of Computer Dependability (on the right) found in the BNC corpus (on the left):

```
9647    error                          37    3.68    error
15    | administrative error           32    3.83    | soft error
12    | logical error                  12    4.81    | unidirectional error
9     | system error                   4     5.91    | uncorrectable error
9     | systematic error               3     6.20    | administrative error
7     | data error                     3     6.20    | single error
7     | run-time error                 2     6.60    | bite error
6     | occasional error               2     6.60    | | single bite error
5     | severe error                   1     7.30    | | triple bite error
3     | single error                   2     6.60    | effective error
3     | transient error                2     6.60    | functional error
2     | hardware error                 2     6.60    | injectable error
1     | accidental error               2     6.60    | latent error
1     | bit error                      2     6.60    | multiple error
1     | correctable error              2     6.60    | radiation-induced error
1     | early error                    1     7.30    | accidental error
1     | effective error                1     7.30    | application-aware error
1     | sequence error                 1     7.30    | arbitrary error
1     | tolerable error                1     7.30    | asymmetric error
1     | uncorrectable error            1     7.30    | bit error
1     | undetected error               1     7.30    | | unidirectional bit error
                                       1     7.30    | computational error
                                       1     7.30    | correctable error
                                       1     7.30    | data error
                                       1     7.30    | | effective data error
                                       1     7.30    | | pure data error
                                       1     7.30    | early error
                                       1     7.30    | hardware error
                                       1     7.30    | hardware-based error
                                       1     7.30    | implementation-level error
                                       1     7.30    | logical error
                                       1     7.30    | mean-square error
                                       1     7.30    | multibit error
                                       1     7.30    | occasional error
                                       1     7.30    | rate error
                                       1     7.30    | run-time error
                                       1     7.30    | | observable run-time error
                                       1     7.30    | sequence error
                                       1     7.30    | severe error
                                       1     7.30    | symmetric error
                                       1     7.30    | system error
                                       1     7.30    | systematic error
                                       1     7.30    | tolerable error
                                       1     7.30    | transient error
                                       1     7.30    | undetected error
                                       1     7.30    | unpredictable error
                                       1     7.30    | visible error
                                       1     7.30    | undefined state error
                                       1     7.30    | human-induced configuration error
                                       1     7.30    | human-made configuration error
                                       1     7.30    | transient SEU error
                                       1     7.30    | latent sector error
                                       1     7.30    | soft memory error
                                       2     6.60    | unidirectional byte error
                                       1     7.30    | single byte error
                                       1     7.30    | partial disk error
                                       1     7.30    | cache-aided rollback error
                                       1     7.30    | unrecoverable ECC error
                                       1     7.30    | correct single-bit error
                                       1     7.30    | online software error
```

The manual evaluation on 10% of extracted terminology of Computer Dependability domain was performed by experts of the domain. The precision of term extraction was 67%.

The evaluation of term extraction methodology revealed several tendencies in the analyzed domains:

1. Most of the domain-specific terms are two-word or three-word phrases.
2. The majority of the terms are very rare, therefore using only statistical modeling based on explored domain corpora for term detection would have been not reliable, since the size of both corpora is rather small. Thus linguistically based term candidate detection was the optimal solution for the given task.
3. However, statistical termhood modeling by contrasting general language corpora and domain specific corpora can help to make judgments on a term's usage, even for a given small domain corpora.

7.2 Experimental Results of Synonymy Relationship Learning

In this section we describe the results of unsupervised synonymy learning. The experiments have been carried out on two domains: Computer Dependability and Cancer Research.

7.2.1 Corpus and Sentence Alignment

Two different corpora on scientific domains built from abstracts of publications were used:

-   The Corpus of Computer Dependability domain (COCD) a collection of 4854 abstracts on computer dependability from IEEE database. The corpus contains 18974 sentences (over 400000 tokens), which led to 589 aligned sentence pairs.
-   The corpus of cancer research (COCR) contains 3334 domain specific abstracts of scientific publications on three types of cancer:

    (1) COCR1 - *mammary carcinoma* register made of 1500 abstracts; 15195 sentences; 994 aligned sentence pairs obtained.

    (2) COCR2 - *nephroblastoma (Wilms' tumour)* register made of 1500 abstracts; 10575 sentences; 511 aligned sentence pairs gained.

    (3) COCR3 - *rhabdoid tumour* register made of 334 abstracts; 2321 sentences; 125 aligned sentence pairs gained.

    COCR abstracts were extracted from Pubmed[152]. The corpus contains 610437 tokens.

The summary of the corpora is presented in Table 15.

---

[152] http://www.ncbi.nlm.nih.gov/pubmed

Table 15. The summary of the corpora.

Corpus	COCD	COCR1	COCR2	COCR3
Tokens	412265	336745	227477	46215
Sentences	18974	15195	10575	2321
Aligned sentence pairs	589	994	511	125

An example of an aligned sentence[153]:

Example 86

```
In addition , it was shown that with preoperative chemotherapy about 45% of an
In addition , it was shown that ____ _____ _____ _____ 43% of an

unselected population of patients with Wilms ' tumour      can be treated and
unselected population of patients with Wilms ' tumor   could ___ be treated ___

cured without any                             irradiation and
_____ without any radiotherapy when chemotherapy _____ had been given

          its well-known sequelae .
preoperatively ___ _____ _____ .
```

We have run four sentence alignment experiments for each of the corpora:

- **Sumo_85** setting: lexical connection strength function [154] $S(x, y, \lambda)$ is calculated with λ value being the number of lexical links among sentences; weighing factor $\alpha=0.85$;

- **SumoWsize_85** setting: lexical connection strength function $S(x, y, \lambda)$ is calculated with λ value being the sum of connected word lengths; weighing factor $\alpha=0.85$;

- **SumoWsize_mwu_85** setting: lexical connection strength function $S(x, y, \lambda)$ is calculated with λ value being the sum of connected word lengths; weighing factor $\alpha=0.85$; additionally, the alignment function tries to align sentences that contain previously extracted terms of the domain[155].

- **SumoWsize_mvu_65** setting: lexical connection strength function $S(x, y, \lambda)$ is calculated with λ value being the sum of connected word lengths; alignment function aligns sentences that contain extracted terms of the domain; weighing factor $\alpha=0.65$. This choice allows this experimental setting to generate more alignments.

Aligned sentence pairs were checked for paraphrase twist pattern (described in section 6.4.1). Examples of found twist patterns include[156]:

---

[153] More examples of aligned sentences are given in Appendix D1.
[154] As described in section 6.4.1.
[155] Term extraction results presented in section 7.1.
[156] Note: only the snippets of sentences are presented.

Example 87

adjuvant ___ **treatment** of early breast

adjuvant **CNF** _____ for early breast

in _____ **advanced** breast cancer

in **metastatic** _____ breast cancer

antibody _____ **against** the

antibody **targeting** _____ the

this _____ **approach** in

the **method** _____ in

an _____ **association** between

a **relationship** _____ between

The _____ **average** tumor size

The **mean** _____ tumor size

of _____ **axillary** nodes

of **lymph** _____ nodes

received _____ **intensive** chemotherapy

received **multiagent** _____ chemotherapy

The _____ **histology** of the

The **pathology** _____ of the

the _____ **study** group

the **comparison** _____ group

The _____ **purpose** of this

The **objective** _____ of this

```
with _____ HR-negative breast cancer

with hormone-non-responsive _____ breast cancer


the _____ individual agents

the chemotherapy _____ agents


invasive _____ lobular carcinoma

invasive ductal _____ carcinoma


adjuvant ____ chemotherapy treatment

adjuvant CNF _____ treatment
```

The patterns that include punctuation marks and number were filtered out:

Example 88

```
[ _ 10 ] .

[ 4 __ ] .

, __ and propose

, we ___ propose
```

Additionally only the unique *twist pairs* were selected. The summary of *twist* pattern acquired for all corpora is given in the Table 16.

Table 16. The summary of extracted paraphrase twist pairs from different corpora.

Corpus		COCD	COCR1	COCR2	COCR3
# of twist pairs	Sumo_85	2538	10217	2520	621
	SumoWsize_85	323	509	214	62
	SumoWsize_mwu_85	320	376	155	48
	SumoWsize_mwu_65	559	656	280	77
# of filtered twist pairs	Sumo_85	238	361	292	70
	SumoWsize_85	90	70	53	23
	SumoWsize_mwu_85	87	67	37	16
	SumoWsize_mwu_65	130	107	52	25

7.2.2 Acquired Synonymy Examples

From aligned sentences, using *twist paraphrase* pattern, we have obtained synonymic multi-word units and single synonymous word pairs. All of the pairs were treated assuming that their overall frequency was equal to one. Although most of pairs were synonymous, the others were not just errata, but lexically related words, including antonymy, hyperonymy-hyponymy and associations. Some of the examples are presented in Table 17., and Table 18.

Table 17. Examples of acquired synonymous pairs.

COCD	COCR
faulty tiles – faulty scan cells	progression-free survival - overall survival
attack consequences - attack impact	event-free survival - overall survival
error-free operation - error free operation	distant metastases - regional metastasis
unaffected register - not corrupted register	neoplasia - malignancy
tolerance - resilience	highly malignant - extremely malignant
package loss - message loss	common renal tumour - frequent renal tumour
Qos properties - Qos composition	renal tumor - renal neoplasm
adjustable algorithm - context-aware algorithm	renal tumor - renal malignancy
cover - briefly describe	of childhood - in children
attacker can compromise -attack is successful	null - unsuccessful
new message - incoming message	tumour - tumor
enhance - improve	her2-negative tumor - her2-positive tumor
minimize - decrease	endocrine-responsive breast_cancer - hormone-
approach - algorithm	responsive breast_cancer
multicasting - broadcasting	analysis - trial
invulnerable – robust	neoplasm - tumor
	undergo surgery - receive surgery

In the evaluation we have focused on the *precision* of the method. Evaluation of extracted pairs was manually performed by domain experts. Sumo_85 metrics gave most of the related pairs, however it also had the highest error rate (see Figure 48.). The evaluation of all four experimental settings is summarized in Table 19. The overall performance for both corpora (COCD and COCR) of four methods in terms of precision is illustrated in Figure 49.

Table 18. Examples of acquired non-synonymous pairs.

Relationship type	Example
Antonyms	Toxicity – safety
	Incoming throughput – outgoing throughput
	Higher bits – lower bits
	Older version – newer version
Hypernyms-hyponyms	Children – patients
	Adults – patients
	Chemotherapy – therapy
	Human – user
Associations	A challenge – rare event
	Response – treatment
	Performance – reliability

Table 19. The evaluation of precision of four experimental methods.

Corpora	Sumo_85	SumoWsize_85	SumoWsize_mwu_85	SumoWsize_mwu_65
COCD	54%	72%	**77%**	77%
COCR1	69%	**74%**	68%	62%
COCR2	61%	84%	**89%**	82%
COCR3	72%	**86%**	75%	72%

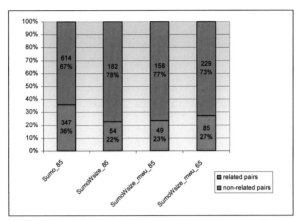

Figure 48. The overall performance of four experimental methods.

Precision wise *SumoWsize_85* and *SumoWsize_mvu_85* methods perform the best. 72-89% of *paraphrase twist* pairs are indeed related words or MWUs (see Figure 49.). However the drawback of these methods is that smaller number of sentences get aligned, thus yielding fewer twist patterns. With *Sumo_85* setting many more sentences get aligned and thus more twist pairs can be discovered (see Figure 48., and Figure 49.). The *Sumo_85* method generates a lot of unrelated word or MWU pairs. In COCD corpus with Sumo_85 method 54% of aligned pairs are related words or MWUs, whereas in COCR corpora precision value varies from 61% to 72% (see Figure 49.).

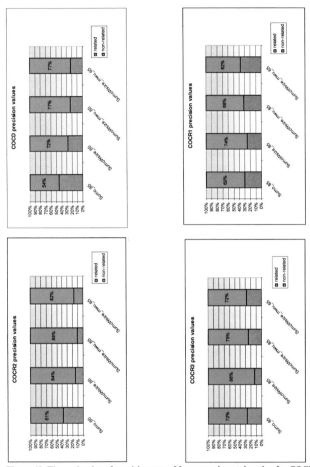

Figure 49. The evaluation of precision rate of four experimental setting for COCD, COCR1, COCR2, and COCR3 corpora.

The summary of the numbers of pairs of related words and MVUs acquired with four experimental settings is presented in Table 20., and Figure 50.

Table 20. The numbers of pairs of related words or MVUs acquired with four experimental settings.

Corpora	Sumo_85	SumoWsize_85	SumoWsize_mwu_85	SumoWsize_mwu_65
COCD	**130**	65	67	**101**
COCR1	**252**	52	46	**67**
COCR2	**181**	**45**	33	43
COCR3	**51**	**20**	12	18

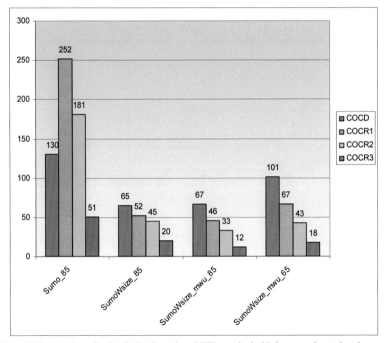

Figure 50. The numbers of pairs of related words or MVUs acquired with four experimental settings.

The above presented approach proved to be promising for extracting synonymous words and multi-word units. Its strength is an ability to fruitfully utilize small domain corpora, without supervised training and without using language processing tools. Four different experimental settings were used to evaluate the paraphrase alignment methods for relationship extraction. *Sumo_85* detects the highest number of related word pairs and multi-word unit pairs. *Sumo_Wsize_85* and *Sumo_Wsize_mvu_85* generates fewer non-related pairs. The method of synonymy detection proved to be efficient for both research domains. Further improvement of the method should include automatic differentiation between the acquired types of semantically related pairs, since *paraphrase twist* pattern applies for hypernym-hyponym, association and antonym relations. Possible solutions could be:

- context based classification of acquired *twist pairs*. Turney (Turney (2008)) tackled the problem of classifying different lexical information such as synonymy, antonymy, hypernymy and association by employing context words. His classifier was trained on a huge web data corpus and performed with 97.5 % accuracy on a TOEFL test.
- tuning constraints for the "strength of context" of paraphrase twists. Consider the example:

Example 89

```
             Let Ti be the           incoming throughput of the
Similarly, let To be the outgoing _____ throughput of the

server , measured as the number of client          _
server , measured as the number of client requests a

                             connection demands per second .
server is able to handle _____ _____ per second .
```

In this example, the context on the right side of the twist pair *(incoming throughput, outgoing throughput)* indicates that aligned pair is not synonymous. However, differences occur after 8 words!

- adding linguistic knowledge, e.g., linguistic annotation for noticing complex sentence constructions, like coreference. Consider the example:

Example 90

```
This is _____ illustrated _____ ___ ___ ___
This is consistent _____ with the energy plot shown

in Figure 7.
in Figure 7.
```

7.3   Experimental Results of Extracting SVO Triplets

In this section we will describe the results of acquiring SVO triplets using MPRO and KURD software packages. The methodology of SVO triplets extraction is described in section 6.5. The summary of SVO triplets extraction is presented in Table 21.

Table 21. The summary of the extraction of SVO triplets.

Corpora	COCD	COCR1	COCR2	COCR3
Tokens	412265	336745	227477	46215
Acquired SVO patterns	5908	5271	3682	830
Filtered SVO patterns	509	629	384	226

The general linguistic pattern of predicate argument structure has helped to detect many SVO groups, however the entire majority of those examples contain numerals, personal pronouns, names, etc. After linguistic filtering the acquired SVO patterns were pruned down to 9-27% (see Figure 51.).

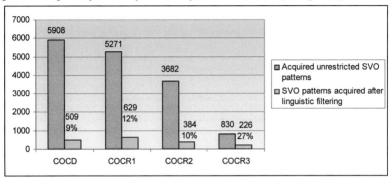

Figure 51. The distribution of acquired SVO patterns for all domain corpora.

An example of extracted SVO patterns from the Cancer Research domain:
Example 91

{histology_S is_V an important prognostic factor_O}

{Nephroblastomas_S are_V embryonal tumors_O}

{pulmonary irradiation_S did not clearly improve_V the four-year relapse-free survival percentage_O}

{Thrombocytopenia_S was_V the most frequent toxicity_O}

{Gender_S was found to be_V the only significant prognostic variable_O}

{Older age_S is_V an adverse prognostic factor_O}

{chemotherapy_S is_V hepatotoxicity_O}

{Neoadjuvant chemotherapy_S allowed to decrease_V the intraoperative stage_O}

{Neutropenia_S was_V the dose-limiting toxicity_O}

{Other significant toxicities_S were_V anemia_O}

{All children_S received_V whole lung radiation therapy_O}

{pulmonary irradiation_S did not clearly improve_V the four-year relapse-free survival percentage_O}

{Bone marrow cytokeratin 19 mRNA level_S is_V an independent predictor_O}

{abdominal radiation_S seems to damage_V gonadal function_O}

{Abdominal recurrence_S included_V all infradiaphragmatic tumor recurrences_O}

{Abdominal mass_S was_V the main symptom_O}

{Angiography_S showed_V an enlarged right gonadal artery_O}

{Aniridia_S is_V an autosomal dominant eye anomaly_O}

{another patient_S had_V chronic renal insufficiency_O}

{DNA sequencing detects WT1 mutation}

Formed SVO triplets:
Example 92

is (histology; prognostic factor)

is (thrombocytopenia; toxicity)

is (aniridia; autosomal dominant eye anomaly)

is (gender; prognostic variable)

is (older age; adverse prognostic factor)

is (Abdominal mass; main symptom)

is (Bone marrow cytokeratin 19 mRNA level; independent predictor)

is (surgery; adverse factor)

is (carboplatin; drug)

is (nephroblastoma;

is (aCGH; cytogenetic technique)

decreases (neoadjuvant chemotherapy; intraoperative stage)

receives (children; lung radiation theraphy)

receives (patient; preoperative irradiation)

not_improves (pulmonary irradiation; relapse-free survival)

shows (sacrococcygeal region; immature teratoma)

shows (Angiography; enlarged right gonadal artery)

defines (mitotic atypia; anaplasia)

detects (DNA sequencing; WT1 mutation)

damages (abdominal radiation; gonadal function)

has (patient; tumor)

has (patient; chronic renal insufficiency)

includes (chemotherapy regimen; dactinomycin)

includes (Abdominal recurrence; infradiaphragmatic tumor recurrence}

An example of extracted SVO patterns from the Computer Dependability domain:
Example 93

{A database_S is_V a collection_O}

{CuriOS_S is_V a new operating operating system_O}

{Fault injection_S is_V a widely used technique_O}

{Fault tolerance_S is_V a key issue_O}

{GRID_S is_V a Coordination Action_O}

{Model checking_S is_V a formal verification technique_O}

{Modularity_S is_V a desirable property_O}

{OMG DDS_S is_V a middleware standard_O}

{targeted application_S is_V a VoIP communication system_O}

{Tempest_S is_V a system_O}

{The EAST - ADL1_S is_V an architecture description language_O}

{topology_S is_V an important factor_O}

{periodic rejuvenation_S alters_V the lifetime distribution_O}

{Connectors_S are_V reliable software components_O}

{Defects_S are_V a major problem_O}

{The solution_S assumes_V a parallel architecture_O}

{online-upgrade protocol_S avoids_V data staleness_O}

{software bugs_S can crash_V the system_O}

{a single faulty node_S can degrade_V the performance_O}

{microarchitecture-level fault checks_S can detect_V many arbitrary faults_O}

{TierFS_S can provide_V better recoverability_O}

{proposed technique_S can tolerate_V concurrent multiple failures_O}

{the system_S can tolerate_V multibit errors_O}

{an error_S causes_V the failure_O}

{The Reconciliation Action_S changes_V the values_O}

{most file systems_S check_V consistency_O}

{architecture-centred solution_S comprises_V a rigorous approach_O}

{Microprocessors_S contain_V many large array structures_O}

{Section 3_S contextualises_V the proposed approach_O}

{each process_S copies_V its checkpoint data_O}

{measurement_S could evaluate_V the impact_O}

{NBTI_S degrades_V PMOS transistors_O}

{providers_S deploy_V specialized detection_O}

{the unstructured logs_S do not have_V a structure_O}

{asynchronous signaling protocols_S embed_V data validity_O}

{TCPScript_S embeds_V messages_O}

{data data_S follows_V a statistical model_O}

{The paper_S gives_V an overview_O}

{the model checking_S has_V difficulties_O}

{The run_S has_V 3 API usages_O}

{The Network security systems_S have_V unique testing
requirements_O}

{Application performance issues_S have_V an immediate impact_O}

{Botnets_S have become_V a severe global Internet threat_O}

{sensors_S have become_V an invaluable tool_O}

{researchers_S have proposed_V statistical methods_O}

{researchers_S have proposed_V statistical methods_O}

{an attacker_S impairs_V the effectiveness_O}

{a 9 - node in-memory tier_S improves_V performance_O}

{System 1_S includes_V the following components_O}

Formed SVO triplets:
Example 94

is (database; collection)

is (CuriOS; operating system)

is (fault injection; technique)

is (fault tolerance; key issue)

is (GRID; coordination action)

is (model checking; formal verification technique)

is (modularity; property)

is (OMG DDS; middleware standard)

is (targeted application; VoIP communication system)

is (Tempest; system)

is (EAST - ADL1; architecture description language)

is (topology; factor)

```
is (connector; reliable software component)

alter (periodic rejuvenation; lifetime distribution)

avoid (online-upgrade protocol;     data staleness)

crash (software bug; system)

degrade (single faulty node; performance)

detect (microarchitecture-level fault check; arbitrary fault)

provide (TierFS; recoverability)

tolerate (technique; concurrent multiple failure)

tolerate (system; multibit error)

cause (error; failure)

check (file system; consistency)

contain (microprocessor; large array structure)
```

To summarize, the SVO pattern detection technique has revealed more types of relationships between domain terms, than previously introduced paraphrase sentence alignment technique (see section 7.2). However the drawback is the need of NLP tools and predefined linguistic rules. SVO pattern detection technique compares to lexico-syntactic pattern acquisition approaches. Naturally the same patterns can by found by applying lexico-syntactic rules like:

Example 95

```
X has Y

X is a Y

X includes Y
```

Possible improvements of the SVO triplet detection function in KURD could include automatic labeling/classification of detected triples, i.e., according to the verb class, or to the semantic relationship the verb implies. As for instance *contain, include, have* – part-of relationship.

7.4 Experimental Results of Ontology Evaluation

In this section we concentrate on the results of using the domain thesaurus to validate the domain coverage of the ACGT MO. The results of building the thesaurus of the Cancer Research domain are described in section 6.1.

Mappings of thesaurus terms to the ontology is not a straightforward evaluation measure since the aim of an ontology is not to provide one class per term. However, retrieving the knowledge about these kinds of missing mappings can serve to raise the awareness of ontologists to possible data loss, given that the knowledge behind the terms cannot be expressed by the ontology.

The evaluation of ACGT MO with respect to the coverage of the domain[157] showed that 53% of 2028 ontology concepts map with the terms of the domain thesaurus. See Table 22.

Table 22. The summary of the ACGT MO ontology evaluation.

The number of terms in the reference thesaurus	13663
The number of ACGT MO ontology concepts	2028
Domain coverage of the ACGT MO ontology	53%

The examples of such mappings between ontology concepts and the terms of the domain thesaurus include complete mappings as for instance:

Example 96

```
Renal_Cell_Carcinoma <==> Renal_Cell_Carcinoma

Disease <==> Disease
```

and partial mappings as for instance:

Example 97

```
Clinical_Trial_Identifier <==> Clinical_Trial

Hemorrhage_Grade2 <==> Hemorrhage
```

Some of the mappings between domain terms and ontology concepts are presented in Tables 23-26. More examples are given in Appendix E1.

Most of the mappings between the ontology and domain terms are direct and partial mappings of single word terms. Figure 52., illustrates the distribution of single word terms, two-word terms and three-word terms of the domain terminology that was mapped with ontology concepts. In sections 3.2 and 7.1 we discussed the fact that domain specific terminology is mostly two-worded or three-worded phrases. From the figure x. we see that 60 % of the ACGT MO ontology concepts are not single word concepts (see Figure 53.). Mapping only 53% of 2028 ontology concepts with a larger than 13000 terms domain thesaurus indicates that unmapped lexicalizations of concepts are arbitrary. Thus the pragmatic property of ontology, i.e., to what extent ontological concepts relate to the source of reference, is low. Arbitrary concepts are not explanatory, which diminishes the accessibility and usability of the ontology to the domain experts. Consider for instance:

Example 98

```
CapecitabineDocetaxelChemo

CarboplatinEtoposideChemo

CisplatinFluorouracilChemo

DeGramontChemo

DHAPandARDHAPChemo
```

---

[157] Coverage of the domain is calculated as the *lexical overlap* between the domain thesaurus and the ontology.

```
DocetaxelCisplatinChemo

DoxorubicinIfosfamideChemo

ESHAPandR-ESHAPChemo

EtoposideCisplatinChemo

GemCapChemo

GemCarboChemo

GemicitabineCisplatinChemo

GemTaxolChemo

OralMaintainanceChemo

PaclitaxelCarboplatinChemo

PemetrexedCisplatinChemo

PMitCEBOChemo

PostOpChemo

PreOpChemo

VinorelbineCarboplatinChemo

VinorelbineCisplatinChemo

TEOralMaintainanceChemo

TIOralMaintainanceChemo

TMZOralMaintainanceChemo

SIOPPostOpChemo

SIOPPreOpChemo

Week1PreOpChemo

Week2PreOpChemo

Week3PreOpChemo

Week4PreOpChemo
```

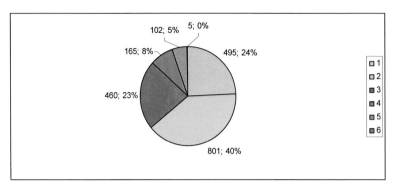

Figure 52. The distribution of the length (in tokens) of the ACGT ontology concepts.

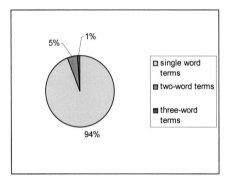

Figure 53. The distribution of ontology concept mappings with domain terms (single word terms, two-word terms, three-word terms).

Table 23. Examples of partial mappings between domain terms and ontology concepts.

Ontology class	Thesaurus term	Term count in domain corpus
StandardPartialNephrectomy	partial nephrectomy	3
ChronicViralInfection	viral infection	2
ImmatureTeratomaGCTDisease	immature teratoma	4
LateEffectRole	late effect	8
SkinResponse	response	6
SkeletonLateEffect	late effect	8
LiverCancer	cancer	93

Table 24. Examples of complete mappings between domain terms and ontology concepts.

Ontology class	Thesaurus term	Term count in domain corpus
RenalVein	renal vein	2
NephrogenicRest	nephrogenic rest	2
TreatmentCycle	treatment cycle	3
ClinicalTrial	clinical trial	17
SurgicalApproach	surgical approach	1
PartialNephrectomy	partial nephrectomy	3
BacterialInfection	bacterial infection	2
ViralInfection	viral infection	2
CongenitalSyndrome	congenital syndrome	3
LateEffect	late effect	5
TumorRegression	tumor regression	4
RenalCellCarcinoma	renal cell carcinoma	1
Diagnosis	diagnosis	6
Protocol	protocol	12
Report	report	4
Infection	infection	9
Infiltration	infiltration	2
Anaplasia	anaplasia	6

The examples in Table 25., clearly indicate 'problematic' classes in ontology. For instance, the fact that "pN2a" cannot be mapped stresses that class names either should not be abbreviations and acronyms, or a lexical description of the name of a class should exist. The last two classes in Table 25., present specific grading which does not frequently occur in scientific publications, but may well occur in patient documentation.

Table 25. An example of ontology concepts that remain unmapped.

Ontology class
EndOfBloodPressureMeasuringProcess
pN2a
FeverGrade4
ECOGPerformanceRating

Naturally, a lot of domain specific terms remain unmapped. Those particularly frequently occurring terms should draw attention of ontology evaluators (see Table 26.).

Table 26. An example of thesaurus terms that were found in the domain text register, but are not present in ontology.

Thesaurus term	Term count in domain corpus
Cortical lesion	1
contralateral biopsy	3
intracranial hemorrhage	2
survival	414

The evaluation of ontologies against reference terminologies help to highlight two major issues:

- The clarity of the lexicalizations of the ontology concepts. The fact that concepts are not mapped indicates the need for changes with respect to the class names used, or at least to additional labels supplied within the ontology.
- The developers of the ontology are informed of possibly missing classes in the representation of the domain.

Table 26., lists some of the examples of domain terms that are not present in the ontology. For instance *survival* is a very frequent term in COCR corpora, as most of the publications present research on improving the *survival* of cancer patients. The ACTG MO ontology models concepts like *death*, but there is no hint at a concept regarding *survival*. The proposed ontology evaluation methodology can indicate classes that are not present in an evaluated ontology of the domain.

8. Conclusions

In this thesis I have discussed the validity and theoretical background of knowledge acquisition from natural language. I have also presented the theoretical and experimental framework for NLP- driven ontology building and evaluation tasks. This section summarizes the contributions to the field of ontology learning and outlines the directions of further research in the area.

8.1 Summary and Contributions

This thesis reports the contributions to the state-of-art of NLP-driven ontology learning and evaluation. First, the framework for automatic detection of ontology building blocks: domain terms and their semantic relationships is presented. In addition, the approach of thesaurus-based evaluation of the pragmatic quality of ontologies is reported. Finally, the experimental investigation of proposed methodology has been evaluated on two different domains.

Section 1 briefly discusses the motivation of ontology building. Ontology is perceived differently, depending on the point of view of the research domain, as presented in section 2 that outlines the main perspectives on ontology derived from domains of philosophy, computer science and linguistics. The major interest of the thesis is to investigate the task of ontology building and evaluation from the standpoint of linguistics and an NLP perspective. Section 3 summarizes theoretical premises of a bottom-up ontology building approach and presents the arguments defending this perspective.

Additionally, section 4 overviews the techniques of NLP that have proved to be sufficient for the tasks of term extraction and semantic relationship extraction. Domain terms and their semantic interrelations are building blocks of an ontology. Section 5 reports state-of-art ontology evaluation approaches and explains how NLP can contribute to the strategy of the glass-box ontology evaluation.

Section 6 presents the hybrid methodology for domain terminology extraction and termhood assessment, which is based on linguistic NP pattern preprocessing and statistical termhood filtering. The proposed method achieved 79% of accuracy and has improved the baseline AUTOTERM approach (Hong et al. (2001), Haller (2006)) by 4%. In addition, the proposed method organizes domain terms into hypernym-hyponym hierarchies .

Regarding automatic relationship extraction, a novel method for utilizing monolingual paraphrase alignments and detecting synonymy has been developed. The approach does not use any language processing tools. The extended Cordeiro et al. (2007) method showed 72%-89% performance of accuracy in extracting synonymous word pairs, and synonymous MWU (multi-word unit) pairs.

In addition to unsupervised synonymy detection section 6 presents an SVO pattern matching approach that extends the KURD (Carl and Schmidt-Wigger (1998)) procedure.

The tasks of domain term extraction and semantic relationship extraction are major contributions to ontology building from NLP-driven standpoint. Yet another field where the role of natural language and NLP recently started to be explored is the evaluation of domain ontologies. A methodology for evaluation of a pragmatic property of domain ontologies is proposed. Evaluation of domain coverage of an ontology with specialized domain thesauri is an innovative attempt to assess other than syntactic properties of the quality of domain ontologies.

Ultimately, section 7 demonstrates that the developed methodology has proved to be useful because it was successfully applied and evaluated in two different research domains.

A thorough overview of related work is introduced throughout all the sections.

8.2   Discussion and Outlook

This thesis takes the standpoint that meaning is not a psychological phenomenon but rather a social phenomenon that is represented in textual discourse. Hence the proposed methodology for ontology building is a bottom-up approach. Domain specific knowledge can be mined from domain specific discourse. In fact, according to Teubert (2007) only textual discourse can be empirically analyzed. Moreover, "[…] there is no content unless it is represented." (Teubert (2007:67)) Consequently, the main assumption is that the domain specific discourse is a place where the meaning resides.

The thesis portrays the task of ontology building as a step-by-step process where supervision and verification by domain experts plays an important role. NLP contributions to this task are domain terminology extraction and semantic relationship detection. A similar approach was taken by state-of-art ontology learning systems like Kyoto[158], Terminae (Gilles et al. (2008)), Theseus Medico[159], and the pioneer Text-to-Onto (Maedche and Staab (2000)). Further extension of this research could be event extraction, which has been partially achieved by extracting SVO triplets. Obviously, NLP-driven ontology learning is related to state-of-art language analysis. Current capability of language analysis[160] halts at the semantic layer of language, as shown by Girju (2008). Therefore, a full competence of language analysis in the layers of discourse, pragmatics and knowledge remains a project for the future. Nevertheless,

---

[158] http://www.kyoto-project.eu/
[159] http://www.theseus-programm.de/was-ist-theseus/default.aspx
[160] Note: most of the state-of-the-art experiments were applied only to commonly used languages.

this fact does not diminish the importance of successful approaches that suggest a partial automation of the ontology learning task.

This thesis proposes the automated approach of extracting terminology (Grigonytė and Haller (2008)) and semantic relationships (Grigonytė et al. (2010a)) from domain specific corpora.

The terminology extraction task adopts a hybrid terminology extraction technique (Hong et al. (2001), Haller (2006)). Recent information extraction techniques related to terminology extraction show a tendency to become independent of language analysis. Among examples are Isozaki (2001), Quasthoff et al. (2002), Zhou and Su (2005), Kim et al. (2006), Funayama et al. (2009), Hasan et al. (2009), Lefever et al. (2009). However, the most reliable performance still is achieved by merging linguistic language analysis and statistical termhood assessing techniques (Maynard and Ananiadou (2000), Gilles et al. (2000), Dias (2003), Ji et al. (2007), Wong et al. (2007)).

The evaluation of term extraction methodology revealed several properties in both domains (computer dependability and cancer research) that were analyzed:

1. Most of the domain specific terms are two-word or three-word phrases.
2. The majority of the terms are very rare, therefore only using statistical modeling based on the two explored domain corpora for term detection would not have been reliable. Thus linguistically based term candidate detection was the optimal solution for both application domains that were analyzed.

A larger size of domain corpora would allow more reliable statistical termhood modeling. The problem of the size of domain corpora can be overcome by using Internet as a reference corpus. Such investigation was described by Buttler et al. (2001), Zhang et al. (2005).

Statistical modeling of terms proved to be a better approach than the approach of stop-word lists filtering to improve the performance of terminology extraction. This thesis shows that termhood modeling that contrasts general language corpora and domain specific corpora can help to make judgments on the usage of terms, even for given small domain specific corpora. The evaluation of termhood with the BNC corpus helped to reveal the multitude of usages of single words or multi-word units. This fact is theoretically supported by Zielinski's (2002) observation that the multitude of usages reveal the vagueness of a term. We found this observation valid by comparing the frequency of a domain term in the corpus of the domain and in the general language corpus.

The detection of noun phrases which normally embody term candidates is already quite reliable according to the measures of recall and precision. However, the biggest problem remains to determine which term is domain specific and which is general. Obviously, at this point statistical measures of distributional information are the most helpful.

Relationship extraction has been tackled by a number of researchers as presented in section 4.3.2. Pattern based techniques yield high precision but low recall, due to the fact that patterns can target only predefined and rule-encoded relationships. Semantic relatedness approaches that make use of lexical resources, are applicable to many ontology engineering methodologies, due to the reuse factor. WordNet (Fellbaum (1998)) is frequently given as an example of such a resource. However as reported by Roark and Charniak (1998), around 60% of domain specific terms cannot be found in WordNet. Low coverage with respect to the specific domains makes lexical resources difficult to adapt. This raises a need of different relationship detection techniques such as machine learning approaches, as presented by Pereira et al. (1993), Yangarber et al. (2000) Stevenson and Joanis (2003), Girju et al. (2004), Evert (2005), Cimiano (2005), Baroni (2008).

The results are reasonably good in learning particular semantic relationships like part-whole, causality, synonymy, etc. The drawback of such techniques is a need to prepare training data for each type of semantic relationship to be learned. As a solution Turney (2008) shows how learning can be done more efficiently by using SVM learner and training data for four kinds of semantic relationships: synonymy, antonymy, association, hypernymy. With regard to the problem of retraining for each task, Baroni and Lenci (2009) have presented yet another perspective that is very much worth considering: instead of preparing training data for each task, NLP researchers should consider gathering preprocessed linguistic resources that can assist all NLP tasks. An attempt of such a resource is *distributional semantic memory* (Baroni and Lenci (2009)) – a graph of weighted links between words. Depending on a task, different tuples of features can be extracted from this graph, and thus multiple semantic spaces can be derived.

Unsupervised learning (Sahlgren (2006), Hjelms (2009)) overcomes the problem of creating training data, however, relationships learned in the semantic relationship learning task need to be distinguished later.

A similar experience has been reported in this thesis. An unsupervised technique of learning relationships by using paraphrase domain corpora has been proposed.

On one hand, we were employing a similar method as presented in Cordeiro et al. (2007) for paraphrase extraction and alignment, yet with additional alignment constraints, such as using multi-word units, and stressing left and right context of a paraphrase. On the other hand, a new type of aligned sentence segments – *twists* – for synonymy evidence searching was explored. The proposed approach takes a corpus as input, and extracts a set of synonymic expressions for that domain. The major premise for this approach has been that two context frames that are aligned are similar or the same, therefore the non-aligned parts probably will be synonymous. This assumption has been shown to work in practice. Synonymous words have indeed been detected. However, semantic relationships other than synonymy have been detected as well.

This observation shows that the above mentioned premise has merged unrevealed properties of semantic relationships into one. For instance, hypernymy-hyponymy and antonymy have been treated as synonymy. In fact some linguistics theories explain this phenomenon.

As in *lexical gradient* theory (Vokhidova (2009)) where no distinct line between synonym and antonym exists to begin with, it follows that both relationships get merged in our approach. Additionally we could not claim that hypernym-hyponym, or holonym-meronym word pairs are synonymous. However, words that were paired in our approach share some synonymous properties that must be encoded in the context. This observation correlates with Sinclair's (1991, 1996) theory that *lexical unit* and *unit of meaning* are not equal. Thus even when words have autonomous meanings, their collocates reveal different semantic aspects of those meanings. In our case, similar contexts made word pairs look like synonyms.

The proposed method is promising in its potential, however it definitely needs to be more elaborated in order to bring more precision when discriminating between synonymous and non-synonymous pairs. Possible solutions could be:

- context based classification of acquired *twist pairs*. Turney (Turney (2008)) tackled the problem of classifying different lexical information such as synonymy, antonymy, hypernymy and association by employing context words. His classifier was trained on a huge web data corpus and performed with 97.5 % accuracy on a TOEFL test.
- tuning constraints for the "strength of context" of paraphrase twists.
- adding linguistic knowledge, e.g., linguistic annotation for noticing complex sentence constructions, like coreference.

To conclude, the presented approach proved to be promising for extracting synonymous words and multi-word units. Its strength is an ability to utilize small domain corpora, without supervised training and without using language processing tools. The method of synonymy detection is domain and application oriented. Further improvement of the method should include differentiation between acquired types of semantically related pairs.

With regards to *SVO triplet* extraction, SVO patterns help to mine explicitly visible relations from domain texts. With regards to ontology learning, argument structure patterns are referred to as *facts* (Kyoto project), or in information extraction – as *events* (Ahn (2006)), or *inference rules* (Lin and Pantel (2001a)).

In this thesis the linguistically-driven methodology for extracting SVO phrases was used. It is a standard approach used in many state-of-art systems, as in Lin and Pantel (2001a), Ramshaw et al. (2001), Gilles et al. (2008), Buyko et al. (2009), Hahn et al. (2009), Kilicoglu and Bergler (2009). The improvement of the above approach is dependent on the quality of syntactic analysis, i.e., the ability to deal with complex syntactic structures, as well as with discourse related bottleneck of coreference and anaphora. Yet another solution could be the machine learning approach (Piskorski et al. (2008), Naughton et al. (2008), Chen and Ji (2009), Ji (2009)), which also needs to take the discourse layer into account.

Yet another contribution of NLP that was investigated in this thesis is domain thesauri-driven ontology evaluation. The proposed evaluation technique follows the glass-box strategy and extends ontology evaluation to a different semiotic level (Burton-Jones et al. (2005)) which is called pragmatic metrics. Pragmatic quality of ontology determines to what extent ontological concepts relate to the source of reference, in our case to the domain terminology. This approach is different from other data-driven approaches such as Brewster et al. (2004), Daelemans and Reinberger (2004), Gangemi et al. (2006) that aim at evaluating syntactic quality of ontologies.

The proposed technique shows that using domain thesauri to validate domain coverage of an ontology is a highly promising approach. The checking of the ontologies for class names or labels that are actually used by domain experts is a highly important step because it fosters accessibility and usability of the ontology to the domain experts.

The impact of the analysis regarding the modification and improvement of an ontology is twofold:

- First, the clarification of term usage helps to determine whether it is necessary to implement changes with respect to the class names used, or at least with respect to additional labels supplied within an ontology.
- Second, the developers of the ontology can get an insight about possibly missing classes in their representation of the domain. The domain experts who build the ontology can be aided to determine which of the areas identified by the present study are of relevance and ought to be represented by the ontology.

A possible extension of the approach could be the evaluation of how well the shallow hierarchies of thesaurus i.e., hypernym-hyponym, map to an ontology. For now it is concluded, that the mapping between ontology and terminology should not be used to change or extend the structure of the ontology, since *terminological subsumptions* do not necessarily indicate *ontological subsumption* (Grigonytė et al. (2010)). With regards to the evaluation of the ontology structure, Hicks and Herold (2009) introduced a novel approach for assessing the property of *rigidity* in ontologies. The method makes use of patterns of semantic relations found in texts.

To summarize, we want to quote Cimiano's (2006) rhetorical question: "to what extent can knowledge actually be extracted from text?" That appears to correspond with the aims of *language analysis levels* (Girju (2008)). The work presented in this thesis can be significantly improved when more complex layers of language such as discourse or pragmatics will be addressed in research.

Bibliography

Abney, S. P. 2008. *Semisupervised learning in computational linguistics.* CRC Press.

Adam, P. 2007. *Formal representation of concepts: The Suggested Upper Merged Ontology and its use in linguistics. Ontolinguistics.* Mouton de Gruyter, p.103-114.

Agirre, E. & Rigau, G. 1996. *Word Sense Disambiguation using Conceptual Density.* Proceedings of the 16th Conference on Computational Linguistics (COLING '96), p.16-22.

Ahmad, K. 1995. *Pragmatics of Specialist Terms: The Acquisition and Representation of Terminology.* Proceedings of the Third International EAMT Workshop on Machine Translation and the Lexicon, p.51-76.

Ahn, D. 2006. *The stages of event extraction.* ARTE '06: Proceedings of the Workshop on Annotating and Reasoning about Time and Events, p.1-8.

Aires, J.; Lopes, G. & Silva, J. F. 2008. *Efficient multi-word expressions extractor using suffix arrays and related structures.* iNEWS '08: Proceeding of the 2nd ACM workshop on Improving non english web searching, p.1-8.

Albertazzi, L. 2007. *At the Roots of Consciousness: Intentional Presentations.* Journal of Consciousness Studies. Vol. 14(1), p.94-114.

Altmann, G. 1981. *Funktionsanalyse in der Linguistik.* Esser, J. & Hübler, A. (Ed.). *Forms and Functions.* Sprachwissenschaftliches Institut Universitat Bochum, p.25-32.

Ananiadou, S. 1994. *A Methodology For Automatic Term Recognition.* COLING 15th International Conference on Computational Linguistics, p.1034-1038.

Andreopoulos, B.; Alexopoulou, D. & Schroeder, M. 2008. *Word Sense Disambiguation in biomedical ontologies with term co-occurrence analysis and document clustering.* International Journal of Data Mining in Bioinformatics. Vol. 2(3), p.193-215.

Antoniou, G. & Harmelen, F. v. 2008. *A Semantic Web Primer, 2nd Edition (Cooperative Information Systems).* The MIT Press.

Appelt, D. E. & Israel, D. 1999. *Introduction to Information Extraction Technology*, IJCAI-99 Tutorial.

Arieti, J. A. 2005. *Philosophy in the ancient world: an introduction.* Rowman & Littlefield Publishers, Inc.

Aristotle 2005. *Metaphysics - Aristotle.* NuVision Publications, LLC.

Arppe, A. 1995. *Term extraction from unrestricted texts.* Proceedings of NODALIDA 95.

Aussenac, N.; Bourigault, D.; Condamines, A. & Gros, C. 1995. *How can Knowledge Acquisition benefit From Terminology.* Proceedings of the 9th Knowledge Acquisition for Knowledge Based System Workshop (KAW '95).

Aussenac-Gilles, N.; Biebow, B. & Szulman, S. 2000. *Revisiting Ontology Design A Methodology Based on Corpus Analysis.* Knowledge Acquisition, Modeling and Management, 12th

International Conference, EKAW 2000, Springer. Lecture Notes in Computer Science, p.172-188.

Aussenac-Gilles, N.; Despres, S. & Szulman, S. 2008. *The TERMINAE Method and Platform for Ontology Engineering from Texts*. Proceeding of the 2008 conference on Ontology Learning and Population: Bridging the Gap between Text and Knowledge, p.199-223.

Aussenac-Gilles, N. & Soergel, D. 2005. *Text analysis for ontology and terminology engineering.* Applied Ontology. Vol. 1(1), p.35-46.

Avižienis, A. 2008. *On representing knowledge in the dependability domain: a panel discussion.* Proceedings of the DSN, p.440-441.

Avižienis, A.; Grigonytė, G.; Haller, J.; von Henke, F. W.; Liebig, T. & Noppens, O. 2009. *Organizing Knowledge as an Ontology of the Domain of Resilient Computing by Means of Natural Language Processing - An Experience Report.* Proceedings of FLAIRS 22, AAAI press, p.474-479.

Avižienis, A.; Laprie, J.-C.; Randell, B. & Landwehr, C. 2004. *Basic concepts and taxonomy of dependable and secure computing.* IEEE Journal on Dependable and Secure Computing. Vol. 1(1), p.11-33.

Avižienis, A.; Čulo, O.; Grigonytė, G. & Marcinkevičienė, R. 2007. *Building a Thesaurus and an Ontology of the Concepts of Dependability and Security.* In proc. of 37th IEEE/IFIP International Conference on Dependable Systems and Networks, p.420-421.

Baroni, M. 2008. *Distributional Semantics: From Ad Hoc Solutions to Persistent Models,* http://nl.ijs.si/is-ltc08/IS-LTC08-MarcoBaroni.pdf

Baroni, M. & Lenci, A. 2009. *One distributional memory, many semantic spaces.* GEMS '09: Proceedings of the Workshop on Geometrical Models of Natural Language Semantics, p.1-8.

Barzilay, R. & Lee, L. 2003. *Learning to Paraphrase: An Unsupervised Approach Using Multiple-Sequence Alignment.* HLT-NAACL 2003: Main Proceedings, p.16-23.

Bendaoud, R.; Napoli, A. & Toussaint, Y. 2008. *A proposal for an Interactive Ontology Design Process based on Formal Concept Analysis.* FOIS. Frontiers in Artificial Intelligence and Applications, p.311-323.

Bernaras, A.; Laresgoiti, I. & Corera, J. 1996. *Building and Reusing Ontologies for Electrical Network Applications.* Proceedings of the 12th European Conference on Artificial Intelligence (ECAI 96), p.298-302.

Berners-Lee, T. 1999. *Weaving the Web: The Original Design and Ultimate Destiny of the World Wide Web by Its Inventor.* Harper San Francisco.

Berners-Lee, T. 2005. *WWW at 15 years: looking forward.* WWW '05: Proceedings of the 14th international conference on World Wide Web, p.1-1.

Biber, D. 1990. *Methodological Issues Regarding Corpus-based Analyses of Linguistic Variation.* Literary and Linguistic Computing. Vol. 5(4), p.257-269.

Biber, D. 1993. *Representativeness in Corpus Design.* Literary and Linguistic Computing. Vol. 8(4), p.243-257.

Biber, D.; Conrad, S. & Reppen, R. 1998. *Corpus Linguistics.* Cambridge University Press, Cambridge.

Bloom, L.; Hood, L. & Lightbown, P. 1974. *Imitation in language development: If, when, and why.* Cognitive Psychology. Vol. 6(3), p.380 - 420.

Borst, P.; Akkermans, H. & Top, J. 1997. *Engineering ontologies*. International Journal of Human Computer Studies. Vol. 46(2-3), p.365-406.

Bourigault D.; Jacquemin, C. & L'Homme, M. 2001. *Recent Advances in Computational Terminology*. John Benjamins Publishing Company.

Bourigault, D. 1992. *Surface Grammatical Analysis for the Extraction of Terminological Noun Phrases*. Proc. of 14th International Conference on Computational Linguistics (COLING), p.977-981.

Bourigault, D. 1994. *LEXTER, un Logiciel d'Extraction de TERminologie, Application à l'acquisition des connaissances à partir de textes*. Translated: *LEXTER, Terminology Extraction Software, Application to acquire knowledge from texts*, Paris: Ecole des Hautes Etudes en Sciences Sociales.

Brank, J.; Grobelnik, M. & Mladenić, D. 2005. *A Survey of Ontology Evaluation Techniques*. In In Proceedings of the Conference on Data Mining and Data Warehouses, p.166-169.

Brewster, C.; Alani, H.; Dasmahapatra, S. & Wilks, Y. 2004. *Data Driven Ontology Evaluation*. Proceedings of the International Conference on Language Resources and Evaluation (LREC-04), p.641-644.

Brown, P. F.; Pietra, S. A. D.; Pietra, V. J. D. & Mercer, R. L. 1991. *Word-sense disambiguation using statistical methods*. Proceedings of the 29th annual meeting on Association for Computational Linguistics, p.264-270.

Brown, R. 1973. *A first language: The early stages*. Oxford, England: Harvard U. Press.

Budanitsky, A. & Hirst, G. 2006. *Evaluating WordNet-based Measures of Lexical Semantic Relatedness*. Computational Linguistics. Vol. 32(1), p.13-47.

Budin, G. 1996. *Wissensorganisation und Terminologie: die Komplexität und Dynamik wissenschaftlicher Informations- und Kommunikationsprozesse. Band 28 von Forum für Fachsprachen-Forschung*. Gunter Narr Verlag.

Buetow, K. H. 2005. *Cyberinfrastructure: Empowering a third way in biomedical research*. Science. Vol. 308(5723), p.821-824.

Buitelaar, P. 2004. *OntoSelect: Towards the Integration of an Ontology Library, Ontology Selection and Knowledge Markup*. In: Proc. of the Workshop on Knowledge Markup and Semantic Annotation (Semannot2004) at the ISWC 2004, p.127-128.

Buitelaar, P. & Cimiano, P. 2008. *Ontologies and Lexical Semantics in Natural Language Understanding*, course at Saarland University WS2008, http://people.aifb.kit.edu/pci/ESSLLI07/

Buitelaar, P.; Cimiano, P. & Magnini, B. 2005. *Ontology Learning from Text: Methods, Evaluation and Applications*. IOS press.

Burkhardt, H. & Smith, B. 1991. *Handbook of Metaphysics and Ontology*. München, Hamden, Wien: Philosophia.

Burton-Jones, A.; Storey, V. C.; Sugumaran, V. & Ahluwalia, P. 2005. *A semiotic metrics suite for assessing the quality of ontologies*. Data and Knowledge Engineering. Vol. 55(1), p.84-102.

Buttler, D.; Liu, L. & Pu, C. 2001. *A Fully Automated Object Extraction System for the World Wide Web*. ICDCS '01: Proceedings of the The 21st International Conference on Distributed Computing Systems, p.361.

Buyko, E.; Faessler, E.; Wermter, J. & Hahn, U. 2009. *Event extraction from trimmed dependency graphs*. BioNLP '09: Proceedings of the Workshop on BioNLP, p.19-27.

Bybee, J. L. 1985. *Morphology: A study of the relation between meaning and form*. John Benjamins, Amsterdam.

Cabre-Castellvi, T.; Estopa, R. & Vivaldi-Palatresi, J. 2001. *Automatic Term Detection: A Review of Current Systems*. Bourigault, D.; Jacquemin, C. & LHomme, M. (Ed.). *Recent Advances in Computational Terminology*. John Benjamins, p.53-88.

Cal, A. 2004. *Reasoning in Data Integration Systems: why LAV and GAV are Siblings*. Proceedings of SEBD, p.282-289.

Calzolari, N. & Zampolli, A. 1990. *Methods and Tools for Lexical Acquisition*. EAIA. Lecture Notes in Computer Science, p.4-24.

Caraballo, S. A. 1999. *Automatic construction of a hypernym-labeled noun hierarchy from text*. Proceedings of the 37th annual meeting of the Association for Computational Linguistics on Computational Linguistics, p.120-126.

Cardoso, J. & Miltiadis, L. 2008. *Semantic Web Engineering in the Knowledge Society*. Idea Group, Hershey.

Carl, M. & Schmidt-Wigger, A. 1998. *Shallow post morphological processing with KURD*. NeMLaP3/CoNLL '98: Proceedings of the Joint Conferences on New Methods in Language Processing and Computational Natural Language Learning, p.257-265.

Carnap, R. 1942. *Introduction to Semantics*. Cambridge, Massachusetts.

Charles, W. G. 2000. *Contextual correlates of meaning*. Applied Psycholinguistics. Vol. 21, p.505-524.

Chen, J.; Yeh, C.-H. & Chau, R. 2006. *A Multi-word Term Extraction System*. PRICAI. Lecture Notes in Computer Science, p.1160-1165.

Chen, Z. & Ji, H. 2009. *Can one language bootstrap the other: a case study on event extraction*. SemiSupLearn '09: Proceedings of the NAACL HLT 2009 Workshop on Semi-Supervised Learning for Natural Language Processing, p.66-74.

Chimienti, M.; Dassisti, M.; Nicola, A. D. & Missikoff, M. 2009. *Evaluation of Ontology Building Methodologies - A Method based on Balanced Scorecards*. Proceedings of the KEOD conference, p.141-146.

Chomsky, N. 1965. *Aspects of the Theory of Syntax*. MIT Press, Cambridge.

Church, K.; Gale, W.; Hanks, P. & Hindle, D. 1991. *Using statistics in lexical analysis*. Lexical Acquisition: Exploiting On-Line Resources to Build a Lexicon, p.115-164.

Church, K. & Hanks, P. 1990. *Word Association Norms, Mutual Information, and Lexicography*. Computational Linguistics. Vol. 16(1), p.22-29.

Church, K. W. & Hanks, P. 1989. *Word association norms, mutual information, and lexicography*. In Proceedings of the 27th Annual Meeting of the Association for Computational Linguistics, p.76-83.

Cimiano, P. 2006. *Ontology Learning and Population from Text: Algorithms, Evaluation and Applications*. Springer.

Cimiano, P.; Handschuh, S. & Staab, S. 2004. *Towards the self-annotating web*. WWW '04: Proceedings of the 13th international conference on World Wide Web, p.462-471.

Cimiano, P.; Hotho, A. & Staab, S. 2005. *Learning concept hierarchies from text corpora using formal concept analysis*. Journal of Artificial Intelligence Research. Vol. 24(1), p.305-339.

Cimiano, P.; Maedche, A.; Staab, S. & Volker, J. 2003. *Ontology Learning*. Staab, S. & Studer, R. (Ed.). *Handbook on Ontologies in Information Systems*. Springer, p.245-268.

Cimiano, P. & Wenderoth, J. 2005. *Automatically Learning Qualia Structures from the Web.* Proceedings of the ACL-SIGLEX Workshop on Deep Lexical Acquisition, p.28-37.

Corcho, O.; Fernández-López, M. & Gómez-Pérez, A. 2003. *Methodologies, tools and languages for building ontologies: where is their meeting point?.* Data and Knowledge Engineering. Vol. 46(1), p.41-64.

Cordeiro, J.; Dias, G. & Brazdil, P. 2007. *Learning Paraphrases from WNS Corpora.* 20th International FLAIRS Conference.

Cordeiro, J.; Dias, G. & Cleuziou, G. 2007. *Biology Based Alignments of Paraphrases for Sentence Compression.* In Proceedings of the Workshop on Textual Entailment and Paraphrasing (ACL-PASCAL/ACL2007), p.177-184.

Cordeiro, J.; Dias, G. & P, B. 2009. *Unsupervised Induction of Sentence Compression Rules.* Proceedings of the Workshop on Language Generation and Summarisation (ACL-IJCNLP 2009), p.15-22.

Cunningham, C. *2004, Notes on Plato 1-13-04; lecture notes, http://cuip.uchicago.edu/~cac/depaul/winter2004/index.htm*

Čulo, O.; Grigonytė, G.; Hernandez, M.; Avižienis, A.; Haller, J. & Marcinkevičienė, R. 2007. *Building a Thesaurus of Dependability and Security: a Corpus Based Approach.* In Proc. Of 3rd Baltic Conf. on Human Language Technologies, p.71-76.

Dagan, I. & Itai, A. 1994. *Word sense disambiguation using a second language monolingual corpus.* Computational Linguistics. Vol. 20(4), p.563-596.

Dagan, I.; Marcus, S. & Markovitch, S. 1993. *Contextual Word Similarity and Estimation from Sparse Data.* Meeting of the Association for Computational Linguistics, p.164-171.

Dagan, I.; Pereira, F. & Lee, L. 1994. *Similarity-based estimation of word co-occurrence probabilities.* Proc. of the 32nd Annual Meeting of the Association for COmputational Linguistics (ACL'94), p.272-278.

Daille, B. 2003. *Conceptual structuring through term variations.* Proceedings of the ACL 2003 workshop on Multiword expressions, p.9-16.

Daille, B.; Gaussier, É. & Langé, J.-M. 1994. *Towards Automatic Extraction of Monolingual and Bilingual Terminology.* COLING, p.515-524.

Daraselia, N.; Yuryev, A.; Egorov, S.; Novichkova, S.; Nikitin, A. & Mazo, I. 2004. *Extracting human protein interactions from MEDLINE using a full-sentence parser.* Bioinformatics. Vol. 20(5), p.604-611.

Daudaravičius, V. & Marcinkevičienė, R. 2004. *Gravity Counts for the Boundaries of Collocations.* International Journal of Corpus Linguistics. Vol. 9(2), p.321-348.

Davidov, D. & Rappoport, A. 2008. *Unsupervised Discovery of Generic Relationships Using Pattern Clusters and its Evaluation by Automatically Generated SAT Analogy Questions.* Proceedings of the 46th Annual Meeting of the ACL and HLT (ACL-HLT-08), p.692-700.

Deane, P. & Wheeler, R. 1984. *On the Use of Syntactic Evidence in the Analysis of Word Meaning.* Papers from the Parasession on Lexical Semantics, Chicago Linguistic Society, ETATS-UNIS, p.95-106.

Debowski, L. 2009. *A link between the number of set phrases in a text and the number of described facts.* Qualico: Text and Language: Structures - Functions - Interrelations.

Dellschaft, K. & Staab, S. 2008. *Strategies for the Evaluation of Ontology Learning.* Proceeding of the 2008 conference on Ontology Learning and Population: Bridging the Gap between Text and Knowledge, p.253-272.

Diab, M. 2000. *An unsupervised method for multilingual word sense tagging using parallel corpora: a preliminary investigation.* Proceedings of the ACL-2000 workshop on Word senses and multi-linguality, p.1-9.

Dias, G. 2003. *Multiword unit hybrid extraction.* Proceedings of the ACL 2003 workshop on Multiword expressions, p.41-48.

Dias, G.; Mukelov, R. & Cleuziou, G. 2008. *Mapping General-Specific Noun Relationships to WordNet Hypernym/Hyponym Relations.* EKAW '08: Proceedings of the 16th international conference on Knowledge Engineering, p.198-212.

Dimitrova, V.; Denaux, R.; Hart, G.; Dolbear, C.; Holt, I. & Cohn, A. G. 2008. *Involving Domain Experts in Authoring OWL Ontologies.* ISWC '08: Proceedings of the 7th International Conference on The Semantic Web, p.1-16.

Dorow, B. & Widdows, D. 2003. *Discovering corpus-specific word senses.* EACL '03: Proceedings of the tenth conference on European chapter of the Association for Computational Linguistics, p.79-82.

Dunning, T. 1993. *Accurate methods for the statistics of surprise and coincidence.* Computational Linguistics. Vol. 19(1), p.61-74.

Dyvik, H. 2004. *Translations as semantic mirrors: from parallel corpus to wordnet.* Language and Computers. Vol. 49, p.311-326.

Eaton, J. E. 1940. *Theory of cogroups.* Duke Mathematical Journal. Vol. 6(1), p.101-107.

Edmonds, P. G. 1999. *Semantic representations of near-synonyms for automatic lexical choice,* University of Toronto.

Ehrig, M. 2007. *Ontology Alignment: Bridging the Semantic Gap.* Springer.

Enguehard, C. & Pantera, L. 1994. *Automatic Natural Acquisition of a Terminology.* Journal of Quantitative Linguistics. Vol. 2(1), p.27-32.

Evert, S. 2005. *The Statistics of Word Cooccurrences: Word Pairs and Collocations,* Institut für maschinelle Sprachverarbeitung, University of Stuttgart.

Evert, S. & Krenn, B. 2001. *Methods for the Qualitative Evaluation of Lexical Association Measures.* In Proceedings of the 39th Annual Meeting of the Association for Computational Linguistics, p.188-195.

Fahmi, I.; Bouma, G. & van der Plas, L. 2007. *Improving Statistical Method using Known Terms for Automatic Term Extraction.* Computational Linguistics in the Netherlands, Vol. 17.

Faure, D. & Nédellec, C. 1999. *Knowledge Acquisition of Predicate Argument Structures from Technical Texts Using Machine Learning The System ASIUM.* Proceedings of the 11th European Workshop on Knowledge Acquisition, Modeling and Management (EKAW-99), p.329-334.

Fellbaum, C. 2007. *The Ontological Loneliness of Idioms.* Schalley, A. & Zaefferer, D. (Ed.). *Ontolinguistics.* Mouton de Gruyter, p.419-434.

Fellbaum, C. D. 1998. *WordNet: An Electronic Lexical Database.* MIT Press, Cambridge, MA.

Fensel, D. 2004. *Ontologies: a silver bullet for knowledge management and electronic commerce.* Springer-Verlag, Berlin.

Fernandez-Lopez, M.; Gomez-Perez, A. & Juristo, N. 1997. *METHONTOLOGY: from Ontological Art towards Ontological Engineering.* Proceedings of the AAAI97 Spring Symposium, p.33-40.

Fillmore, C. 1976. *Frame semantics and the nature of language.* In Annals of the New York Academy of Sciences: Conference on the Origin and Development of Language and Speech. Vol. 280, p.20-32.

Fillmore, C. J.; Kay, P. & O'Connor, M. C. 1988. *Regularity and Idiomaticity in Grammatical Constructions: The Case of Let Alone.* Language. Vol. 64(3), p.510-538.

Finkel, J. R. & Manning, C. D. 2008. *Enforcing transitivity in coreference resolution.* HLT '08: Proceedings of the 46th Annual Meeting of the Association for Computational Linguistics on Human Language Technologies, p.45-48.

Finkelstein-Landau, M. & Morin, E. 1999. *Extracting Semantic Relationships between Terms: Supervised vs. Unsupervised Methods.* Proceedings of the International Workshop on Ontological Engineering on the Global Information Infrastructure, p.71-80.

Firth, J. 1957. *A Synopsis of Linguistic Theory 1930-1955.* Philological Society, Oxford.

Floridi, L. 2004. *The Blackwell guide to the Philosophy of Computing and Information.* Blackwell Publishing.

Fox, M. S.; Barbuceanu, M. & Gruninger, M. 1995. *An organisation ontology for enterprise modelling: preliminary concepts for linking structure and behaviour.* 4th Workshop on Enabling Technologies: infrastructure For Collaborative Enterprises. IEEE Computer Society, p.71-81.

Frank, E.; Paynter, G. W.; Witten, I. H.; Gutwin, C. & Nevill-Manning, C. G. 1999. *Domain-Specific Keyphrase Extraction.* IJCAI '99: Proceedings of the Sixteenth International Joint Conference on Artificial Intelligence, p.668-673.

Frantzi, K.; Ananiadou, S. & Mima, H. 2000. *Automatic recognition of multi-word terms:. the C-value/NC-value method.* International Journal on Digital Libraries. Vol. 3(2), p.115-130.

Frantzi, K. T. & Ananiadou, S. 1999. *The C/NC value domain independent method for multi-word term extraction.* Journal of Natural Language Processing. Vol. 6(3), p.145-180.

Frege, G. 1892. *Über Begriff und Gegenstand.* Vierteljahresschrift für wissenschaftliche Philosophie. Vol. 16, p.192-205.

Freitag, D. & McCallum, A. 1999. *Information Extraction with HMMs and Shrinkage.* Proceedings of the AAAI-99 Workshop on Machine Learning for Information Extraction, p.31-36.

Fries, C. C. 1952. *The Structure of English.* New York: Harcourt, Brace.

Funayama, H.; Shibata, T. & Kurohashi, S. 2009. *Bottom-up named entity recognition using a two-stage machine learning method.* MWE '09: Proceedings of the Workshop on Multiword Expressions, p.55-62.

Gabrilovich, E. & Markovitch, S. 2007. *Computing semantic relatedness using Wikipedia-based explicit semantic analysis.* IJCAI'07: Proceedings of the 20th international joint conference on Artifical intelligence, p.1606-1611.

Gale, W.; Church, K. W. & Yarowsky, D. 1992. *Estimating upper and lower bounds on the performance of word-sense disambiguation programs.* Proceedings of the 30th annual meeting on Association for Computational Linguistics, p.249-256.

Gamallo, P.; Gonzalez, M.; Agustini, A.; Lopes, G. & deLima, V. 2002. *Mapping Syntactic Dependencies onto Semantic Relations.* Proceedings of the ECAI Workshop on Machine Learning and Natural Language Processing for Ontology Engineering, p.15-22.

Gangemi, A.; Catenacci, C.; Ciaramita, M. & Lehmann, J. 2006. *Modelling Ontology Evaluation.*
    Proceedings of the 3rd ESWC, p.140-154.
Gangemi, A.; Steve, G. & Giacomelli, F. 1996. *ONIONS: An Ontological Methodology for Taxonomic*
    Knowledge Integration. Proceedings of the ECAI-1996, Workshop on Ontological Engineering,
    p.29-40.
Genesereth, M. R. & Nilsson, N. J. 1987. *Logical foundations of artificial intelligence.* Morgan
    Kaufmann Publishers Inc., San Francisco, CA, USA.
Gilbert, M. & Williams, D. 2008. *A Systems Approach to User Evaluation of Biomedical Ontologies.*
    ONTORACT '08: Proceedings of the 2008 First International Workshop on Ontologies in
    Interactive Systems, p.97-102.
Gildea, D. & Jurafsky, D. 2002. *Automatic Labeling of Semantic Roles.* Computational Linguistics. Vol.
    28(3), p.245-288.
Girju, R. 2003. *Automatic detection of causal relations for Question Answering.* Proceedings of the ACL
    2003 workshop on Multilingual summarization and question answering, p.76-83.
Girju, R. 2006. *Out-of-context noun phrase semantic interpretation with cross-linguistic evidence.*
    CIKM '06: Proceedings of the 15th ACM international conference on Information and
    knowledge management, p.268-276.
Girju, R. 2008. *Semantic Relation Extraction and its Applications*, ESSLLI course
    http://www.illc.uva.nl/ESSLLI2008/schedule.html
Girju, R.; Badulescu, A. & Moldovan, D. 2003. *Learning semantic constraints for the automatic*
    discovery of part-whole relations. NAACL '03: Proceedings of the 2003 Conference of the
    North American Chapter of the Association for Computational Linguistics on Human Language
    Technology, p.1-8.
Girju, R.; Badulescu, A. & Moldovan, D. 2006. *Automatic Discovery of Part-Whole Relations.*
    Computational Linguistics. Vol. 32(1), p.83-135.
Girju, R.; Giuglea, A.-M.; Olteanu, M.; Fortu, O.; Bolohan, O. & Moldovan, D. 2004. *Support vector*
    machines applied to the classification of semantic relations in nominalized noun phrases. CLS
    '04: Proceedings of the HLT-NAACL Workshop on Computational Lexical Semantics, p.68-75.
Goddard, C. 2001. *Lexico-semantic universals: A critical overview.* Linguistic Typology. Vol. 5, p.1-65.
Goddard, C. & Wierzbicka, A. 2002. *Meaning and universal grammar : theory and empirical findings.*
    Goddard, C.; Wierzbicka, A. (Ed.). John Benjamins Pub., Amsterdam; Philadelphia.
Goertzel, B.; Goertzel, I. F.; Pinto, H.; Ross, M.; Heljakka, A. & Pennachin, C. 2006. *Using dependency*
    parsing and probabilistic inference to extract relationships between genes, proteins and
    malignancies implicit among multiple biomedical research abstracts. BioNLP '06 proceedings,
    p.104-111.
Goldberg, A. 2006. *Constructions at Work: the nature of generalization in language.* Oxford University
    Press.
Goldberg, A. E. 2003. *Constructions: a new theoretical approach to language.* Trends in Cognitive
    Sciences. Vol. 7(5), p.219 - 224.
Gomez-Perez, A. 1995. *Some ideas and examples to evaluate ontologies.* Artificial Intelligence for
    Applications. Vol. 1, p.299.

Gomez-Perez, A.; Fernández-López, M. & Corcho, O. 2004. *Ontological Engineering: with examples from the areas of Knowledge Management, e-Commerce and the Semantic Web.* Springer-Verlag, London.

Grüninger, M. & Fox, M. 1995. *Methodology for the Design and Evaluation of Ontologies.* Proceedings of IJCAI'95, Workshop on Basic Ontological Issues in Knowledge Sharing, April 13, 1995.

Graefen, G. 1997. *Der Wissenschaftliche Artikel - Textart und Textorgnisation. Reden und Schreiben in der Wissenschaft, Vol 27.,* Peter Lang.

Greenwood, M.; Stevenson, M.; Guo, Y.; Harkema, H. & Roberts, A. 2005. *Automatically Acquiring a Linguistically Motivated Genic Interaction Extraction System.* Proceedings of the 4th Learning Language in Logic Workshop (LLL05), Bonn, Germany.

Grefenstette, G. 1994. *Explorations in Automatic Thesaurus Discovery.* Kluwer Academic Publishers, Norwell, MA, USA.

Grigonytė, G.; Avižienis, A.; von Henke, F.; Liebig, T. & Noppens, O. 2009. *D34 Resilience Ontology,* http://www.resist-noe.org/Publications/Deliverables/D34-Resilience_Ontology_Final.pdf, the ReSIST project deliverable.

Grigonytė, G. & Haller, J. 2008. *Domain Independent Automatic Term Extraction Framework.* Proceedings of the second Swedish Language Technology Conference (SLTC-08), p.11-12.

Grigonytė, G.; Cordeiro, J. P.; Moraliyski, R.; Dias, G. & Brazdil, P. 2010a. *Paraphrase Alignment for Synonym Evidence Discovery,* Proceedings of the 23rd Int. Conf. on Computational Linguistics, COLING 2010, p.403-411.

Grigonytė, G.; Brochhausen, M.; Martín, L.; Tsiknakis, M. & Haller, J. 2010. *Evaluating ontologies with NLP-based terminologies: A case study on ACGT and its master ontology.* Vol. 209 IOS Press (2010), p.331-342.

Grigonytė, G.; Čulo, O.; Avižienis, A. & Marcinkevičienė, R. 2008. *Dependability and Security: Thesauri Creation and Clustering Experiments – an Overview and an Outlook.* Proceedings of EDCC 7, p.49-52.

Grishman, R. & Sundheim, B. 1996. *Message understanding conference - 6: A brief history.* Proceedings of the International Conference on Computational Linguistics, p.466-471.

Gruber, T. R. 1993. *A translation approach to portable ontology specifications.* Knowledge Acquisition. Vol. 5(2), p.199-220.

Grzybek, P. 2004. *A Quantitative Approach to Lexical Structure of Proverbs.* Journal of Quantitative Linguistics. Vol. 11(1-2), p.79-92.

Grzybek, P. & Stadlober, E. 2002. *Project Report: The Graz Project on Word Length (Frequencies).* Journal of Quantitative Linguistics. Vol. 9(2), p.187-192.

Grüninger, M. & Fox, M. 1995. *Methodology for the Design and Evaluation of Ontologies.* IJCAI'95, Workshop on Basic Ontological Issues in Knowledge Sharing, April 13, 1995.

Guarino, N. 1997. *Understanding, building and using ontologies.* International Journal of Human Computer Studies. Vol. 46(2-3), p.293-310.

Guarino, N. 1998. *Formal Ontology in Information Systems: Proceedings of the 1st International FOIS Conference,* IOS Press, p.3-18.

Guarino, N. 2008. *Ontologies and Ontological Analysis,* FOIS 2008 tutorial, http://fois08.dfki.de/presentations/FOIS2008-Tutorial1-Guarino.pdf

Guarino, N.& Welty, C. 2000. *Ontological analysis of taxonomic relationships.* In Proceedings of the 19th international Conference on Conceptual Modeling. Lecture Notes In Computer Science. Springer, Berlin, p. 210-224.

Guarino, N. & Welty, C. 2002. *Evaluating ontological decisions with OntoClean.* Communications of ACM. Vol. 45(2), p.61-65.

Guarino, N. & Welty, C. A. 2004. *An Overview of OntoClean.* Staab, S. & Studer, R. (Ed.). *Handbook on Ontologies.* Springer, Berlin, p.151-172.

Guizzardi, G. 2007. *On Ontology, ontologies, Conceptualizations, Modeling Languages, and (Meta)Models.* Proceeding of the 2007 conference on Databases and Information Systems IV, p.18-39.

Guo, W. & Diab, M. T. 2009. *Improvements to monolingual English word sense disambiguation.* DEW '09: Proceedings of the Workshop on Semantic Evaluations: Recent Achievements and Future Directions, p.64-69.

Gurevych, I. 2005. *Using the structure of a conceptual network in computing semantic relatedness.* Proceedings of the 2nd International Joint Conference on Natural Language Processing, p.767–787.

Gómez-Pérez, A. 1999. *Evaluation of Taxonomic Knowledge in Ontologies and Knowledge Bases.* Proceedings of the 12th Banff Knowledge Acquisition for Knowledge-Based Systems Workshop, p.611-618.

Hagiwara, M.; Ogawa, Y. & Toyama, K. 2005. *PLSI Utilization for Automatic Thesaurus Construction.* IJCNLP. Lecture Notes in Computer Science, p.334-345.

Hahn, U. & Markó, K. G. 2002. *An integrated, dual learner for grammars and ontologies.* Data and Knowledge Engineering. Vol. 42(3), p.273-291.

Hahn, U. & Schulz, S. 2002. *Massive bio-ontology engineering for NLP.* Proceedings of the second international conference on Human Language Technology Research, p.68-75.

Hahn, U.; Tomanek, K.; Buyko, E.; Kim, J.-j. & Rebholz-Schuhmann, D. 2009. *How feasible and robust is the automatic extraction of gene regulation events?: a cross-method evaluation under lab and real-life conditions.* BioNLP '09: Proceedings of the Workshop on BioNLP, p.37-45.

Hajicová, E. 2008. *What We Are Talking about and What We Are Saying about It.* CICLing. Lecture Notes in Computer Science, p.241-262.

Haller, J. 2006. *AUTOTERM - automatische Terminologieextraktion Spanisch-Deutsch.* Multiperspektivische Fragestellungen der Translation in der Romania. Sabest 14, Peter Lang Verlag, p.229-242.

Halliday, M. & Hasan, R. 1989. *Language, Context, and Text: Aspects of Language in a Social-Semiotic Perspective (Language Education).* Oxford University Press.

Hanks, P. 2000. *Do word meanings exist?* Computers and the Humanities. Vol. 34(1-2), p.205-215.

Hanks, P. 2004. *The Syntagmatics of Metaphor and Idiom.* International Journal of Lexicography. Vol. 17(3), p.245-274.

Hanks, P. 2007. *Lexicography, lexicology, and corpus analysis,* http://www.lumii.lv/ngslt/hanks/

Harris, R. A. 1993. *The linguistics wars.* Oxford University Press.

Harris, Z. 1958. *Linguistic Analysis for Information Retrieval.* Int. Conf. on Scientific Information, Washington, D.C.

Harris, Z. S. 1970. *Papers in structural and transformational linguistics.* Reidel.

Harris, Z. S. & Hiz, H. 1981. *Papers on Syntax*. Springer.

Hartmann, J.; Spyns, P.; Giboin, A.; Maynard, D.; Cuel, R.; Suarez-Figueroa, M. C. & Sure, Y. 2005. *D1.2.3 Methods for ontology evaluation*, EU-IST Network of Excellence (NoE) IST-2004-507482 KWEB deliverable.

Hasan, K. S.; ur Rahman, A. & Ng, V. 2009. *Learning-based named entity recognition for morphologically-rich, resource-scarce languages*. EACL '09: Proceedings of the 12th Conference of the European Chapter of the Association for Computational Linguistics, p.354-362.

Heaps, H. S. 1978. *Information Retrieval: Computational and Theoretical Aspects*. Academic Press, Inc., Orlando, FL, USA.

Hearst, M. A. 1992. *Automatic acquisition of hyponyms from large text corpora*. Proceedings of the 14th conference on Computational linguistics, p.539-545.

Hearst, M. A. 1998. *Automated discovery of WordNet relations*. *WordNet: An Electronic Lexical Database*. MIT Press, CambridgeMA, p.131–152.

van Heijst, G.; Schreiber, A. T. & Wielinga, B. J. 1997. *Using explicit ontologies in KBS development*. International Journal of Human Computer Studies. Vol. 46(2-3), p.183-292.

Hicks, A. & Herold, A. 2009. *Evaluating Ontologies with Rudify*. Proceedings of the KEOD conference, p.5-12.

Hirst, G. 1987. *Semantic interpretation and the resolution of ambiguity*. Cambridge University Press, New York, NY, USA.

Hjelm, H. 2009. *Cross-language Ontology Learning*, Stockholm University.

Hong, M.; Fissaha, S. & Haller, J. 2001. *Hybrid Filtering for Extraction of Term Candidates from German Technical Texts*. Proceedings of TIA'2001.

Hovy, E. 2001. *Comparing Sets of Semantic Relations in Ontologies*. Green, R.; Bean, C. A. & Myaeng, S. H. (Ed.). *Semantics of Relationships*. Kluwer, p.91-110.

Hovy, E. H. 2005. *Methodologies for the Reliable Construction of Ontological Knowledge*. ICCS, p.91-106.

IFOMIS 2010a. *ACGT Master Ontology*, http://www.ifomis.org/wiki/ACGT_Master_Ontology_%28MO%29

IFOMIS 2010b. *BFO*, http://www.ifomis.org/bfo

Inwood, M. A. 1992. *Hegel Dictionary*. Blackwell Publishers Ltd.

Isozaki, H. 2001. *Japanese named entity recognition based on a simple rule generator and decision tree learning*. ACL '01: Proceedings of the 39th Annual Meeting on Association for Computational Linguistics, p.314-321.

Jacquemin, C. 1999. *Syntagmatic and paradigmatic representations of term variation*. Proceedings of the 37th annual meeting of the Association for Computational Linguistics on Computational Linguistics, p.341-348.

Jain, R. 2008. *Multimedia information retrieval: watershed events*. MIR '08: Proceeding of the 1st ACM international conference on Multimedia information retrieval, p.229-236.

Ji, H. 2009. *Cross-lingual predicate cluster acquisition to improve bilingual event extraction by inductive learning*. UMSLLS '09: Proceedings of the Workshop on Unsupervised and Minimally Supervised Learning of Lexical Semantics, p.27-35.

Ji, L.; Sum, M.; Lu, Q.; Li, W. & Chen, Y. 2007. *Chinese Terminology Extraction Using Window-Based Contextual Information*. CICLing '07: Proceedings of the 8th International Conference on Computational Linguistics and Intelligent Text Processing, p.62-74.

Jimenez-Ruiz, E. & Berlanga, R. 2006. *A View-Based Methodology for Collaborative Ontology Engineering: An Approach for Complex Applications (VIMethCOE)*. WETICE '06: Proceedings of the 15th IEEE International Workshops on Enabling Technologies: Infrastructure for Collaborative Enterprises, p.376-381.

Justeson, J. S. & Katz, S. M. 1995. *Technical Terminology Some Linguistic Properties and an Algorithm for Identification in Text*. Natural Language Engineering. Vol. 1(1), p.9-27.

Kaji, H. 2003. *Word sense acquisition from bilingual comparable corpora*. Proceedings of the NAACL '03, p.32-39.

Kanellopoulos, D. N. 2009. *ODELO: an ontology-driven model for the evaluation of learning ontologies*. International Journal of Learning Technology. Vol. 4(1-2), p.73-99.

Katz, J. 1972. *Semantic Theory*. Harper New York.

Kilgarriff, A. 1997. *Evaluating Word Sense Disambiguation Programs: progress report*. Proc. of SALT Workshop in Speech and Language Technology, p.114-120.

Kilicoglu, H. & Bergler, S. 2009. *Syntactic dependency based heuristics for biological event extraction*. BioNLP '09: Proceedings of the Workshop on BioNLP, p.119-127.

Kim, S.; Song, Y.; Kim, K.; Cha, J.-W. & Lee, G. 2006. *MMR-based active machine learning for bio named entity recognition*. NAACL '06: Proceedings of the Human Language Technology Conference of the NAACL, Companion Volume: Short Papers, p.69-72.

Kjellmer, G. 1994. *A dictionary of English collocations: based on the Brown corpus: in three volumes*. Oxford University Press, USA.

Koeva, S. 2007. *Multi-word term extraction for Bulgarian*. ACL '07: Proceedings of the Workshop on Balto-Slavonic Natural Language Processing, p.59-66.

Krifka, M. 1999. *Manner in dative alternation*. Proceedings of the Eighteenth West Coast Conference on Formal Linguistics, p.1-14.

Köhler, R. & Naumann, S. 2005. *An extension of the synergetic-linguistic model and its application to word frequency*. Proceedings of the Worksshop The Science of Language: Structures of Frequencies and Relations at Graz University.

Köhler, R. & Naumann, S. 2007. *Quantitative analysis of co-refenrence structures in texts*. Grzybek, P. & Köhler, R. (Ed.). *Exact Methods in the Study of Language and Text*. de Gruyter, p.317-330.

Künne, W. 2003. *Conceptions of Truth*. Oxford: Oxford University Press.

López, M. F.; Gómez-Pérez, A.; Sierra, J. P. & Sierra, A. P. 1999. *Building a Chemical Ontology Using Methontology and the Ontology Design Environment*. IEEE Intelligent Systems. Vol. 14(1), p.37-46.

Lakoff, G. 1968. *Instrumental Adverbs and the Concept of Deep Structure*. Foundations of Language, Springer. Vol. 4(1), p.4-29.

Lakoff, G. 1987. *Women, Fire and Dangerous Things: What Categories Reveal about the Mind*. Chicago Press, Chicago.

Langacker, R. 1987. *Foundations of Cognitive Grammar*. Stanford University Press, Stanford.

Lapata, M. 2002. *The disambiguation of nominalizations*. Computational Linguistics. Vol. 28(3), p.357-388.

Lapata, M. & Brew, C. 2004. *Verb class disambiguation using informative priors*. Computational Linguistics. Vol. 30(1), p.45-73.

Laprie, J.-C. 1992. *Dependability*. Springer.

Lauer, M. 1995. *Corpus Statistics Meet the Noun Compound*. ACL-95, p.47-54.

Leacock, C. & Chodorow, M. 1998. *Combining local context and WordNet similarity for word sense identification*. Fellbaum (Ed.), MIT Press, p.265-283.

Leacock, C.; Towell, G. & Voorhees, E. 1993. *Corpus-based statistical sense resolution*. HLT '93: Proceedings of the workshop on Human Language Technology, p.260-265.

Lee, J. H.; Kim, M. H. & Lee, Y. J. 1993. *Information retrieval based on conceptual distance in IS-A hierarchies*. Journal of Documentation. Vol. 49(2), p.188-207.

Lee, L. & Pereira, F. 1999. *Distributional similarity models: clustering vs. nearest neighbors*. Proceedings of the 37th annual meeting of the Association for Computational Linguistics on Computational Linguistics, p.33-40.

Lefever, E.; Macken, L. & Hoste, V. 2009. *Language-independent bilingual terminology extraction from a multilingual parallel corpus*. EACL '09: Proceedings of the 12th Conference of the European Chapter of the Association for Computational Linguistics, p.496-504.

Lenat, D. B. 1995. *CYC: a large-scale investment in knowledge infrastructure*. Communications of ACM. Vol. 38(11), p.33-38.

Lenat, D. B.; Guha, R. V.; Pittman, K.; Pratt, D. & Shepherd, M. 1990. *Cyc: toward programs with common sense*. Communications of ACM. Vol. 33(8), p.30-49.

Lenci, A. 2008. *SIABO PhD school lecture notes*, http://www.cbs.dk/forskning/konferencer/siabo/menu/program/program/presentations.

Lendvai, P. 2009. *Towards acquisition of taxonomic inference*. IWCS-8 '09: Proceedings of the Eighth International Conference on Computational Semantics, p.291-294.

Lesk, M. 1986. *Automatic sense disambiguation using machine readable dictionaries: how to tell a pine cone from an ice cream cone*. SIGDOC '86: Proceedings of the 5th annual international conference on Systems documentation, p.24-26.

Levenshtein, V. I. 1966. *Binary codes capable of correcting deletions, insertions and reversals*. Soviet Physics Doklady. Vol. 10(8), p.707-710.

Levin, B. 1993. *English Verb Classes and Alternations A Preliminary Investigation*. University of Chicago Press, Chicago and London.

Lin, D. 1998. *Automatic retrieval and clustering of similar words*. Proceedings of the 17th international conference on Computational linguistics, p.768-774.

Lin, D. & Pantel, P. 2001. *Induction of semantic classes from natural language text*. KDD '01: Proceedings of the seventh ACM SIGKDD international conference on Knowledge discovery and data mining, p.317-322.

Lin, D. & Pantel, P. 2001a. *DIRT @SBT@discovery of inference rules from text*. KDD '01: Proceedings of the seventh ACM SIGKDD international conference on Knowledge discovery and data mining, p.323-328.

Lin, D.; Zhao, S.; Qin, L. & Zhou, M. 2003. *Identifying synonyms among distributionally similar words*. IJCAI'03: Proceedings of the 18th international joint conference on Artificial intelligence, p.1492-1493.

Liu, H. & Singh, P. 2004. *ConceptNet: A Practical Commonsense Reasoning Toolkit.* BT Technology Journal. Vol. 22(4), p.211-226.

Lorge, I. 1949. *The semantic count of the 570 commonest English words.* Institute of Psychological Research, Teachers College, Columbia University.

Lozano-Tello, A. & Gómez-Pérez, A. 2004. *ONTOMETRIC: A Method to Choose the Appropriate Ontology.* Journal of Database Management. Vol. 15(2), p.1-18.

Maas, H.-D.; Rösener, C.; Theofilidis, A. 2009. *Morphosyntactic and Semantic Analysis of Text: The MPRO Tagging Procedure.* State of the art in computational morphology. Proceedings of the workshop on Systems and frameworks for computational morphology, p.76-87.

Maedche, A. 2002. *Ontology learning for the Semantic Web.* Kluwer, Dordrecht, NL.

Maedche, A. & Staab, S. 2000. *The TEXT-TO-ONTO Ontology Learning Environment,*

Maedche, A. & Staab, S. 2001. *Ontology Learning for the Semantic Web.* IEEE Intelligent Systems. Vol. 16(2), p.72-79.

Maedche, A. & Staab, S. 2002. *Measuring Similarity between Ontologies.* EKAW '02: Proceedings of the 13th International Conference on Knowledge Engineering and Knowledge Management. Ontologies and the Semantic Web, p.251-263.

Manber, U. & Myers, G. 1990. *Suffix arrays: a new method for on-line string searches.* SODA '90: Proceedings of the first annual ACM-SIAM symposium on Discrete algorithms, p.319-327.

Manning, C. D. & Schütze, H. 1999. *Foundations of statistical natural language processing.* MIT Press, Cambridge, MA, USA.

Martn, L.; Bonsma, E.; Anguita, A.; Vrijnsen, J.; Garca-Remesal, M.; Crespo, J.; Tsiknakis, M. & Maojo, V. 2007. *Data Access and Management in ACGT: Tools to Solve Syntactic and Semantic Heterogeneities Between Clinical and Image Databases.* ER Workshops, p.24-33.

Maynard, D. & Ananiadou, S. 1999a. *Term Extraction using a Similarity-based Approach.* Bourigault, D.; Jacquemin, C. & Lhomme, M.-C. (Ed.). *Recent Advances in Computational Terminology.* John Benjamins, p.261-278.

Maynard, D. & Ananiadou, S. 1999b. *Term Sense Disambiguation Using a Domain-Specific Thesaurus.* Proceedings of the LREC 1999, p.681-687.

Maynard, D. & Ananiadou, S. 2000. *Identifying terms by their family and friends.* Proceedings of the 18th conference on Computational linguistics, p.530-536.

Maynard, D.; Tablan, V.; Ursu, C.; Cunningham, H. & Wilks, Y. 2001. *Named Entity Recognition from Diverse Text Types.* In proceedings of the Recent Advances in Natural Language Processing conference, Tzigov Chark, Bulgaria.

Maynard, D.; Funk, A. & Peters, W. 2009. *Using Lexico-Syntactic Ontology Design Patterns for Ontology Creation and Population.* Proceedings of the Workshop on Ontology Patterns (WOP 2009), p.39-52.

McDonald, R.; Pereira, F.; Kulick, S.; Winters, S.; Jin, Y. & White, P. 2005. *Simple algorithms for complex relation extraction with applications to biomedical IE.* ACL '05: Proceedings of the 43rd Annual Meeting on Association for Computational Linguistics, p.491-498.

McEnery, T. & Wilson, A. 2005. *Corpus linguistics: an introduction.* Edinburgh Univ. Press, Edinburgh.

Mccallum, A. & Jensen, D. 2003. *A Note on the Unification of Information Extraction and Data Mining using Conditional-Probability, Relational Models.* IJCAI'03 Workshop on Learning Statistical Models from Relational Data.

Medelyan, O. & Witten, I. H. 2006. *Thesaurus based automatic keyphrase indexing.* JCDL '06: Proceedings of the 6th ACM/IEEE-CS joint conference on Digital libraries, p.296-297.

Mel'chuk, I. & Xolodovic, A. 1970. *Towards a theory of grammatical voice.* Narody Azii i Afriki. Vol. 4, p.111-124.

Meyer, I. 2001. *Extracting knowledge-rich contexts for terminography.* Bourigault, D.; Jacquemin, C. & Lhomme, M.-C. (Ed.). *Recent Advances in Computational Terminology.* John Benjamins, p.279-302.

Michiels, A. & Noël, J. 1982. *Approaches to thesaurus production.* Proceedings of the 9th conference on Computational linguistics, p.227-232.

Miller, G. 1995. *WordNet a Lexical Database for English.* Communications of ACM. Vol. 38(11), p.39-41.

Miller, G. A. 1990. *Wordnet: an online lexical database.* International Journal of Lexicography. Vol. 3(4), p.235-244.

Miller, G. A. & Charles, W. G. 1991. *Contextual correlates of semantic similarity.* Language and Cognitive Processes. Vol. 6(1), p.1-28.

Miller, G. A.; Leacock, C.; Tengi, R. & Bunker, R. T. 1993. *A semantic concordance.* HLT '93: Proceedings of the workshop on Human Language Technology, p.303-308.

Mima, H.; Ananiadou, S. & Nenadic, G. 2001. *The ATRACT Workbench: Automatic Term Recognition and Clustering for Terms.* TSD '01: Proceedings of the 4th International Conference on Text, Speech and Dialogue, p.126-133.

Mima, H.; Ananiadou, S.; Nenadic, G. & ichi Tsujii, J. 2002. *A Methodology for Terminology-based Knowledge Acquisition and Integration.* Proceedings of the COLING 2002, p.1-7.

Mitchell, T. M. 1997. *Machine Learning.* McGraw-Hill.

Mitkov, R. 2002. *Anaphora Resolution.* Longman (Pearson Education), Edinburgh, UK.

Moldovan, D.; Badulescu, A.; Tatu, M.; Antohe, D. & Girju, R. 2004. *Models for the semantic classification of noun phrases.* CLS '04: Proceedings of the HLT-NAACL Workshop on Computational Lexical Semantics, p.60-67.

Muller, P.; Hathout, N. & Gaume, B. 2006. *Synonym extraction using a semantic distance on a dictionary.* TextGraphs '06: Proceedings of TextGraphs: the First Workshop on Graph Based Methods for Natural Language Processing on the First Workshop on Graph Based Methods for Natural Language Processing, p.65-72.

Nagakawa, H. 2001. *Experimental Evaluation of Ranking and Selection Methods in Term Extraction.* Bourigault, D.; Jacquemin, C. & L'Homme, M.-C. (Ed.). *Recent Advances in Computational Terminology.* John Benjamins, p.303-326.

Naughton, M.; Stokes, N. & Carthy, J. 2008. *Investigating statistical techniques for sentence-level event classification.* COLING '08: Proceedings of the 22nd International Conference on Computational Linguistics, p.617-624.

Navigli, R. 2009. *Word sense disambiguation: A survey.* ACM Computing Surveys. Vol. 41(2), p.1-69.

Nedellec, C. 2005. *Learning Language in Logic - Genic Interaction Extraction Challenge.* Proceedings of the 4th Learning Language in Logic Workshop (LLL05), Bonn, Germany.

Needleman, S. B. & Wunsch, C. D. 1970. *A general method applicable to the search for similarities in the amino acid sequence of two proteins.* Journal of Molecular Biology. Vol. 48(3), p.443 - 453.

Ng, H. T. & Lee, H. B. 1996. *Integrating multiple knowledge sources to disambiguate word sense: an exemplar-based approach.* Proceedings of the 34th annual meeting on Association for Computational Linguistics, p.40-47.

Ng, V. 2008. *Unsupervised models for coreference resolution.* EMNLP '08: Proceedings of the Conference on Empirical Methods in Natural Language Processing, p.640-649.

Nickles, M.; Pease, A.; Schalley, A. & Zaefferer, D. 2006. *Ontologies across disciplines.* Schalley, Andrea C. & Zaefferer, D. (Ed.). *Ontolinguistics. How Ontological Status Shapes the Linguistic Coding of Concepts.* Mouton de Gruyter, p.23-70.

Niwa, Y. & Nitta, Y. 1994. *Co-occurrence vectors from corpora vs. distance vectors from dictionaries.* Proceedings of the 15th International Conference On Computational Linguistics, p.304-309.

Bennet, N. A.; He, Q.; Powell, K. & Schatz, B. R. 1999. *Extracting noun phrases for all of MEDLINE.* Proceedings of the AMIA Symposium, p.671-675.

Oakes, M. P. 1998. *Statistics for corpus linguistics.* Edinburgh Univ. Press, Edinburgh.

Ogden, C. & Richards, I. 1923. *The Meaning of Meaning - A Study of the Influence of Language upon Thought and of the Science of Symbolism.* Routledge.

Oh, J.-H.; Lee, K. & Choi, K.-S. 2000. *Term recognition using technical dictionary hierarchy.* ACL '00: Proceedings of the 38th Annual Meeting on Association for Computational Linguistics, p.496-503.

Ohshima, H. & Tanaka, K. 2009. *Real time extraction of related terms by bi-directional lexico-syntactic patterns from the web.* ICUIMC '09: Proceedings of the 3rd International Conference on Ubiquitous Information Management and Communication, p.441-449.

Ottens, K.; Aussenac-Gilles, N.; Gleizes, M. P. & Camps, V. 2007. *Dynamic Ontology Co-Evolution from Texts: Principles and Case Study.* ESOE. CEUR Workshop Proceedings, p.70-83.

Ozdowska, S. 2004. *Identifying correspondences between words: an approach based on a bilingual syntactic analysis of French/English parallel corpora.* MLR '04: Proceedings of the Workshop on Multilingual Linguistic Ressources, p.55-62.

Padó, S. & Lapata, M. 2007. *Dependency-Based Construction of Semantic Space Models.* Computational Linguistics. Vol. 33(2), p.161-199.

Pantel, P. A. 2003. *Clustering by committee*, University of Alberta.

Pantel, P. & Pennacchiotti, M. 2008. *Automatically harvesting and ontologizing semantic relations.* Buitelaar, P. & Cimiano, P. (Ed.). *Ontology Learning and Population: Bridging the Gap between Text and Knowledge.* IOS Press, p.171-195.

Pantel, P. & Pennacchiotti, M. 2006. *Espresso: leveraging generic patterns for automatically harvesting semantic relations.* ACL-44: Proceedings of the 21st International Conference on Computational Linguistics and the 44th annual meeting of the Association for Computational Linguistics, p.113-120.

Park, Y.; Byrd, R. J. & Boguraev, B. K. 2002. *Automatic glossary extraction: beyond terminology identification.* Proceedings of the 19th international conference on Computational linguistics, p.1-7.

Patel, C.; Supekar, K.; Lee, Y. & Park, E. 2003. *OntoKhoj A Semantic Web Portal for Ontology Searching, Ranking, and Classification*. Proceedings of the 5th ACM Int. Workshop on Web Information and Data Management, p.58-61.

Paulo, J. L.; Correia, M.; Mamede, N. J. & Hagège, C. 2002. *Using Morphological, Syntactical, and Statistical Information for Automatic Term Acquisition*. Advances in Natural Language Processing. Springer, p.69-75.

Pearson, J. 1998. *Terms in Context*. John Benjamins Publishing Company.

Pedersen, T. 2000. *A simple approach to building ensembles of Naive Bayesian classifiers for word sense disambiguation*. Proceedings of the 1st North American chapter of the Association for Computational Linguistics conference, p.63-69.

Pekar, V. & Staab, S. 2002. *Taxonomy learning: factoring the structure of a taxonomy into a semantic classification decision*. Proceedings of the 19th international conference on Computational linguistics, p.1-7.

Pereira, F.; Tishby, N. & Lee, L. 1993. *Distributional clustering of English words*. Proceedings of the 31st annual meeting on Association for Computational Linguistics, p.183-190.

Phillips, W. & Riloff, E. 2002. *Exploiting strong syntactic heuristics and co-training to learn semantic lexicons*. EMNLP '02: Proceedings of the ACL-02 conference on Empirical methods in natural language processing, p.125-132.

Piao, S. S. L.; Rayson, P.; Archer, D.; Wilson, A. & McEnery, T. 2003. *Extracting multiword expressions with a semantic tagger*. Proceedings of the ACL 2003 workshop on Multiword expressions, p.49-56.

Pinto, H. S. & Martins, J. P. 2001. *A Methodology for Ontology Integration*. Proceedings of the First International Conference on Knowledge Capture 2001, p.131-138.

Piskorski, J.; Tanev, H.; Atkinson, M. & Van Der Goot, E. 2008. *Cluster-Centric Approach to News Event Extraction*. Proceeding of the Int. Conf. on New Trends in Multimedia and Network Information Systems, p.276-290.

Plante, P. & Dumas, L. 1998. *Le Dépoulliment terminologique assisté par ordinateur. Translated: The terminology extraction assisted by computer*. Terminogramme. Vol. 46, p.24-28.

van der Plas, L. & Tiedemann, J. 2006. *Finding synonyms using automatic word alignment and measures of distributional similarity*. Proceedings of the COLING/ACL on Main conference poster sessions, p.866-873.

Platt, J. C. 1999. *Fast training of support vector machines using sequential minimal optimization*. Advances in kernel methods: support vector learning. MIT Press, p.185-208.

Porzel, R. & Gurevych, I. 2003. *Contextual Coherence in Natural Language Processing*. Blackburn, P.; Ghidini, C.; Turner, R.; Giunchiglia, F. (Ed.). *Modeling and Using Context*. Springer, p.272-285.

Procter, P. 1978. *Longman Dictionary of Contemporary English*. Longman Group.

Pustejovsky, J. 1991. *The Generative Lexicon*. Computational Linguistics. Vol. 17(4), p.409-441.

Pustejovsky, J. 1995. *The Generative Lexicon*. The MIT Press, Cambridge, MA.

Pustejovsky, J.; Bergler, S. & Anick, P. G. 1993. *Lexical Semantic Techniques for Corpus Analysis*. Computational Linguistics. Vol. 19(2), p.331-358.

Putnam, H. 1975. *Mind, Language and Reality. Philosophical Papers*. Cambridge University Press.

Qiu, Y. & Frei, H. 1993. *Concept Based Query Expansion*. Proceedings of the 16th Annual International ACM SIGIR Conference on Research and Development in Information Retrieval (SIGIR-93), p.160-169.

Quasthoff, U.; Biemann, C. & Wolff, C. 2002. *Named entity learning and verification: expectation maximization in large corpora*. COLING-02: proceedings of the 6th conference on Natural language learning, p.1-7.

Quinlan, J. R. 1993. *C4.5: Programs for Machine Learning*. Morgan Kaufman, San Mateo, CA.

Rada, R. & Bicknell, E. 1989. *Ranking Documents with a Thesaurus*. JASIS. Vol. 40(5), p.304-310.

Rada, R.; Mili, H.; Bicknell, E. & Blettner, M. 1989. *Development and Application of a Metric on Semantic Nets*. IEEE Transactions on Systems Management and Cybernetics. Vol. 19(1), p.17-30.

Ramshaw, L.; Boschee, E.; Bratus, S.; Miller, S.; Stone, R.; Weischedel, R. & Zamanian, A. 2001. *Experiments in multi-modal automatic content extraction*. HLT '01: Proceedings of the first international conference on Human language technology research, p.1-5.

Resnik, P. 1995. *Using information content to evaluate semantic similarity in a taxonomy*. Proceedings of the 14th Int'l. Joint Conf. on Artificial Intelligence (AAAI), p.448-453.

Resnik, P. 1999. *Semantic Similarity in a Taxonomy: An Information-Based Measure and its Application to Problems of Ambiguity in Natural Language*. Journal of Artificial Intelligence Research. Vol. 11, p.95-130.

Reymonet, A.; Thomas, J. & Aussenac-Gilles, N. 2007. *Modélisation de Ressources Termino-Ontologiques en OWL. (Translation: Modelling ontological and terminological resources in OWL)*. Actes d'IC, p.169-181.

Richardt, S. 2004. *Metaphors in expert and common-sense reasoning*. Zelinsky-Wibbelt, C. (Ed.). *Text, Context, Concepts*. de Gruyter Mouton, p.243-298.

Riloff, E. & Jones, R. 1999. *Learning dictionaries for information extraction by multi-level bootstrapping*. AAAI '99/IAAI '99: Proceedings of the sixteenth national conference on Artificial intelligence and the eleventh Innovative applications of artificial intelligence conference innovative applications of artificial intelligence, p.474-479.

Ritter, A.; Downey, D.; Soderland, S. & Etzioni, O. 2008. *It's a contradiction - no, it's not: a case study using functional relations*. EMNLP '08: Proceedings of the Conference on Empirical Methods in Natural Language Processing, p.11-20.

Roark, B. & Charniak, E. 1998. *Noun-phrase co-occurrence statistics for semiautomatic semantic lexicon construction*. Proceedings of the 17th international conference on Computational linguistics, p.1110-1116.

Roberts, A. 2005. *Learning meronyms from biomedical text*. ACL '05: Proceedings of the ACL Student Research Workshop, p.49-54.

Roche, C.; Calberg-Challot, M.; Damas, L. & Rouard, P. 2009. *Ontoterminology - A New Paradigm for Terminology*. KEOD, p.321-326.

Roget, P. M. 1852. *Thesaurus of English Words and Phrases Classified and Arranged so as to Facilitate the Expression of Ideas and Assist in Literary composition*. Longman, Brown, Green and Longmans, London.

Ross, S. M. 2002. *A First course in probability*. Prentice Hall, Upper Saddle River, NJ.

Rubenstein, H. & Goodenough, J. B. 1965. *Contextual correlates of synonymy.* Communications of ACM. Vol. 8(10), p.627-633.

Rudolph, S. 2006. *Relational Exploration - Combining Description Logics and Formal Concept Analysis for Knowledge Specification,* Universitaet Karlsruhe.

Rudolph, S. & Völker, J. 2008. *Formal Concept Analysis for the Semantic Web: ISWC 2008 tutorium slides,* http://www.aifb.uni-karlsruhe.de/WBS/jvo/fca4sw/

Rudolph, S.; Völker, J. & Hitzler, P. 2008. *Supporting Lexical Ontology Learning by Relational Exploration.* Conceptual Structures: Knowledge Architectures for Smart Applications, Proc. ICCS 2007. LNAI, p.488-491.

Ruiz-Casado, M.; Alfonseca, E. & Castells, P. 2005. *Automatic Assignment of Wikipedia Encyclopedic Entries to WordNet Synsets.* Proceedings of the Atlantic Web Intelligence Conference, AWIC-2005. Volume 3528 of Lecture Notes in Computer Science, p.380-386.

Sabou, M.; Lopez, V. & Motta, E. 2006. *Ontology Selection for the Real Semantic Web: How to Cover the Queen's Birthday Dinner?* Staab, S.; Svatek, V. (Ed.). *Managing Knowledge in a World of Networks.* Springer, p.96 -111.

Schalley, A. C. & Zaefferer, D. (Ed.) 2007. *Ontolinguistics.* De Gruyter Mouton, Berlin.

Sager, N. 1981. *Natural Language Information Processing.* Addison-Wesley, Reading, MA.

Sahlgren, M. 2006. *The Word-Space Model: Using distributional analysis to represent syntagmatic and paradigmatic relations between words in high-dimensional vector spaces,* Department of Linguistics, Stockholm University.

Salton, G. & Buckley, C. 1988. *Term-weighting approaches in automatic text retrieval.* Information Processing and Management. Vol. 24(5), p.513-523.

Sasano, R. & Kurohashi, S. 2008. *Japanese named entity recognition using structural natural language processing.* Proceedings of IJCNLP, p.212-235.

de Saussure, F.Bally, C. & Sechehaye, A. (Ed.) 1916. *Cours de linguistique gènèrale.* Lausanne, Paris.

Schiller, A. 1996. *Multilingual Finite-State Noun Phrase Extraction.* In Proceedings of the ECAI'96, p.9-6.

Schreiber, G.; Wielinga, B. & Jansweijer, W. 1995. *The KAKTUS view on the 'O' word.* 14th Int. Joint Conf. Artificial Intelligence (IJCAI95), Workshop on Basic Ontological Issues in Knowledge Sharing, Canada.

Schubert, L. & Tong, M. 2003. *Extracting and evaluating general world knowledge from the Brown corpus.* Proceedings of the HLT-NAACL 2003 workshop on Text meaning, p.7-13.

Schwarz, U. & Smith, B. 2008. *Ontological Relations.* Munn, K.; Smith, B. (Ed.). *Applied Ontology An Introduction.* Ontos Verlag, p.219-234.

Schütze, H. & Pedersen, J. O. 1997. *A co-occurrence-based thesaurus and two applications to information retrieval.* Information Processing and Management. Vol. 33(3), p.307-318.

Schütze, H. 1993. *Word Space.* Advances in Neural Information Processing Systems 5, p.895-902.

Segaran, T. 2007. *Programming collective intelligence: building smart web 2.0 applications.* O'Reilly Media, Inc.

Shamsfard, M. & Abdollahzadeh Barforoush, A. 2003. *The state of the art in ontology learning: a framework for comparison.* Knowledge Engineering Review. Vol. 18(4), p.293-316.

Sharman, R.; Kishore, R. & Ramesh, R. 2007. *Ontologies: A Handbook of Principles, Concepts and Applications in Information Systems.* Springer.

Simpson, J. A. & Weiner, E. S. C. 1989. *The Oxford English Dictionary*. Oxford University Press, Oxford.

Sinclair, J. 1996. *The Empty Lexicon*. International Journal of Corpus Linguistics. Vol. 1(1), p.99-119.

Sinclair, J. M. 1991. *Corpus, Concordance, Collocation*. Oxford University Press, Oxford.

Sinclair, J. (Ed.) 1987. *Look Up An account of the COBUILD project in lexical computing*. Collins COBUILD, London.

Smadja, F. 1993. *Retrieving Collocations from Text: Xtract*. Computational Linguistics. Vol. 19(1), p.143-177.

Smith, B. 2009. *An Introduction to Ontology: From Aristotle to the Universal Core*, http://ontology.buffalo.edu/smith/IntroOntology_Course.html

Smith, B.; Kusnierczyk, W.; Schober, D. & Ceusters, W. 2006. *Towards a Reference Terminology for Ontology Research and Development in the Biomedical Domain*. Proceedings of KR-MED, p.57-66.

Smith, B. & Welty, C. 2001. *FOIS introduction: Ontology -towards a new synthesis*. FOIS '01: Proceedings of the Int. Conf. on Formal Ontology in Information Systems, p.3-9.

Smith, T. & Waterman, M. 1981. *Identification Of Common Molecular Subsequences*. Journal of Molecular Biology. Vol. 147, p.195–197.

Snow, R.; Jurafsky, D. & Ng, A. Y. 2006. *Semantic taxonomy induction from heterogenous evidence*. ACL-44: Proceedings of the 21st International Conference on Computational Linguistics, p.801-808.

Sommerville, I. 2007. *Software Engineering*. Addison-Wesley, Harlow, England.

Sonderland, S. 1999. *Learning Information Extraction Rules for Semi-structured and Free-text*. Machine Learning. Vol. 34, p.1-44.

Sowa, J. F. 2000. *Ontology, Metadata, and Semiotics*. ICCS, p.55-81.

Sowa, J. F. 2000a. *Knowledge representation: logical, philosophical and computational foundations*. Brooks/Cole Publishing Co., Pacific Grove, CA, USA.

Spyns, P. & Hogben, G. 2005. *Validating an Automated Evaluation Procedure for Ontology Triples in the Privacy Domain*. Proceeding of the 2005 conference on Legal Knowledge and Information Systems, p.127-136.

Staab, S.; Gomez-Perez, A.; Daelemana, W.; Reinberger, M.-L. & Noy, N. 2004. *Why evaluate ontology technologies? Because it works!* IEEE Intelligent Systems. Vol. 19, p.74- 81.

Staab, S. & Studer, R. 2004. *Handbook on Ontologies (International Handbooks on Information Systems)*. SpringerVerlag.

Stamper, R.; Liu, K.; Hafkamp, M. & Ades, Y. 2000. *Understanding the roles of signs and norms in organizations - a semiotic approach to information systems design*. Behaviour & Information Technology. Vol. 19, p.15-27.

Stevenson, M. & Greenwood, M. A. 2005. *A Semantic Approach to IE Pattern Induction*. In Proceedings of the 43rd Annual Meeting of Association for Computational Linguistics, p.379-386.

Stevenson, M. & Greenwood, M. A. 2006. *Comparing information extraction pattern models*. IEBeyondDoc '06: Proceedings of the Workshop on Information Extraction Beyond the Document, p.12-19.

Stevenson, M. & Wilks, Y. 2001. *The interaction of knowledge sources in word sense disambiguation.* Computational Linguistics. Vol. 27(3), p.321-349.

Stevenson, S. & Joanis, E. 2003. *Semi-supervised verb class discovery using noisy features.* Proceedings of the 7th conference on Natural language learning at HLT-NAACL 2003, p.71-78.

Steyvers, M. & Griffiths, T. 2007. *Probabilistic topic models.* Landauer, T.; McNamara, S. D. & Kintsch, W. (Ed.). *Latent Semantic Analysis: A Road to Meaning.* Laurence Erlbaum, p.427-445.

Stubbs, M. 1996. *Text and corpus analysis.* Blackwell.

Sudo, K.; Sekine, S. & Grishman, R. 2001. *Automatic pattern acquisition for Japanese information extraction.* HLT '01: Proceedings of the first international conference on Human language technology research, p.1-7.

Sudo, K.; Sekine, S. & Grishman, R. 2003. *An improved extraction pattern representation model for automatic IE pattern acquisition.* Proceedings of the ACL '03, p.224-231.

Suomela, S. & Kekäläinen, J. 2006. *User evaluation of ontology as query construction tool.* Information Retrieval. Vol. 9(4), p.455-475.

Sure, Y.; Gómez-Pérez, A.; Daelemans, W.; Reinberger, M.-L.; Guarino, N. & Noy, N. F. 2004. *Why Evaluate Ontology Technologies? Because It Works!* IEEE Intelligent Systems. Vol. 19(4), p.74-81.

Talmy, L. 2000. *Toward a cognitive semantics : concept structuring systems (language, speech and communication).* The MIT Press, Cambridge, MA.

Tan, P.-N.; Steinbach, M. & Kumar, V. 2006. *Introduction to Data Mining.* Pearson Education.

Teubert, W. 2007. *Parole-linguistics and the diachronic dimension of the discourse.* Hoey, M.; Mahlberg, M.; Stubbs, M. & Teubert, W. (Ed.). *Text, discourse and corpora: Theory and analysis.* Continum, p.57-88.

Thelen, M. & Riloff, E. 2002. *A bootstrapping method for learning semantic lexicons using extraction pattern contexts.* Proceedings of the 2002 Conference on Empirical Methods in Natural Language Processing (EMNLP 2002), p.214-221.

Tsiknakis, M. 2006. *Building a European Biomedical Grid on Cancer, Challenges and Opportunities of HealthGrids.* Procs. of the HealthGrid 2006 conference, p.247-258.

Tsiknakis, M.; Brochhausen, M.; Nabrzyski, J.; Pucacki, J.; Sfakianakis, S.; Potamias, G.; Desmedt, C. & Kafetzopoulos, D. 2008. *A Semantic Grid Infrastructure Enabling Integrated Access and Analysis of Multilevel Biomedical Data in Support of Postgenomic Clinical Trials on Cancer.* IEEE Transactions on Information Technology in Biomedicine. Vol. 12(2), p.205-217.

Tsurumaru, H.; Hitaka, T. & Yoshida, S. 1986. *An attempt to automatic thesaurus construction from an ordinary Japanese language dictionary.* Proceedings of the 11th coference on Computational linguistics, p.445-447.

Turney, P. D. 2006. *Expressing Implicit Semantic Relations without Supervision.* Proceedings of the 21st International Conference on Computational Linguistics, p.313-320.

Turney, P. D. 2008. *A uniform approach to analogies, synonyms, antonyms, and associations.* COLING '08: Proceedings of the 22nd International Conference on Computational Linguistics, p.905-912.

Uschold, M. 1996. *Building Ontologies: Towards a Unified Methodology.* In 16th Annual Conf. of the British Computer Society Specialist Group on Expert Systems, p.16-18.

Uschold, M. & Gruninger, M. 1996. *Ontologies: Principles, methods and applications.* Knowledge
  Engineering Review. Vol. 11, p.93-136.

Uschold, M.; King, M.; Moralee, S. & Zorgios, Y. 1998. *The Enterprise Ontology.* The Knowledge
  Engineering Review. Vol. 13(1), p.31-89.

Völker, J.; Haase, P. & Hitzler, P. 2008. *Learning Expressive Ontologies.* Proceeding of the 2008
  conference on Ontology Learning and Population: Bridging the Gap between Text and
  Knowledge, p.45-69.

Völker, J.; Vrandečić, D.; Sure, Y. & Hotho, A. 2008. *AEON - An approach to the automatic evaluation
  of ontologies.* Applied Ontology. Vol. 3(1-2), p.41-62.

Vapnik, V. N. 1995. *The nature of statistical learning theory.* Springer-Verlag New York, Inc.

Vela, M. & Declerck, T. 2009. *Concept and Relation Extraction in the Finance Domain.* Proceedings of
  the Eighth International Conference on Computational Semantics (IWCS-8), p.346-350.

Vokhidova, N. 2009. *Lexikalisch-semantische Graduonymie*, Dissertation an der Universität Mannheim
  (Prof. Dr. Stefan Engelberg).

Waterman, S. 1996. *Distinguished Usage.* Boguraev, B.; Pustejovsky, J. (Ed.). *Corpus Processing for
  Lexical Acquisition.* MIT Press, p.143-174.

Wei, X.; Peng, F.; Tseng, H.; Lu, Y. & Dumoulin, B. 2009. *Context sensitive synonym discovery for web
  search queries.* CIKM '09: Proceeding of the 18th ACM conference on Information and
  knowledge management, p.1585-1588.

Weibel, S. 1998. *The Dublin Core: A simple content description model for electronic resources.* Bulletin
  of the American Society for Information Science and Technology. Vol 24(1), p.9-11.

Welty, C. 2006. *OntOWLClean: Cleaning OWL ontologies with OWL.* Proceeding of the 2006
  conference on Formal Ontology in Information Systems, p.347-359.

Wennerberg, P.; Zillner, S.; Möller, M.; Buitelaar, P. & Sintek, M. 2008. *KEMM: A Knowledge
  Engineering Methodology in the Medical Domain.* Proceeding of the 2008 conference on
  Formal Ontology in Information Systems, p.79-91.

Wierzbicka, A. 1972. *Semantic Primitives.* Atheneum, Frankfurt.

Wierzbicka, A. 1985. *Lexicography and Conceptual Analysis.* Karoma Publishers, Inc.

Wierzbicka, A. 1989. *Semantics, Culture and Cognition.* Oxford University Press.

Wierzbicka, A. 1996. *Semantics: Primes and Universals.* Oxford University Press, New York.

Wilks, Y. 1996. *Homography and part-of-speech tagging*, Presentation at the MikroKosmos Workshop.

Wilks, Y.; Fass, D.; ming Guo, C.; McDonald, J. E.; Plate, T. & Slator, B. M. 1990. *Providing machine
  tractable dictionary tools.* Machine Translation. Vol. 5(2), p.99-154.

Witten, I. H. & Frank, E. 2001. *Data mining.* Morgan Kaufmann, San Francisco.

Wittgenstein, L. 1953. *Philosophical Investigations.* Anscombe, G. & Rhees, R. (Ed.) 1953. Oxford:
  Blackwell.

Wong, W.; Liu, W. & Bennamoun, M. 2007. *Determining termhood for learning domain ontologies
  using domain prevalence and tendency.* AusDM '07: Proceedings of the 6th Australasian
  conference on Data mining and analytics, p.47-54.

Wu, H. & Zhou, M. 2003. *Optimizing synonym extraction using monolingual and bilingual resources.*
  Proceedings of the second international workshop on Paraphrasing, p.72-79.

Wu, Z. & Palmer, M. 1994. *Verbs semantics and lexical selection.* Proceedings of the 32nd annual
  meeting of ACL, p.133-138.

Yan, Y.; Okazaki, N.; Matsuo, Y.; Yang, Z. & Ishizuka, M. 2009. *Unsupervised relation extraction by mining Wikipedia texts using information from the web.* ACL-IJCNLP '09: Proceedings of the Joint Conference of the 47th Annual Meeting of the ACL and the 4th International Joint Conference on Natural Language Processing of the AFNLP: Vol. 2, p.1021-1029.

Yangarber, R. 2003. *Counter-training in discovery of semantic patterns.* ACL '03: Proceedings of the 41st Annual Meeting on Association for Computational Linguistics, p.343-350.

Yangarber, R.; Grishman, R.; Tapanainen, P. & Huttunen, S. 2000. *Automatic acquisition of domain knowledge for Information Extraction.* Proceedings of the 18th conference on Computational linguistics, p.940-946.

Yarowsky, D. 1992. *Word-sense disambiguation using statistical models of Roget's categories trained on large corpora.* Proceedings of the 14th conference on Computational linguistics, p.454-460.

Yarowsky, D. 1995. *Unsupervised word sense disambiguation rivaling supervised methods.* Proceedings of the 33rd annual meeting on Association for Computational Linguistics, p.189-196.

Yu, J.; Thom, J. A. & Tam, A. 2009. *Requirements-oriented methodology for evaluating ontologies.* Information Systems. Vol. 34(8), p.686-711.

Zelinsky-Wibbelt, C. 2000. *Discourse and the Continuity of Reference. Representing Mental Categorization.* de Gruyter Mouton.

Zhang, Y.; Huang, F. & Vogel, S. 2005. *Mining translations of OOV terms from the web through cross-lingual query expansion.* SIGIR '05: Proceedings of the 28th annual international ACM SIGIR conference on Research and development in information retrieval, p.669-670.

Zhang, Z. 2008. *Mining relational data from text: From strictly supervised to weakly supervised learning.* Information Systems. Vol. 33(3), p.300-314.

Zhou, G. & Su, J. 2005. *Machine learning-based named entity recognition via effective integration of various evidences.* Natural Language Engineering. Vol. 11(2), p.189-206.

Zhou, L. 2007. *Ontology learning: state of the art and open issues.* Information Technology and Management. Vol. 8(3), p.241-252.

Zielinski, D. 2002. *Computergestützte Termextraktion aus technischen Texten (Italienisch).* Diplomarbeit FR 4.6, UdS,, http://fr46.uni-saarland.de/download/publs/haller/zielinski.pdf

Zielinski, D. 2007. *Terminologieextraktion, Lecture notes,* http://fr46.uni-saarland.de/?L=0

Zipf, G. K. 1945. *The Meaning-Frequency Relationship of Words.* Journal of General Psychology. Vol. 1945(33), p.251-256.

Zipf, G. K. 1949. *Human Behavior and the Principle of Least Effort.* Addison-Wesley, Reading MA (USA).

Øhrstrøm, P.; Schärfe, H. & Uckelman, S. L. 2008. *Jacob Lorhard's Ontology: A 17th Century Hypertext on the Reality and Temporality of the World of Intelligibles.* ICCS '08: Proceedings of the 16th international conference on Conceptual Structures, p.74-87.

Appendices

Appendix A1

An example of the abstract of the scientific publication extracted from PubMed:
http://www.ncbi.nlm.nih.gov/pubmed/20367206

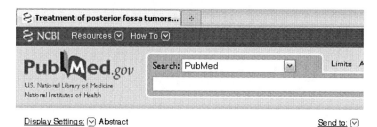

Expert Rev Neurother. 2010 Apr;10(4):525-46.

Treatment of posterior fossa tumors in children.

Muzumdar D, Ventureyra EC.

Division of Neurosurgery, Children's Hospital of Eastern Ontario, 401 Smyth Road, Ottawa, Ontario K1H 8L1, Canada.

Abstract
The most common posterior fossa tumors in children are medulloblastoma, astrocytoma and ependymoma. Atypical rhabdoid teratoid tumors and brain stem gliomas are relatively rare. As the posterior fossa is a limited space, the tumors presenting in this region cause symptoms early on and require prompt treatment to avoid potential morbidity and mortality. Early detection and diagnosis of these tumors and prompt neurosurgical consultation is crucial in the optimum management of pediatric infratentorial brain tumors. Surgery is the mainstay of treatment, as it provides biopsy and decompression of the tumor. Adjuvant therapy is required in the majority of cases. Recent advances in the field of radiation biology and pharmacology have improved dose and delivery techniques of chemoradiation therapy. In the current era, advances in translational research and molecular genetics have assumed a major role in the pursuit of achieving a 'cure' for these potentially malignant tumors.

PMID: 20367206 [PubMed - in process]

Appendix A2

An example of abstract of the scientific publication extracted from ReSIST project knowledge base ieee.rkbexplorer.com http://ieee.rkbexplorer.com/description/publication-00534618

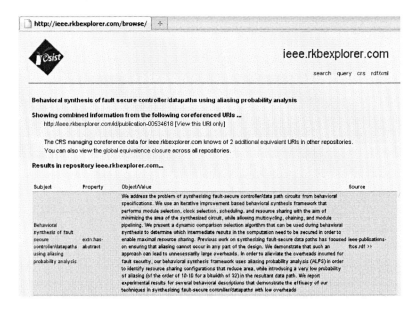

Appendix B1

An example of MPRO software output:

(1) Operating system is a kind of system.

```
{ori=Operating,wnra=9,wnrr=1,snr=3,osaw=$iaibl$sm,pctr=no,last=no,pctl=yes,offset=53,lw=no,gra=c
ap,vtyp=ing,ds=operate,ls=operate,w=1,cs=v,c=verb,s=nil,ew=1,ews=.,lu=operate,ts=operate,t=opera
te,saw=&b,mlu=operate}
{ori=Operating,wnra=9,wnrr=1,snr=3,osaw=$iaibl$sm,pctr=no,last=no,pctl=yes,offset=53,lw=no,gra=c
ap,nb=sg,case=acc;nom,s=vn,ds=operate~ing,ss=vn,ls=operate,w=1,c=noun,ew=1,ews=.,lu=operating,ts
=operating,t=operating,ehead={case=acc;nom,nb=sg},saw=&b,mlu=operating}
{ori=Operating,wnra=9,wnrr=1,snr=3,osaw=$iaibl$sm,pctr=no,last=no,pctl=yes,offset=53,lw=no,gra=c
ap,s=va,ds=operate~ing,ss=va,ls=operate,w=1,c=adj,deg=base,ew=1,ews=.,lu=operating,ts=operating,
t=operating,ehead={case=nom;acc,nb=sg;plu},saw=&b,mlu=operating}
{ori=system,wnra=10,wnrr=2,snr=3,osaw=$iaibl$sm,pctr=no,last=no,pctl=no,offset=60,lw=no,gra=smal
l,nb=sg,case=acc;nom,s=set,ss=set,ds=system,ls=system,w=1,cs=n,c=noun,ew=0,lu=system,ts=system,t
=system,ehead={case=acc;nom,nb=sg},saw=&b,mlu=system}
{ori=is,wnra=11,wnrr=3,snr=3,osaw=$iaibl$sm,pctr=no,last=no,pctl=no,offset=63,lw=no,gra=small,c=
verb,vtyp=fiv,tns=pres,mode=ind,per=3,nb=sg,end=s,s=be,subl={reg=0,dom=0,loc=no,freq=0},ds=be,ls
=be,w=1,ew=0,lu=be,saw=&b,mlu=be}
```

```
{ori=is,wnra=11,wnrr=3,snr=3,osaw=$iaibl$sm,pctr=no,last=no,pctl=no,offset=63,lw=no,gra=small,c=
w,sc=verb,vtyp=fiv,auxtype=ptc2;ing;zu,tns=pres,mode=ind,per=3,nb=sg,end=s,s=aux,subl={reg=0,dom
=0,loc=no,freq=0},ds=be,ls=be,w=1,ew=0,lu=be,saw=&b,mlu=be}
{ori=a,wnra=12,wnrr=4,snr=3,osaw=$iaibl$sm,pctr=no,last=no,pctl=no,offset=65,lw=no,gra=small,c=w
,sc=art,dtype=n,nb=sg,subl={reg=0,dom=0,loc=no,freq=0},ds=a,ls=a,w=1,s=nil,ew=0,lu=a,saw=&b,mlu=
a}
{ori=kind,wnra=13,wnrr=5,snr=3,osaw=$iaibl$sm,pctr=no,last=no,pctl=no,offset=70,lw=no,gra=small,
nb=sg,case=acc;nom,s=type,ss=type,ds=kind,ls=kind,w=1,cs=n,c=noun,ew=0,lu=kind,ts=kind,t=kind,eh
ead={case=acc;nom,nb=sg},saw=&b,mlu=kind}
{ori=kind,wnra=13,wnrr=5,snr=3,osaw=$iaibl$sm,pctr=no,last=no,pctl=no,offset=70,lw=no,gra=small,
s=manner,ss=manner,ds=kind,ls=kind,w=1,cs=a,deg=base,c=adj,ew=0,lu=kind,ts=kind,t=kind,ehead={ca
se=nom;acc,nb=sg;plu},saw=&b,mlu=kind}
{ori=of,wnra=14,wnrr=6,snr=3,osaw=$iaibl$sm,pctr=no,last=no,pctl=no,offset=73,lw=no,gra=small,c=
w,sc=p,ptype=pre,subl={reg=0,dom=0,loc=no,freq=0},ds=of,ls=of,w=1,s=nil,ew=0,lu=of,saw=&b,mlu=of
}
{ori=system,wnra=15,wnrr=7,snr=3,pctr=yes,last=no,pctl=no,offset=80,gra=small,nb=sg,case=acc;nom
,s=set,ss=set,ds=system,ls=system,w=1,cs=n,c=noun,ew=0,lu=system,ts=system,t=system,ehead={case=
acc;nom,nb=sg},mlu=system,lw=yes}
{ori=.,wnra=16,wnrr=8,snr=3,osaw=$iainl$sm,pctr=no,pctl=no,offset=81,gra=other,lu=.,c=w,sc=punct
,pc=se;.,s=nil,subl={reg=0,dom=0,loc=no,freq=0},ds=.,ls=.,w=1,ew=0,saw=&n,mlu=.,last=yes,lw=no}
```

Appendix B2

An example of KURD software output:

(1) Operating system is a kind of system.

```
{ori=Operating,lu=operate,mlu=operate,snr=3,wnra=9,wnrr=1,offset=53,saw=&b,osaw=$iaibl$sm,ew=1,l
w=no,last=no,ews=.,pctr=no,pctl=yes,c=verb,sc=main,vtyp=ing,per=3,gra=cap,error=nil,partner=nil,
dtype=nil,ptype=nil,atype=nil,advtype=nil,w=1,cs=v,ds=operate,ts=operate,t=operate,ls=operate,en
d=nil,s=nil,tag=@dv1dv4d0_219inp1b1pre2b1bd0_219susV1susV2mS152mS168mS176,sem=nil;vn;va,vtype=ni
l,grup={c=vg,sc=ing,b=1,e=1,sure=yes},cl={i=1154,c=ns,sc=nsNof,form=ing,b=1,e=2,of=3,sure=ob,f=s
ubj},markcoord=nil,markclause=1094,markval=compl,aatype=pre;pred,pro,conf=0.5000}
,{ori=system,lu=system,mlu=system,snr=3,wnra=10,wnrr=2,offset=60,saw=&b,osaw=$iaibl$sm,ew=0,lw=n
o,last=no,pctr=no,pctl=no,c=noun,sc=nil,vtyp=nil,ehead={nb=sg,per=3,case=acc;nom},nb=sg,case=acc
;nom,per=3,gra=small,error=nil,partner=nil,dtype=nil,ptype=nil,atype=nil,advtype=nil,subjtype=ni
l,w=1,cs=n,ds=system,ts=system,t=system,ls=system,ss=set,s=set,chunked=system,headnoun=yes,tag=@
dv1dv4inp1inp2inp2ainp6mnp24ab1db2bbIabIbb0_0af6f9bmS168mS176,sem=set,fc=no,displaced=poss,vtype
=nil,ntype=nil,phr={c=np,sc=no,e=2,sure=no,f=obj},ephr={nb=sg,case=acc;nom,per=3,s=set},cl={i=11
54,c=ns,sc=nsNof,form=ing,b=1,e=2,of=3,sure=ob,f=subj},markcoord=nil,np_cand=n,markclause=1094,m
arkphr=np,markval=compl,lwcl=yes,ncand=yes,singdet=yes,style=simpl,bstyle=simpl,estyle=simpl,fla
ga=subj1}
,{ori=is,lu=be,mlu=be,snr=3,wnra=11,wnrr=3,offset=63,saw=&b,osaw=$iaibl$sm,ew=0,lw=no,last=no,pc
tr=no,pctl=no,c=verb,sc=main,vtyp=fiv,ehead={nb=sg,per=3},nb=sg,per=3,tns=pres,mode=ind,gra=smal
l,error=nil,partner=nil,dtype=nil,atype=nil,advtype=nil,auxtype=nil,w=1,ds=be,ls=be,end=s,s=be,s
ubl={reg=0,dom=0,loc=no,freq=0},tag=@dv1dv4d0_219inp1d0_219mS128mSi140d1_3mS128mSi140mS183d1_3mS
128mSi140mS183mS128mSi140mS183,sem=be;aux,displaced=no,vtype=np,vvtype=np;ap;that,aauxtype=ptc2;
ing;zu,grup={c=vg,sc=fiv,b=3,e=3,sure=yes},cl={c=hs,sc=hs,b=3,e=5},markverb=fiv,markfiv=onefiv,m
arkcoord=nil,markclause=1668,markgruppe=fiv,markval=compl,flaga=verb1}
,{ori=a,lu=a,mlu=a,snr=3,wnra=12,wnrr=4,offset=65,saw=&b,osaw=$iaibl$sm,ew=0,lw=no,last=no,pctr=
no,pctl=no,c=det,sc=det,spec=indef,vtyp=nil,ehead={nb=sg,per=3},nb=sg,per=3,gra=small,error=nil,
dtype=n,atype=nil,advtype=nil,w=1,ds=a,ls=a,s=nil,subl={reg=0,dom=0,loc=no,freq=0},chunked=a#kin
d,tag=@dv1dv4inp1mnp24ab1pre3b1bb1cb2bf4f9mS128mSi140d1_3b1pre3b1bb1cb2bmS128mSi140d1_3b1pre3b1b
b1cb2bb1pre3b1bb1cb2bmS128mSi140mS128mSi140,sem=nil,vtype=nil,phr={i=948,c=np,sc=indef,b=4,e=5,o
f=3,mod_ok=rel,sure=yes,f=obj},ephr={nb=sg,case=acc;nom,per=3,s=type},cl={c=hs,sc=hs,b=3,e=5,sur
e=yes},markcoord=nil,markclause=1668,markphr=np,ddtype=n,det_nb=sg,flaga=obj1}
,{ori=kind,lu=kind,mlu=kind,snr=3,wnra=13,wnrr=5,offset=70,saw=&b,osaw=$iaibl$sm,ew=0,lw=no,last
=no,pctr=no,pctl=no,c=noun,sc=nil,vtyp=nil,ehead={nb=sg,per=3,case=acc;nom},nb=sg,case=acc;nom,p
er=3,gra=small,error=nil,partner=nil,dtype=nil,ptype=nil,atype=nil,advtype=nil,subjtype=nil,w=1,
```

```
cs=n,ds=kind,ts=kind,t=kind,ls=kind,ss=type,s=type,chunked=a#kind,headnoun=yes,tag=dl_m1dv1dv4d0
_7d0_8inp1inp2inp2binp6mnp24ab1cb2bf0f4f9d0_7d0_8mS128mSi140d0_7d0_8d1_3inp2inp2binp6b1cb2bf0mS1
28mSi140d1_3inp2inp6b1cb2bf0inp2inp6b1cb2bf0mS128mSi140f0mS128mSi140,sem=type,fc=no,vtype=nil,nt
ype=nil,phr={i=948,c=np,sc=indef,b=4,e=5,of=3,mod_ok=rel,sure=yes,f=obj},ephr={nb=sg,case=acc;no
m,per=3,s=type},cl={c=hs,sc=hs,b=3,e=5,sure=yes},markcoord=nil,np_cand=n,markclause=1668,markphr
=np,lwcl=yes,ncand=yes,det_nb=sg,style=simpl,bstyle=simpl,estyle=simpl,flaga=obj1}
,{ori=of,lu=of,mlu=of,snr=3,wnra=14,wnrr=6,offset=73,saw=&b,osaw=$iaibl$sm,ew=0,lw=no,last=no,pc
tr=no,pctl=no,c=w,sc=p,vtyp=nil,gra=small,error=nil,dtype=nil,ptype=pre,atype=nil,advtype=nil,w=
1,ds=of,ls=of,s=nil,subl={reg=0,dom=0,loc=no,freq=0},chunked=of#system,tag=@dv1dv4inp1susKde49d1
_3pp1b3b4bf7f7bsusKde49mS126,sem=nil,vtype=nil,phr={i=1267,c=pp,sc=no,form=of,b=6,e=7,of=4,f=mod
},ephr={nb=sg,case=acc,per=3,s=set},cl={c=hs,sc=hs,b=3},markcoord=nil,markclause=1356,pptype=pre
,pcand=yes}
,{ori=system,lu=system,mlu=system,snr=3,wnra=15,wnrr=7,offset=80,ew=0,lw=yes,last=no,pctr=yes,pc
tl=no,c=noun,sc=nil,vtyp=nil,nb=sg,case=acc;nom,per=3,gra=small,error=nil,partner=nil,dtype=nil,
ptype=nil,atype=nil,advtype=nil,subjtype=nil,w=1,cs=n,ds=system,ts=system,t=system,ls=system,ss=
set,s=set,chunked=of#system,headnoun=yes,tag=@dv1dv4inp1inp2inp4inp6mnp24ab1bb2bf6f9susKde49d1_3
pp9inp2inp4inp6b1bb2bpp1b3b4bsusKde49mS126,sem=set,fc=no,vtype=nil,ntype=nil,phr={i=1267,c=pp,sc
=no,form=of,b=6,e=7,of=4,sure=yes,f=mod},ephr={nb=sg,case=acc;nom,per=3,s=set},cl={c=hs,sc=hs,b=
3},markcoord=nil,np_cand=n,markclause=1356,markphr=np,lwcl=yes,ncand=yes,pcand=yes,singdet=yes,s
tyle=simpl,bstyle=simpl,estyle=simpl}
,{ori=.,lu=.,mlu=.,snr=3,wnra=16,wnrr=8,offset=81,saw=&n,osaw=$iainl$sm,ew=0,lw=no,last=yes,pctr
=no,pctl=no,c=w,sc=punct,pc=se;.,vtyp=nil,gra=other,error=nil,dtype=nil,atype=nil,advtype=nil,w=
1,ds=.,ls=.,s=nil,subl={reg=0,dom=0,loc=no,freq=0},tag=@dv1dv4inp1d1_3d1_3,sem=nil,vtype=nil,cl=
{c=hs,sc=hs,b=3},markcoord=nil,markclause=1668}
```

Appendix B3

Tagsets used in MPRO and KURD. Resource: "http://legolas/iaiwiki/index.php"

Tag	Meaning
c	Word category
case	Case
cs	Category of the part of word
ctn	Capital to normal
deg	Degree
ds	Derivation of the components
ehead	Advanced head characteristics
error	Incorrect uppercase or lowercase
ew	First word in the sentence object
ews	Last word or character in the preceding sentence object
foreign	Foreign language passage
fsgml	Sentence-representation Tags
g	Gender
gra	Letters, characters inventory
gs	Gender of the components
hsns	Topologic sentence restriction of the finite verb (m. clause/ sub. clause)
hyphen	Hyphenated word
infl	Inflection type
last	Last word in the sentence
lco	End of omission
lng	Origin
lngs	Origin of the components
ls	Stems of the components
lu	Basic form, spelling variants-neutral (lexical units)
lw	Last word in the phrase object
mbc	Capital letter is mandatory (must be capitalized)

```
mlu          Basic form, spelling variants-sensitive
mode         Mode
mori         Original form with spare images
nb           Number
nbrdig       Arity of digits
ns           Correct form (Correction)
offset       Offset
ori          Original form
orth         Spelling problem
osaw         Separator after word in the original coding
pcomp        contracted preposition
pref         Prefix type
ptc          Adjectival participle
rco          Beginning of omission
s            Semantics
saw          Space after word (separator after word)
sc           Subcategory
snr          Record number
ss           Semantics of the components
state        Analysis Status
t            Basic shapes of the components
textinfo     Processing parameters
tns          Tense
ts           Word segments according to the word elements
vtyp         Verb
w            Arity, number of the components
wnra         absolute word number
wnrr         relative word number
zf           Quote Form
```

The list of 'cs' categories:

```
adv := adverb
{ori=soon,c=w,sc=adv,...}
{ori=there,c=w,sc=adv,...}
{ori=today,c=w,sc=adv,...}

art := article
{ori=a,c=w,sc=art,...}
{ori=the,c=w,sc=art,...}

card := cardinal number
{ori=eleven,c=w,sc=card,...}
{ori=two,c=w,sc=card,...}

cit := quote
{ori=«,c=w,sc=cit,...}
{ori=",c=w,sc=cit,...}

clause := expressions like "etc."
{ori=etc.,c=w,sc=clause,...}

comma := comma
```

```
{ori=&cm,c=w,sc=comma,...}

compar := comparative conjunction
{ori=as,c=w,sc=compar,...}

dem := demostrative pronoun
{ori=this,c=w,sc=dem,...}

interr1 := interrrogative pronoun
{ori=what,c=w,sc=interr1,...}
{ori=who,c=w,sc=interr1,...}

itj := interjection, expression
{ori=aha,c=w,sc=itj,...}
{ori=do_it_yourself,c=w,sc=itj,...}

noun := substantive
{ori=name,c=w,sc=noun,...}

p := preposition
{ori=on,c=w,sc=p,pcomp=yes,...}

part := particle
{ori=like,c=w,sc=part,...}
{ori=to,c=w,sc=part,...}

pers := personal pronoun
{ori=you,c=w,sc=pers,...}
{ori=he,c=w,sc=pers,...}

poss := possessive pronoun
{ori=mine,c=w,sc=poss,...}
{ori=his,c=w,sc=poss,...}

pron := pronoun
{ori=somebody,c=w,sc=pron,...}

punct := sentence symbols
{ori=|,c=w,sc=punct,...}
{ori=(,c=w,sc=punct,...}

quant := quantifier
{ori=all,c=w,sc=quant,...}
{ori=both,c=w,sc=quant,...}

unknown := unknown category
{ori=exc.,c=w,sc=unknown,...}

verb := non-regular verb form
{ori=been,c=w,sc=verb,...}
{ori=was,c=w,sc=verb,...}

enum := enumeration
{ori=a),c=w,sc=enum,...}
```

```
{ori=(1),c=w,sc=enum,...}

webadresse := URL, E-Mail
{ori=http://www.daad.de,c=w,sc=webadresse,...}
```

A list of 'c' categories:

```
adj := adjective
{ori=nice,c=adj,...}
{ori=big,c=adj,...}

adv := adverb,
{ori=soon,c=adv,...}

noun := substantive
{ori=house,c=noun,...}
{ori=city,c=noun,...}

verb := verb
{ori=buy,c=verb,...}
{ori=run,c=verb,...}

z := digit
{ori=22,c=z,...}
{ori=22.4,c=z,...}

fromto := interval of digits
{ori=3-5,c=fromto,...}
{ori=3:0,c=fromto,...}

sgml := SGML-Tag;
{ori=sgml,mori=<DOI:>,c=sgml,...}

w := word falling into 'sc' category
{ori=he,c=w,sc=pers,...}
```

Appendix C1

An example of the rules marking NPs:

```
np_pp_ing_det1 =
a{c~=det;adj,phr={c=np;pp,b=_B}}a{agr_np=ok}e{cl={c=_C,sc=_SC,form=_FF}},
Aa{vtyp=ing}e{c=verb}a{grup=_}e{cl={c=_C,sc=_SC,form=_FF}},
a{phr={c=np,sc~=no;rel}}e{phr={b~=_B}}e{cl={c=_C,sc=_SC,form=_FF}}
:Au{c=verb}d{phr=_}c{tag=$.+dI_65}.

np_plu_ing_plu =
Na{c~=det;adj,phr={c=np,b~=_},nb=plu}e{phr={b~=1,f~=subj}}a{subjcand=_}a{agr
_np=ok}e{det_nb=plu}e{cl={c=_C,sc=_SC,form=_FF}},
```

```
Aa{vtyp=ing}e{c=verb}a{subjcand=_}e{cl={c=_C,sc=_SC,form=_FF}},
+Ba{phr={c=np,sc=no},nb=plu,headnoun=yes}e{cl={c=_C,sc=_SC,form=_FF}},
*e{c=adv}a{vtyp~=fiv},
e{vtyp~=fiv}
:Au{c=verb}d{phr=_}c{tag=$.+dI_67},
Nu{phr={f~=subj}}c{tag=$.+dI_67}.
```

Appendix C2

Examples of terms extracted from abstracts:

```
ABS_1002
NP
1        fault-free hypercube
1        software-based fault tolerance
1        redundant hardware
1        graceful degradation
1        physical processor
2        virtual processor
1        fault
1        multiple fault
1        cost


ABS_1015
NP
1        model
1        system
1        reliable system
1        simulation
1        fast Monte_Carlo simulation
1        fast simulation
1        efficient heuristics
1        reliability
PERSON
1        Markov


ABS_256
NP
1        event-driven simulation tool
1        safety-critical system
1        real time application
1        nuclear application
1        dangerous situation
1        non-intrusive analysis
1        injury
1        graphic facility
```

Appendix C3

Most frequent tokens of candidate terms in both domains:

Cancer research domain				Computer security and dependability domain			
#	Token	Freq.	Rel.freq.	#	Token	Freq.	Rel.freq.
1	TUMOUR	608	0,86	1	FAULT	440	0,91

#	Word	Count	Value
2	BREAST	359	0,51
3	CANCER	333	0,47
4	CELL	250	0,36
5	CLINICAL	209	0,30
6	TREATMENT	206	0,29
7	RENAL	150	0,21
8	PATIENT	149	0,21
9	THERAPY	143	0,20
10	RATE	131	0,19
11	DISEASE	130	0,18
12	SIGNIFICANT	125	0,18
13	SURGICAL	125	0,18
14	TISSUE	121	0,17
15	EARLY	116	0,16
16	ANALYSIS	115	0,16
17	FACTOR	113	0,16
18	GROUP	107	0,15
19	DOSE	106	0,15
20	CHEMOTHERAPY	104	0,15
21	NODE	104	0,15
22	MOLECULAR	99	0,14
23	SURGERY	99	0,14
24	EFFECT	97	0,14
25	METASTASIS	97	0,14
26	GENETIC	92	0,13
27	SPECIFIC	91	0,13
28	RISK	89	0,13
29	SINGLE	88	0,13
30	LESION	87	0,12
31	RESPONSE	85	0,12
32	CARCINOMA	80	0,11
33	THERAPEUTIC	80	0,11
34	AXILLARY	77	0,11
35	MASS	77	0,11
36	RECURRENCE	77	0,11
37	TOXICITY	77	0,11
38	CHANGE	75	0,11
39	KIDNEY	75	0,11
40	TRIAL	75	0,11
41	WILMS	74	0,11
42	GROWTH	72	0,10
43	CARDIAC	70	0,10
44	DATA	68	0,10
45	PEDIATRIC	68	0,10
46	RHABDOID	67	0,10
47	FEATURE	66	0,09
48	LYMPH	66	0,09
49	BILATERAL	65	0,09
50	POSTOPERATIVE	65	0,09
51	METASTATIC	64	0,09
52	SUBSEQUENT	64	0,09
53	REGIMEN	62	0,09
54	MARKER	61	0,09
55	FUNCTION	60	0,09
56	PATTERN	60	0,09
57	PRIMARY	60	0,09
58	EXPRESSION	59	0,08
59	LEVEL	59	0,08
60	COMPLETE	58	0,08
61	PROGNOSTIC	58	0,08

#	Word	Count	Value
2	SYSTEM	320	0,72
3	BASED	225	0,50
4	TOLERANT	194	0,46
5	ERROR	158	0,37
6	MODEL	143	0,34
7	FAILURE	123	0,29
8	NETWORK	120	0,28
9	TIME	120	0,28
10	APPLICATION	115	0,27
11	APPROACH	114	0,27
12	SOFTWARE	111	0,26
13	DATA	107	0,25
14	TECHNIQUE	99	0,23
15	PROTOCOL	95	0,22
16	ALGORITHM	94	0,22
17	SINGLE	90	0,21
18	TEST	89	0,21
19	DETECTION	84	0,20
20	ANALYSIS	81	0,19
21	EFFICIENT	81	0,19
22	DESIGN	79	0,19
23	SPECIFIC	78	0,18
24	PERFORMANCE	76	0,18
25	CRITICAL	74	0,18
26	NON	71	0,17
27	CONTROL	70	0,17
28	PROCESS	70	0,17
29	MEMORY	66	0,16
30	SECURE	66	0,16
31	PROCESSOR	63	0,15
32	SECURITY	63	0,15
33	SIGNIFICANT	63	0,15
34	METHOD	61	0,14
35	STATE	61	0,14
36	OPTIMAL	57	0,13
37	RECOVERY	55	0,13
38	SCHEME	55	0,13
39	ARCHITECTURE	54	0,13
40	SELF	54	0,13
41	ATTACK	53	0,13
42	FAULTY	53	0,13
43	SERVICE	53	0,13
44	BEHAVIOUR	52	0,12
45	INFORMATION	52	0,12
46	CODE	51	0,12
47	EFFECTIVE	50	0,12
48	ENVIRONMENT	50	0,12
49	TOLERANCE	50	0,12
50	RELIABLE	49	0,12
51	REDUNDANT	47	0,11
52	COMPONENT	46	0,11
53	CIRCUIT	45	0,11
54	DEPENDABLE	45	0,11
55	LEVEL	45	0,11
56	REAL	45	0,11
57	COMMUNICATION	44	0,10
58	FREE	44	0,10
59	HARDWARE	44	0,10
60	MALICIOUS	44	0,10
61	ONLINE	44	0,10

#	Word	n	Freq
62	SURVIVAL	58	0,08
63	ADJUVANT	57	0,08
64	DIAGNOSIS	57	0,08
65	INVOLVEMENT	57	0,08
66	STAGE	56	0,08
67	TECHNIQUE	56	0,08
68	ONCOLOGY	54	0,08
69	CASE	53	0,08
70	FINDING	53	0,08
71	INTRAOPERATIVE	53	0,08
72	RADIATION	53	0,08
73	BIOLOGICAL	52	0,07
74	HISTOLOGICAL	52	0,07
75	ABDOMINAL	51	0,07
76	CONTROL	51	0,07
77	DIAGNOSTIC	51	0,07
78	EPITHELIAL	51	0,07
79	PATHOLOGICAL	51	0,07
80	RADIOTHERAPY	51	0,07
81	REGION	51	0,07
82	APPROACH	50	0,07
83	LATE	50	0,07
84	SEVERE	50	0,07
85	OUTCOME	49	0,07
86	EVENT	48	0,07
87	ACTIVITY	47	0,07
88	AGENT	47	0,07
89	AGGRESSIVE	47	0,07
90	NUCLEAR	47	0,07
91	OPTIMAL	47	0,07
92	VOLUME	47	0,07
93	EFFECTIVE	46	0,07
94	EVALUATION	46	0,07
95	LEFT	46	0,07
96	BIOPSY	45	0,06
97	CONVENTIONAL	45	0,06
98	EXAMINATION	45	0,06
99	NEOPLASM	45	0,06
100	TYPE	45	0,06

#	Word	n	Freq
62	PATH	44	0,10
63	COMPUTER	43	0,10
64	PHYSICAL	43	0,10
65	PROGRAM	43	0,10
66	SOLUTION	42	0,10
67	FUNCTIONAL	41	0,10
68	GLOBAL	41	0,10
69	MESSAGE	41	0,10
70	OPERATION	41	0,10
71	PROBABILISTIC	41	0,10
72	IMPLEMENTATION	40	0,09
73	NODE	40	0,09
74	LOGIC	39	0,09
75	MAIN	39	0,09
76	SIMULATION	39	0,09
77	DEVICE	38	0,09
78	SERVER	38	0,09
79	TRADITIONAL	38	0,09
80	END	37	0,09
81	PROBLEM	37	0,09
82	STRUCTURE	37	0,09
83	KEY	36	0,09
84	LINE	36	0,09
85	MECHANISM	36	0,09
86	MULTI	36	0,09
87	STATIC	36	0,09
88	USER	36	0,09
89	ARBITRARY	35	0,08
90	COST	35	0,08
91	TO	35	0,08
92	ARRAY	34	0,08
93	POINT	34	0,08
94	CONCURRENT	33	0,08
95	CORRECT	33	0,08
96	EXPERIMENTAL	33	0,08
97	FLOW	33	0,08
98	FORMAL	33	0,08
99	GROUP	33	0,08
100	INJECTION	33	0,08

Appendix C4

The domain term annotation system:

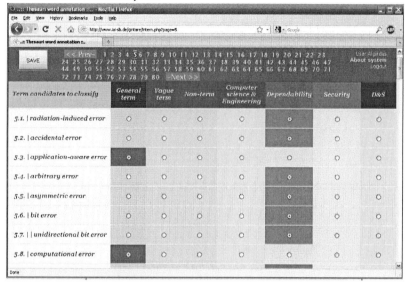

Appendix D1

Examples of aligned sentences:

```
<paraph id="899" alg="NW">
  <nx>(12863, 14927, 0.865882)</nx>
  <s1>The primary end point was progression-free survival; overall survival was a secondary end point.</s1>
  <s2>The primary endpoint was disease-free survival; overall survival was a secondary endpoint.</s2>
  <sa1>The primary end point      was      progression-free survival; overall survival was a secondary end point     .</sa1>
  <sa2>The primary      endpoint was disease-free      survival; overall survival was a secondary      endpoint .</sa2>
</paraph>

<paraph id="467" alg="NW">
  <nx>(5158, 7837, 0.953621)</nx>
  <s1>Breast cancer is the most frequently diagnosed malignancy among American women.</s1>
  <s2>BACKGROUND: Breast cancer is the most common malignancy in women.</s2>
  <sa1>      Breast cancer is the most      frequently diagnosed malignancy      among American women .</sa1>
  <sa2>BACKGROUND : Breast cancer is the most common      malignancy in      women .</sa2>
</paraph>

<paraph id="61" alg="NW">
  <nx>(427, 5541, 0.961789)</nx>
  <s1>Wilms' tumour ( WT ) is the most common solid tumour of childhood.</s1>
  <s2>Much progress has Wilms' tumour ( WT ) is the most common renal tumour in children.</s2>
  <sa1>      Wilms' tumour ( WT ) is the most common      solid tumour      of childhood .</sa1>
  <sa2>Much progress has Wilms ' tumour ( WT ) is the most common renal      tumour in children .</sa2>
</paraph>

<paraph id="87" alg="NW">
  <nx>(703, 5693, 0.937570)</nx>
  <s1>Nephroblastoma is the most common malignant tumor in children.</s1>
  <s2>Nephroblastoma ( Wilms' tumor ) is the most common renal malignancy in childhood.</s2>
  <sa1>Nephroblastoma (      Wilms' tumor ) is the most common      malignant tumor in      children .</sa1>
  <sa2>Nephroblastoma ( Wilms ' tumor ) is the most common renal malignancy      in childhood .</sa2>
</paraph>

<paraph id="60" alg="NW">
  <nx>(796, 1237, 0.989621)</nx>
  <s1>All patients were treated with combined chemotherapy and radiotherapy.</s1>
  <s2>He was treated by surgical resection, chemotherapy, and radiotherapy.</s2>
  <sa1>      All patients were treated      with combined chemotherapy      and radiotherapy .</sa1>
  <sa2>He was      treated by surgical resection ,      chemotherapy , and radiotherapy .</sa2>
</paraph>
```

Appendix D2

Examples of extracted pairs:
(1) synonymous

```
{lymph_node status, lymph_node involvement}
{reduction, decrease}
{clinical partial_response, partial_response}
{er-negative cell_lines, er-negative cells}
{node-negative breast_cancer, early breast_cancer}
{axillary, breast_cancer}
{er-negative_patient, er-positive_patient}
{overall_survival and progression-free_survival, overall and progression-
free_survival}
{experienced objective_responses, achieved objective_responses}
{have febrile_neutropenia, develope febrile_neutropenia}
{suggested, indicated}
{incidence, risk}
{activity, efficacy}
{control_group, controls}
{median_progression-free_survival, median_survival}
{steroidal aromatase_inhibitor, third-generation aromatase_inhibitor}
{primary_endpoint, primary_objective}
{study, meta-analysis}
{investigate, evaluated}
{immediate axillary lymph_node dissection, subsequent axillary lymph_node dissection}
{re-exploration, sln_biopsy}
{observed, detected}
{evaluable, eligible}
{included, enrolled}
{assessable, evaluable}
{eligible, assessable}
{invasive breast_cancer, advanced breast_cancer }
{positive sentinel_nodes, negative sentinel_nodes}
{her2-negative tumor, her2-positive tumor}
{metastatic breast_cancer , her2-negative breast_cancer}
{endocrine-responsive breast_cancer, hormone-responsive breast_cancer}
{analysis, trial}
{trial, study}
{neoplasm, tumor}
{common_cancer, common_malignancy}
{common_cancer in women, common_malignancy in women}
{undergo surgery, receive surgery}
{randomized trial, randomized study}
{purpose, aim}
{sole, only}
{found, identified}
{assessed, assessable}
{estrogen receptor-positive breast_cancer, hormone receptor-positive breast_cancer}
{benefit, use}
{clinicopathologic stages, clinical stage}
{cumulative incidence, cumulative risk}
```

{developmental tumor, developmental malignancy}
{embryonal malignancy, developmental malignancy}
{embryonic tumor, solid tumor}
{evaluated, reviewed}
{follow up, follow-up period}
{genitourinary tract, urinary tract}
{in children, in childhood}
{percentage, rate}
{pulmonary nodules, pulmonary densities}
{radical nephroureterectomy, radical nephrectomy}
{renal tumor, malignant tumor }
{renal tumor, solid tumor}
{renal tumor in children, solid tumors in children}
{reviewed, examined}
{solid tumors, malignant tumor}
{tMK protein, tMK polypeptide}
{calculation, estimate}
{duration, time}
{follow-up duration, follow-up time}
{frequent, common}
{greater, better}
{in childhood, of childhood}
{neoplasm, tumor}
{overall survival , event-free survival}
{renal malignancy in children, renal tumour in children}
{renal neoplasm, renal tumor}
{truncated midkine, truncated MK}

{approach, scheme}
{barrier operator, aggregate operator}
{bundle, isolate}
{client machine, server machine}
{coding packet, data packet}
{communication model, communication implementation}
{connections created, connections closed}
{different, distinct}
{display, show}
{Drop Random Policy, Drop All Policy}
{evaluation method, evaluation methodology}
{fair choice, guided choice}
{generalized horizontal cut, generalized vertical cut}
{good write event, dropped write event}
{hierarchically distributed, fully distributed}
{information part, information bits}
{Java Virtual Machine, Multi-Tasking Virtual Machine}
{leading low-latency anonymous networks, representative low-latency networks}
{Manhattan distance, Euclidean distance}
{Manhattan distance, Mahalanobis distance}
{MAP-AMVA accuracy, MAP-AMVA results}
{message identifier, context identifier}
{methodology, method}
{multiple vehicles, several vehicles}
{organized, done}
{outline, introduce}

{paper, work}
{parent, parent_msg}
{path, branch}
{performance constraint, availability constraint}
{per-packet basis, per-message basis}
{previous work, related work}
{read, write}
{response action, adversary action}
{shop, order}
{single-window join, per-group join}
{system clock, scan clock}
{Telecontrol Testbed, Microgrid Testbed}
{test window, baseline window}
{tool architecture, system architecture}
{training phase, test phase}
{Ttemporal seconds, Tspatial seconds}
{valuable comment, constructive comment}
{wildcard CNAME record, wildcard TXT record}
{working with system administrators, consulting with system administrators}
{adverse effects on dependability, adverse impact on dependability}
{allow, enable}
{current value, current state}
{deduce, derive}
{describe, discuss}
{describe, present}
{evaluate, assess}
{feedback, comments}
{frequency tuning, frequency control}
{helpful comment, valuable comment}
{implement isolation, implement protection}
{incoming message, new message}
{introduce, present}
{listed, given}
{method, technique}
{most read count, maximum read count}
{offer, provide}
{organized, structured}
{performance of the register, reliability of the register}
{processed, executed}
{propose, present}
{pseudo algorithm, pseudo code}
{rest, remainder}
{significantly, substantialy}

(2) non-synonymous

{axillary cancer, breast_cancer}
{effect, difference}
{doxorubicin, docetaxel}
{bendamustine, paclitaxel}
{capecitabine, ixabepilone}
{non-SN, SLN}
{pro-angiogenic level, cytokine level}
{association, combination}

{steroidal aromatase_inhibitor, third-generation aromatase_inhibitor}
{relapse-free_survival, clinical_response}
{dfs, IBTR}
{left-sided breast_cancer, metastatic breast_cancer}
{capecitabine, vinorelbine}
{trastuzumab, vinorelbine}
{promising activity, clear activity}
{enrolled, treated}
{included, treated}
{children, patients}
{CTX, cyclophosphamide}
{difference, result}
{excellent survival, excellent prognosis}
{FNAB smears, aspiration smears}
{KV, MBL}
{month, year}
{partial remission, partial response}
{pathologic features, radiographic features}
{solid tumor, intraabdominal tumor}
{higher level, lower level}
{inversely correlated, directly correlated}
{more, less}
{non-aggressive WT, aggressive tumor}
{weak inverse relationship, significant inverse relationship}

{linearizability, wait-freedom}
{availabilitymaximizing optimal server admission, performancemaximizing optimal
server admission}
{anonymizing packet, anonymizing network}
{availabilitymaximizing feedback controller, performance-maximizing feedback
controller}
{clock distribution overhead, clock routing overhead}
{encoding parameters, encoding performance}
{SQL injection, XPath injection}
{data cache, instruction cache}
{rate-capacity effect, recovery}
{sum, product}
{novel metric, energy-based metric}
{novel dynamic attestation system, application-level dynamic attestation system}
{communication protocol, communication flow}
{distributed Web services, existing Web services}
{report, detect}
{mean vector, test vector}
{test vector, output vector}
{evaluation results, coverage results}
{mean vector, training vector}
{timing vector, training vector}
{empirical results, evaluation results}
{paper, section}
{human, user}

Appendix E1

Mappings between domain terms and lexicalized classes of ACGT MO:
(1) Examples of full mappings.

```
Age <==> Age
Dose <==> Dose
Density <==> Density
Thickness <==> Thickness
Volume <==> Volume
Weight <==> Weight
Malignancy <==> Malignancy
Toxicity <==> Toxicity
Function <==> Function
Patient <==> Patient
Complication <==> Complication
Criterion <==> Criterion
Drug <==> Drug
Marker <==> Marker
Symptom <==> Symptom
Therapy <==> Therapy
Cell <==> Cell
Kidney <==> Kidney
Abdomen <==> Abdomen
Pelvis <==> Pelvis
Urine <==> Urine
Lesion <==> Lesion
Neoplasm <==> Neoplasm
Carcinoma <==> Carcinoma
Nephroblastoma <==> Nephroblastoma
Metastasis <==> Metastasis
Sarcoma <==> Sarcoma
Relapse <==> Relapse
Thrombus <==> Thrombus
Doxorubicin <==> Doxorubicin
Institution <==> Institution
Anemia <==> Anemia
Hypertension <==> Hypertension
Cycle <==> Cycle
Biopsy <==> Biopsy
Chemotherapy <==> Chemotherapy
Radiotherapy <==> Radiotherapy
Resection <==> Resection
Nephrectomy <==> Nephrectomy
Treatment <==> Treatment
Adhesion <==> Adhesion
Bleeding <==> Bleeding
Disease <==> Disease
Neutropenia <==> Neutropenia
Syndrome <==> Syndrome
Nephroblastomatosis <==> Nephroblastomatosis
Infection <==> Infection
```

```
Infiltration <==> Infiltration
Anaplasia <==> Anaplasia
Necrosis <==> Necrosis
Obstruction <==> Obstruction
Rupture <==> Rupture
Death <==> Death
Day <==> Day
Week <==> Week
```

(2) Examples of partial mappings.

```
Clinical_Trial_Protocol       <==>     Clinical_Trial
Clinical_Trial_Identifier <==>     Clinical_Trial
Clinical_Trial_Patient_Number       <==>     Clinical_Trial
Histological_Type     <==>     Histological_Type
Late_Effect_Role     <==>     Late_Effect
Cardiac_Late_Effect_Role   <==>     Late_Effect
Kidney_Late_Effect_Role    <==>     Late_Effect
Skeleton_Late_Effect_Role <==>     Late_Effect
Clinical_Trial_Patient     <==>     Clinical_Trial
Subdivision_Of_Inferior_Vena_Caval_Tree       <==>     Vena_Cava
Renal_Vein   <==>     Renal_Vein
Nephrogenic_Rest     <==>     Nephrogenic_Rest
Treatment_Cycle       <==>     Treatment_Cycle
Clinical_Trial     <==>     Clinical_Trial
Surgical_Approach   <==>     Surgical_Approach
Partial_Nephrectomy       <==>     Partial_Nephrectomy
Standard_Partial_Nephrectomy       <==>     Partial_Nephrectomy
Bacterial_Infection       <==>     Bacterial_Infection
Viral_Infection     <==>     Viral_Infection
Chronic_Viral_Infection   <==>     Viral_Infection
Congenital_Syndrome       <==>     Congenital_Syndrome
Renal_Pelvis_Cancer       <==>     Renal_Pelvis
Immature_TeratomaGCT_Disease     <==>     Immature_Teratoma
Immature_Teratoma_With_Malignant_TransformationGCT_Disease <==>     Immature_Teratoma
Immature_Teratoma_Without_Malignant_TransformationGCT_Disease       <==>
Immature_Teratoma
Late_Effect   <==>     Late_Effect
Cardiac_Late_Effect       <==>     Late_Effect
Kidney_Late_Effect <==>     Late_Effect
Skeleton_Late_Effect       <==>     Late_Effect
Diffuse_Anaplasia     <==>     Diffuse_Anaplasia
Focal_Anaplasia     <==>     Focal_Anaplasia
Relapse_Free_Survival     <==>     Free_Survival
```